Kenneth Burke, arguably the most important American literary theorist of the twentieth century, helped define the theoretical terrain for contemporary cultural studies. His perspectives were literary and linguistic, but his influences ranged across history, philosophy and the social sciences. In this important and original study Robert Wess traces the trajectory of Burke's long career and situates his work in relation to postmodernity. His study is both an examination of contemporary theories of rhetoric, ideology and the subject, and an explanation of why Burke failed to complete his *Motives* trilogy. Burke's own critique of the "isolated unique individual" led him to question the possibility of unique individualism, a strategy which anticipated important elements of postmodern concepts of subjectivity. Robert Wess's study is both a timely and judicious exposition of Burke's massive *œuvre*, and a crucial intervention in current debates on rhetoric and human agency.

❖❖

Kenneth Burke
Rhetoric, Subjectivity, Postmodernism

❖❖

General editors

RICHARD MACKSEY, *The Johns Hopkins University*
and MICHAEL SPRINKER, *State University of New York at Stony Brook*

The Cambridge *Literature, Culture, Theory* Series is dedicated to theoretical studies in the human sciences that have literature and culture as their object of enquiry. Acknowledging the contemporary expansion of cultural studies and the redefinitions of literature that this has entailed, the series includes not only original works of literary theory but also monographs and essay collections on topics and seminal figures from the long history of theoretical speculation on the arts and human communication generally. The concept of theory embraced in the series is broad, including not only the classical disciplines of poetics and rhetoric, but also those of aesthetics, linguistics, psychoanalysis, semiotics, and other cognate sciences that have inflected the systematic study of literature during the past half century.

Kenneth Burke

Rhetoric, subjectivity, postmodernism

ROBERT WESS

Oregon State University

CAMBRIDGE
UNIVERSITY PRESS

Published by the Press Syndicate of the University of Cambridge
The Pitt Building, Trumpington Street, Cambridge CB2 1RP
40 West 20th Street, New York, NY 10011–4211, USA
10 Stamford Road, Oakleigh, Melbourne 3166, Australia

First published 1996

Printed in Great Britain at the University Press, Cambridge

A catalogue record for this book is available from the British Library

Library of Congress cataloguing in publication data
Wess, Robert.
Kenneth Burke, rhetoric, subjectivity, postmodernism / Robert Wess.
p.   cm. – (Literature, culture, theory; 18)
Includes bibliographical references and index.
ISBN 0 521 41049 5 (hardback) – ISBN 0 521 42258 2 (paperback)
1. Burke, Kenneth, 1897–1993 . 2. Literature – Philosophy. 3. Rhetoric. I. Title. II. Series
PN49.W418 1996
818'.5209–dc20   95–12761   CIP

ISBN 0 521 41049 5 hardback
ISBN 0 521 42258 2 paperback

For Sandra

Anybody can do anything for any reason.
Burke, SO

[Humans] build their cultures by huddling together, nervously loquacious,
at the edge of an abyss.
Burke, *PC*

Contents

Preface

In the narrative in these pages of Kenneth Burke's career, the themes of rhetoric, subjectivity, and postmodernism are concentrated in the term "a rhetoric of the subject." Our term rather than Burke's, "a rhetoric of the subject" designates, as it were, the position of the narrator in this narrative.

Offering glimpses of the overall structure of the narrative in passing, chapter 1 introduces a rhetoric of the human subject, placing it in the context of contemporary theory, particularly contemporary theorizing of ideology, here construed as a rhetoricizing of ideology. Chapter 1's argument, in a nutshell, is that contemporary theory needs Burke's rhetorical realism of the act to preserve the theoretical gains of recent decades by warding off the rhetorical idealism that sometimes threatens to undermine them.

A rhetoric of the subject is apart from and a part of Burke's career: a part of it in the sense that we extrapolate this rhetoric from *GM* and *RM*, considered here as constituting a completed rhetorical theory of the subject[1]; apart from it in the sense that Burke seems always to have seen these two books as two parts of a trilogy needing *SM* to be complete. Further, during the final phase of his career, he tends to shy away from the full implications of a rhetoric of the subject, although near the end of his life, there may be one last change in direction. A rhetoric of the subject is thus — as the theoretical point Burke paradoxically both moves toward and resists — the source of the principal tension in our narrative of his preternaturally long career.

---

1 Our extrapolation may be considered an "extension" in the sense designated by the title *Extensions of the Burkeian System*, a volume growing out of the 1990 convention of the Kenneth Burke Society. "Extension" here refers to the practice, encouraged by Burke himself, of using Burke and simultaneously departing from his work in some new direction (Chesebro vii–viii).

Acknowledging my debts upon completing this book became more difficult as I became more aware in the process of writing it of just how overdetermined a book is. I'm responsible for the words on these pages, but for whatever merit they may possess I'm indebted to many others, too many to acknowledge or perhaps even fully comprehend. But I cannot let this opportunity pass without thanking Richard McKeon for starting my education in rhetoric and Kenneth Burke for continuing it; no doubt they would consider me a sometimes wayward student. The Center for the Humanities at Oregon State University provided invaluable time for part of my research and writing; I and my colleagues at Oregon State are indebted to its director, Peter Copek, whose vision and energy brought this Center to our campus. To the reader commissioned by Cambridge University Press, Steven Mailloux, I'm indebted for a critical assessment that helped me make this a better book. Michael Sprinker – all that I could hope for in a reader and more – meticulously read through two complete drafts; I'm indebted to him for innumerable suggestions that saved me from many errors and undoubtedly would have saved me from even more had I been able to heed them all. Finally, for all her support during all our years together, I dedicate this book to Sandra.

Acknowledgments

Acknowledgment is due to the Yale Collection of American Literature, Beinecke Rare Book and Manuscript Library, Yale University, for permission to publish an extract from *The Dial* papers: letter from Kenneth Burke to Alyse Gregory, 20 November 1924; and to Pennsylvania State University Libraries for permission to quote excerpts from three letters dated 22 September 1932, 28 September 1932, and 3 October 1932, from Kenneth Burke to Malcolm Cowley.

Special acknowledgment is also due, for permission to quote from all these letters, to Michael Burke and the KB Literary Trust.

Abbreviations

ACR   "Auscultation, Creation, and Revision: The Rout of the Esthetes – Literature, Marxism, and Beyond." *Extensions of the Burkeian System.* Ed. James W. Chesebro. Tuscaloosa: University of Alabama Press, 1993. 42–172.

ATH1 *Attitudes toward History.* 2 vols. New York: New Republic, 1937.

ATH   *Attitudes toward History.* 1937. 3rd ed. Berkeley: University of California Press, 1984.

CP   *Collected Poems 1915–1967.* Berkeley: University of California Press, 1968.

CS   *Counter-Statement.* 1931. 3rd ed. Berkeley: University of California Press, 1968.

DD   *Dramatism and Development.* Barre: Clark University Press, 1972.

GM   *A Grammar of Motives.* 1945. Berkeley: University of California Press, 1969.

"LR" "Lexicon Rhetoricæ." 1931. *CS* 123–83.

LSA   *Language as Symbolic Action.* Berkeley: University of California Press, 1966.

PC1   *Permanence and Change: An Anatomy of Purpose.* New York: New Republic Books, 1935.

PC   *Permanence and Change: An Anatomy of Purpose.* 1935. 3rd ed. Berkeley: University of California Press, 1984.

PDC   *Poetics, Dramatistically Considered.* Unpublished typescript.

PLF   *The Philosophy of Literary Form: Studies in Symbolic Action.* 1941. 3rd ed. Berkeley: University of California Press, 1973.

"PLF" "The Philosophy of Literary Form." *PLF* 1–137.

RM   *A Rhetoric of Motives.* 1950. Berkeley: University of California Press, 1969.

RR   *The Rhetoric of Religion: Studies in Logology.* 1961. Berkeley: University of California Press, 1970.

SCBC *The Selected Correspondence of Kenneth Burke and Malcolm*

Cowley: 1915–1981. Ed. Paul Jay. New York: Viking, 1988.

SM   *A Symbolic of Motives.* Projected but not completed.

TBL   *Towards a Better Life: Being a Series of Epistles, or Declamations.* 1932. Berkeley: University of California Press, 1966.

WO   *The Complete White Oxen: Collected Short Fiction.* 1924. Rev. and enl. ed. Berkeley: University of California Press, 1968.

The same abbreviations appear in parenthetical page references when necessary. Parenthetical page references to other Burke texts use the following:

AHC   "Art and the Hope Chest." Rev. of *The Ordeal of Mark Twain,* by Van Wyck Brooks. *Vanity Fair* Dec. 1922: 59, 102.

AIWS   "As I Was Saying." *Michigan Quarterly Review* 11 (1972): 9–27.

ARG   "Approaches to Remy de Gourmont." *The Dial* 70 (1921): 125–38.

BCC   "Kenneth Burke and Malcolm Cowley: A Conversation." *Pre/Text* 6 (1985): 181–200.

CDF   "*Coriolanus* – and the Delights of Faction." 1966. *LSA* 81–97.

CF   "The Correspondence of Flaubert." *The Dial* 72 (1922): 147–55.

CR   "On Catharsis, or Resolution." *Kenyon Review* 21 (1959): 337–75.

CSV   "Catharsis – Second View." *Centennial Review* 5 (1961): 107–32.

D67   "Dramatism." *Communication: Concepts and Perspectives.* Ed. Lee Thayer. Second International Symposium on Communication Theory and Research, March 1966. Washington, DC: Spartan Books, 1967. 327–60.

D68   "Dramatism." *International Encyclopedia of the Social Sciences.* Ed. David L. Sills. New York: Macmillan, 1968. 445–51.

DL83   "Dramatism and Logology." *TLS* Aug. 12, 1983: 859.

DL85   "Dramatism and Logology." *Communication Quarterly* 33 (1985): 89–93.

DM   "Definition of Man." 1963–64. *LSA* 3–24.

DOES   "Dramatism as Ontology or Epistemology: A Symposium." With Bernard L. Brock, Parke G. Burgess, and Herbert W. Simons. *Communication Quarterly* 33 (1985): 17–33.

DVI   "A 'Dramatistic' View of 'Imitation.'" *Accent* 12 (1952): 229–41.

DVOL   "A Dramatistic View of the Origins of Language." 1952–53. *LSA* 419–79.

EW   "Engineering with Words." Rev. of *Geography and Plays,* by Gertrude Stein. *The Dial* 74 (1923): 408–12.

FAP   "Freud – and the Analysis of Poetry." 1939. *PLF* 258–92.

FIP   "Fact, Inference, and Proof in the Analysis of Literary Symbolism." *Symbols and Values: An Initial Study*. Thirteenth Symposium of the Conference on Science, Philosophy and Religion. Ed. Lyman Bryson *et al.* New York: Harper and Brothers, 1954. 283–306. Reprinted *Terms for Order*. Ed. Stanley Edgar Hyman. Bloomington: Indiana University Press, 1964. 145–72.

FMT   "Four Master Tropes." 1941. *GM* 503–17.

FPO   "Form and Persecution in the *Oresteia*." 1952. *LSA* 125–38.

FTCG "On the First Three Chapters of Genesis." *Dædalus* 87.3 (1958): 37–64.

IH   "In Haste." *Pre/Text* 6 (1985): 329–77.

IMHS "Is Mr. Hook a Socialist?" *Partisan Review* 4 (1938): 40–44.

L1   Letter to Alyse Gregory. 20 Nov. 1924. Yale Collection of American Literature. Yale University Library.

L2   Letter to Malcolm Cowley. 22 Sept. 1932. Kenneth Burke Collection. Pennsylvania State University Library.

L3   Letter to Malcolm Cowley. 28 Sept. 1932. Kenneth Burke Collection. Pennsylvania State University Library.

L4   Letter to Malcolm Cowley. 3 Oct. 1932. Kenneth Burke Collection. Pennsylvania State University Library.

LAPE "Linguistic Approach to Problems of Education." *Modern Philosophies and Education*. Ed. Nelson B. Henry. University of Chicago Press, 1955. 259–303.

LAR   "Love among the Ruins." Rev. of *Maria Capponi*, by René Schickele. *New York Herald Tribune Books* Mar. 4, 1928: 7.

LWE   "Last Word on the Ephebe." The Literary Review of the *New York Evening Post* Aug. 26, 1922: 897-98.

M/A   "(Nonsymbolic) Motion / (Symbolic) Action." *Critical Inquiry* 4 (1978): 809–38.

MAC   "My Approach to Communism." *New Masses* Mar. 20, 1934: 16, 18–20.

MBU   "Mind, Body and the Unconscious." *LSA* 63–80.

MP   "Methodological Repression and/or Strategies of Containment." *Critical Inquiry* 5 (1978): 401–16.

NAC   "The Nature of Art under Capitalism." 1933. *PLF* 314–22.

OI   "On Interpretation." *The Plowshare: A Literary Periodical of One-Man Exhibits* 10.1 (1934): 1–79.

OSIS   "On Stress, Its Seeking." *Bennington Review* 1 (1967): 32–49.

PAC   "Poetics and Communication." *Perspectives in Education, Religion, and the Arts*. Eds. Howard E. Kiefer and Milton K. Munitz.

New York: State University of New York Press, 1970. 401–18.

PM   "The Poetic Motive." *Hudson Review* 11 (1958): 54–63.

QAP   "Questions and Answers about the Pentad." *College Composition and Communication* 19 (1978): 330–35.

RHB   "The Rhetoric of Hitler's 'Battle.'" 1939. *PLF* 191–220.

RLS   "The Relation between Literature and Science." *The Writer in a Changing World.* Second American Writers' Congress. New York: Equinox Cooperative Press, 1937. 158–71.

RON   "Rhetoric – Old and New." *Journal of General Education* 5 (1951): 202–09.

RPP   "Rhetoric, Poetics, and Philosophy." *Rhetoric, Philosophy, and Literature: An Exploration.* Ed. Don M. Burks. West Lafayette: Purdue University Press, 1978. 15–33, 111–13.

RSA   "Revolutionary Symbolism in America." *American Writers' Congress.* Ed. Henry Hart. New York: International Publishers, 1935. 87–94, 167–71. Reprinted Simons 267–80.

SAK   "Symbolic Action in a Poem by Keats." 1943. *GM* 447–63.

SAU   "*Somnia ad Urinandum*: More Thoughts on Motion and Action." 1965. *LSA* 344–58.

SO   "The Seven Offices." 1958. *ATH* 353–75.

SPM   "Semantic and Poetic Meaning." 1938. *PLF* 138–67.

SPP   "Self-Portrait of a Person." Rev. of *Particulars of a Life*, by B. F. Skinner. *Behaviorism* 4 (1976): 257–71.

SRM   "Symbolism as a Realistic Mode: 'De-Psychoanalyzing' Logologized." *Psychocultural Review* 3 (1979): 25–37.

SSA   "The Study of Symbolic Action." *Chimera* 1 (1942): 7–16.

SW   "Symbolic War." *Southern Review* 2 (1936): 134–47.

TB   "The Thinking of the Body: Comments on the Imagery of Catharsis in Literature." 1963. *LSA* 308–43.

TH   "Toward Helhaven: Three Stages of a Vision." *Sewanee Review* 79 (1971): 151–85.

TP1   "Twelve Propositions on the Relation between Economics and Psychology." *Science and Society* 2 (1938): 242–49.

TP   "Twelve Propositions on the Relation between Economics and Psychology." 1938. *PLF* 305–13.

TS   "Terministic Screens." 1965. *LSA* 44–62.

TYL   "Thirty Years Later: Memories of the First American Writers' Congress." Symposium; with Malcolm Cowley, Granville Hicks, and William Phillips; moderated by Daniel Aaron. *The*

American Scholar 35 (1966): 495–516.

UB   "The Unburned Bridges of Poetics, or, How Keep Poetry Pure?" *Centennial Review* 8 (1964): 391–97.

VLD   "The Virtues and Limitations of Debunking." 1938. *PLF* 168–90.

WC   "The Writers' Congress." *The Nation* May 15, 1935: 571.

WD   "Words as Deeds." *Centrum* 3 (1975): 147–68.

WRC   "War, Response, and Contradiction." 1933. *PLF* 234–57.

WS   "Why Satire, with a Plan for Writing One." *Michigan Quarterly Review* 13 (1974): 307–37.

WW   "What Are the Signs of What? (A Theory of 'Entitlement')." 1962. *LSA* 359–79.

Secondary texts on Burke are cited by reference to the author and, if necessary, to the title as well.

Abbott, Don. "Marxist Influences on the Rhetorical Theory of Kenneth Burke." *Philosophy and Rhetoric* 7 (1974): 217–33.

Allen, Virginia. "Some Implications of Kenneth Burke's 'Way of Knowing' for Composition Theory." *Journal of Advanced Composition* 3 (1982): 10–23.

Baer, Donald M. "A Comment on Skinner as Boy and on Burke as S^Δ." *Behaviorism* 4 (1976): 273–77.

Birdsell, David S. "Ronald Reagan on Lebanon and Grenada: Flexibility and Interpretation in the Application of Kenneth Burke's Pentad." Brock, *et al.*, *Methods* 196–209.

Booth, Wayne. "Kenneth Burke's Way of Knowing." *Critical Inquiry* 1 (1974): 1–22.

    "Kenneth Burke's Comedy: The Multiplication of Perspectives." *Critical Understanding: The Powers and Limits of Pluralism.* University of Chicago Press, 1979. 99–137.

Brock, Bernard L., Robert L. Scott, and James W. Chesebro, eds. *Methods of Rhetorical Criticism: A Twentieth-Century Perspective.* 3rd ed. Detroit: Wayne State University Press, 1989.

Brock, Bernard L. "Epistemology and Ontology in Kenneth Burke's Dramatism." *Communication Quarterly* 33 (1985): 94–104.

    "The Dramatistic Approach: Rhetorical Criticism: A Burkeian Approach Revisited." Brock, *et al.*, *Methods* 183–95.

    "The Evolution of Kenneth Burke's Philosophy of Rhetoric: Dialectic between Epistemology and Ontology." Chesebro, *Extensions* 309–28.

Brummett, Barry. "A Pentadic Analysis of Ideologies in Two Gay

Rights Controversies." *Central States Speech Journal* 30 (1979): 250–61.

Carter, C. Allen. "Logology and Religion: Kenneth Burke on the Metalinguistic Dimensions of Language." *Journal of Religion* 72 (1992): 1–18.

Charland, Maurice. "Constitutive Rhetoric: The Case of the *Peuple Québécois*." *Quarterly Journal of Speech* 73 (1987): 133–50.

Chesebro, James W. "Epistemology and Ontology as Dialectical Modes in the Writings of Kenneth Burke." *Communication Quarterly* 36 (1988): 175–92.

Ed. *Extensions of the Burkeian System*. Tuscaloosa: University of Alabama Press, 1993.

Conklin, Groff. "The Science of Symbology," rev. of *Attitudes toward History*. *New Masses* Aug. 10, 1937: 25–26.

Conrad, Charles. "Phases, Pentads, and Dramatistic Critical Process." *Central States Speech Journal* 35 (1984): 94–104.

Crusius, Timothy. "A Case for Kenneth Burke's Dialectic and Rhetoric." *Philosophy and Rhetoric* 19 (1986): 23–37.

"Kenneth Burke's *Auscultation*: A 'De-struction' of Marxist Dialectic and Rhetoric." *Rhetorica* 6 (1988): 355–79.

Desilet, Gregory. "Nietzsche Contra Burke: The Melodrama in Dramatism." *Speech Communication Association* 75 (1989): 65–83.

Durham, Weldon R. "Kenneth Burke's Concept of Substance." *Quarterly Journal of Speech* 66 (1980): 351–64.

Feehan, Michael. "Kenneth Burke's Discovery of Dramatism." *Quarterly Journal of Speech* 65 (1979): 405–11.

"Oscillation as Assimilation: Burke's Latest Self-Revisions." *Pre/Text* 6 (1985): 319–27.

"Kenneth Burke's Dualistic Theory of Constitutions." *Pre/Text* 12 (1991): 39–59.

"Co-Haggling with Robert Wess." *Pre/Text* 12 (1991): 33–36.

Frank, Armin Paul. *Kenneth Burke*. Twayne's United States Authors Series 160. (New York: Twayne, 1969).

Griffin, Leland. "A Dramatistic Theory of the Rhetoric of Movements." Rueckert, *Critical* 456–78.

Heath, Robert L. "Kenneth Burke's Break with Formalism." *Quarterly Journal of Speech* 70 (1984): 132–43.

Realism and Relativism: A Perspective on Kenneth Burke. Macon: Mercer University Press, 1986.

Heilman, Robert B. "Burke as Political Threat: A Chronicle of the

1950s." *Horns of Plenty: Malcolm Cowley and His Generation* 2.1 (1989): 19–26.

Henderson, Greig E. *Kenneth Burke: Literature and Language as Symbolic Action*. Athens: University of Georgia Press, 1988.

"Aesthetic and Practical Frames of Reference: Burke, Marx, and the Rhetoric of Social Change." Chesebro, *Extensions* 173–85.

Hook, Sidney. "The Technique of Mystification." Rev. of *ATH*. Rueckert, *Critical* 89–97.

"Is Mr. Burke Serious?" Rueckert, *Critical* 97–101.

Jameson, Fredric. "The Symbolic Inference; or, Kenneth Burke and Ideological Analysis," *Critical Inquiry* 4 (1977–78): 507–23.

Jay, Paul. "Modernism, Postmodernism, and Critical Style: The Case of Burke and Derrida." *Genre* 21 (1988): 339–58.

"Kenneth Burke and the Motives of Rhetoric." *American Literary History* 1 (1989): 535–53.

Johnson, Edgar. "The Artist and the World." Rev. of "On Interpretation," by Kenneth Burke. *The New Republic* Sept. 5, 1934: 109–10.

Leff, Michael. "Burke's Ciceronianism." Simons 115–27.

Lentricchia, Frank. *Criticism and Social Change*. University of Chicago Press, 1983.

McWhorter, Ladella, and David Cratis Williams. Rev. of *Kenneth Burke and Martin Heidegger, with a Note against Deconstructionism*, by Samuel B. Southwell. *Philosophy and Rhetoric* 23 (1990): 75–80.

Madsen, Arnie. "Burke's Representative Anecdote as a Critical Method." Chesebro, *Extensions* 208-29.

Melia, Trevor. "Scientism and Dramatism: Some Quasi-Mathematical Motifs in the Work of Kenneth Burke." Simons 55–73.

Murray, Timothy C. "Kenneth Burke's Logology: A Mock Logomachy." *Glyph* 2 (1977): 144–61.

Nelson, Cary. "Writing as the Accomplice of Language: Kenneth Burke and Poststructuralism." Simons 156–73.

Parkes, Henry Bamford. "Kenneth Burke." Essay-rev. of *ATH*. Rueckert, *Critical* 109–22.

Ransom, John Crowe. "Mr. Burke's Dialectic." Rev. of *GM*. Rueckert, *Critical* 159–63.

Roig, Charles. *Symboles et société: Une introduction à la politique des symboles d'après l'œuvre de Kenneth Burke*. Bern: Peter Lang, 1977.

Rosenfeld, Isaac. "Dry Watershed." Rev. of *GM*. *Kenyon Review* 8 (1946): 310–17.

Rueckert, William H., ed. *Critical Responses to Kenneth Burke 1924–1966*.

Minneapolis: University of Minnesota Press, 1969.

Kenneth Burke and the Drama of Human Relations. 2nd ed. Berkeley: University of California Press, 1982.

"A Field Guide to Kenneth Burke – 1990." Chesebro, *Extensions* 3–41.

Schiappa, Edward. "Burkean Tropes and Kuhnian Science: A Social Constructionist Perspective on Language and Reality." *Journal of Advanced Composition* 13 (1993): 401–22.

Schlauch, Margaret. "A Review of *Attitudes toward History.*" Rueckert, *Critical* 105–09.

"A Reply to Kenneth Burke." *Science and Society* 2 (1938): 250–53.

Simons, Herbert W., and Trevor Melia, eds. *The Legacy of Kenneth Burke.* Madison: University of Wisconsin Press, 1989.

Southwell, Samuel B. *Kenneth Burke and Martin Heidegger, with a Note against Deconstruction.* University of Florida Humanities Monograph 60. Gainesville: University of Florida Press, 1987.

Stuart, Charlotte L. "The Constitution as 'Summational Anecdote.'" *Central States Speech Journal* 25 (1974): 111–18.

Tate, Allen. "Mr. Burke and the Historical Environment." Rueckert, *Critical* 62–70.

Thomas, Douglas. "Burke, Nietzsche, Lacan: Three Perspectives on the Rhetoric of Order." *Quarterly Journal of Speech* 79 (1993): 336–55.

Wess, Robert. "Frank Lentricchia's *Criticism and Social Change*: The Literary Intellectual as Pragmatic Humanist." *minnesota review* ns 27 (1986): 123–31.

"Kenneth Burke's 'Dialectic of Constitutions.'" *Pre/Text* 12 (1991): 9–30.

"The Question of Truth Rhetorically Considered." *Pre/Text* 12 (1991): 61–65.

Williams, David Cratis. "Under the Sign of (An)Nihilation: Burke in the Age of Nuclear Destruction and Critical Deconstruction." Simons 196–23.

Wolfe, Cary. "Nature as Critical Concept: Kenneth Burke, the Frankfurt School, and 'Metabiology.'" *Cultural Critique* 18 (1991): 65–96.

Addendum: Unfortunately, Stephen Bygrave's *Kenneth Burke: Rhetoric and Ideology* (London: Routledge, 1993) came to my attention too late to incorporate into the present study.

1

❖❖❖

Ideology as rhetoric

❖❖❖

When a bit of talking takes place, just what is doing the talking? Just where are the words coming from? ... An "ideology" is like a spirit taking up its abode in a body: it makes that body hop around in certain ways; and that same body would have hopped around in different ways had a different ideology happened to inhabit it.

Burke, *LSA*

Rhetoric has assumed a prominence unimaginable a generation ago. True, it is still mentioned pejoratively in everyday conversation and the media. But among theorists one now sometimes runs across the opposite extreme. Stanley Fish, for instance, in *Doing What Comes Naturally*, tells us that its basic message is that "we live in a rhetorical world."[1] Normally not part of the training of contemporary theorists, rhetoric is instead something encountered on the terrain of contemporary discourse, where it sometimes is and sometimes is not recognized by name. Samuel Ijsseling finds appeals to rhetoric − "direct or indirect" − in strategies used to bring traditional philosophy into question in "Nietzsche, Marx and Freud, and ... in Heidegger and the various French authors who have been inspired by these thinkers, e.g. J. Derrida, R. Barthes, M. Foucault, J. Lacan and L. Althusser."[2]

Fish writes in "Rhetoric," published for the first time in *Doing*, of some of the theorists responsible for the current rise of rhetoric, including "Kenneth Burke, whose 'dramatism' anticipates so much of what is considered avant-garde today."[3] Burke has, of course, been depicted as an anticipatory figure by others such as Wayne Booth, Fredric Jameson, Frank Lentricchia, Richard Macksey, and Edward

---

1 *Doing What Comes Naturally: Change, Rhetoric, and the Practice of Theory in Literary and Legal Studies* (Durham: Duke University Press, 1989), p. 25.
2 *Rhetoric and Philosophy in Conflict: An Historical Survey* (The Hague: Martinus Nijhoff, 1976), p. 5.
3 *Doing*, p. 500.

Said.[4] Lentricchia's *Criticism and Social Change*, moreover, takes a pathbreaking step in pitting Burke against Paul de Man that makes Burke a player in contemporary debate.[5] Whatever its differences with Lentricchia's reading of Burke, the present study follows his lead down this path as it stages interactions between Burke and contemporary theory. Nonetheless, it's still true, as Michael Sprinker recently observed, that Burke remains "generally unassimilated" in the field of literary and cultural studies.[6] Perhaps a more general assimilation will finally occur as a by-product of the revival of rhetoric.[7]

Evidence of this possibility appears in John Bender and David E. Wellbery's authoritative narrative of this revival, where Burke appears as their exemplary figure: "Burke's work presents an especially forceful illustration of our argument bearing on rhetoricality ... Although Burke himself named his method 'dramatism,' a term that signals his abiding concern for the place of language in human action and interaction, the rhetorical thrust of his wide-ranging inquiry is evident on every page."[8]

Rhetoric's antagonists in their narrative are the enlightenment and romanticism, conceived less as distinct epochs than as interlocked parts of a single discursive regime: "Perhaps we can grasp here the affinity between the Enlightenment and Romantic destructions of rhetoric. The cogito, the unshakable foundation of certainty, generates at once the impersonal or abstracted subject of science and the creative, self-forming subject of Romanticism. Once these subjective functions took command over the field of discourse and representation, rhetoric

---

4 Booth, "Burke's Way," p. 2; Jameson, pp. 507–08; Lentricchia, *passim*; Macksey, "Concluding Remarks," *The Structuralist Controversy: The Languages of Criticism and the Sciences of Man*, eds. Richard Macksey and Eugenio Donato (Baltimore: Johns Hopkins University Press, 1972), p. 320; Said, "Roads Taken and Not Taken in Contemporary Criticism," *Contemporary Literature* 17 (1976): 331.

5 Lentricchia's book may be contrasted to Samuel B. Southwell's. Both use Burke to attack deconstruction, Lentricchia from the left, Southwell from the right.

6 "The War against Theory," *the minnesota review* n.s. 39 (1992–93), p. 106.

7 Burke has been most fully assimilated in a field where rhetoric has always been central: speech communication. In it, his dramatistic method is a major critical approach (Brock, "Dramatistic"). Speech scholars organized the 1984 conference on Burke, where the Kenneth Burke Society was formed (Simons); subsequently, the Society met in 1990 and 1993 (Chesebro, *Extensions* vii, 342). At the annual conference of the Speech Communication Association, the Society organizes a number of Burke panels; at the 1993 conference, for example, there were seven. In contrast, at the annual conference of the Modern Language Association, panels on Burke have been scheduled only intermittently, and the Society has yet to establish itself there as it has in speech.

8 "Rhetoricality: On the Modernist Return of Rhetoric," *The Ends of Rhetoric: History, Theory, Practice*, eds. Bender and Wellbery (Stanford University Press, 1990), p. 36.

could no longer maintain its cultural predominance."[9] With these in place, language and verbal interaction – the realm of rhetoric – were marginalized to the wings, leaving the stage to enlightenment certainty and romantic authenticity.

Today, of course, objectivism in the sense of scientific neutrality and subjectivism in the sense of totally autonomous creation are routinely dismissed. Terry Eagleton depicts the drama of the subject and the object in a parodic tone that gives it the quality of an outmoded fashion that we can now look back at with smiling condescension: "the drama of subject and object, the fraught narrative of their couplings and splittings, matchings and misalliances...like the tale of two incompatible partners continually warring to gain an edge over each other, who nevertheless cannot relinquish their fatal fascination for one another and resolve yet again, after another painful separation, to make a go of it."[10] Richard Rorty seconds Eagleton in observing that one can easily compile a long list of figures who during the last century have contributed in varying ways "to set[ting] aside the subject-object, representationalist notions of knowledge."[11]

Rhetoric is imposing itself today, not because the classics from the rhetorical tradition have once again become directly influential, but because of a dramatic reversal in which language and verbal interaction have advanced from the wings to take over the stage. One can, for example, see this reversal occur in Fish as rhetoric appears in his text even *avant la lettre*. Consider his well-known "How to Recognize a Poem When You See One," which depicts students construing a list of names as a religious poem in a narrative Fish designs to show that meaning is neither the representation of an object nor the expression of a subject but the construction of an "interpretive community." The closer one looks, Fish concludes, the more one sees "how unhelpful the terms 'subjective' and 'objective' finally are."[12] Marginalizing subject and object on one hand and foregrounding verbal interaction on the other, Fish steps into the world he later, in "Rhetoric," identifies as rhetorical.

It's now commonplace to observe that "objects" and "subjects" are

9 "Rhetoricality," pp. 11–12.
10 *The Ideology of the Aesthetic* (Oxford: Basil Blackwell, 1990), p. 70.
11 "Two Meanings of 'Logocentrism': A Reply to Norris," in *Redrawing the Lines: Analytic Philosophy, Deconstruction, and Literary Theory*, ed. Reed Way Dasenbrock (Minneapolis: University of Minnesota Press, 1989), p. 207.
12 *Is There a Text in This Class? The Authority of Interpretive Communities* (Cambridge: Harvard University Press, 1980), p. 336.

in some sense constructs. Constructionist theorists may disagree sharply: some render constructions visible by historicizing them; others, by deconstructing them. But they come together in agreeing that there is a constructive ingredient in our "realities." It's as if rhetoric on the one hand and subject–object on the other are so related that the constructivist dismantling of the latter entails the revival of the former. In the old paradigm, subject and object interact, the interaction produces a discourse, and enlightenment or romantic criteria determine whether to place trust in the discourse. In the new, trust is placed in the interaction among discourses more than in single discourses, the basis of the trust being neither enlightenment certainty nor romantic authenticity but rhetorical sayability.

The constructionist argument is now widespread. Anything put forward as an essentialist representation that claims transparently to reveal some entity antecedent to language is certain to be exposed as in some way constructing what it purports to represent. Even with the term "nonverbal," one can say that "nonverbal" is itself a word, a word enmeshed, like any other, in relations with other words, relations that make it possible for "nonverbal" to mean. Hence, in the nonverbal there is an ingredient of verbal construction. Burke gives his own picture of a constructionist world in a well-known passage, written over three decades ago:

[C]an we bring ourselves to realize . . . just how overwhelmingly much of what we mean by "reality" has been built up for us through nothing but our symbol systems? Take away our books, and what little do we know about history, biography, even something so "down to earth" as the relative position of seas and continents? . . . In school, as they go from class to class, students turn from one idiom to another. The various courses in the curriculum are in effect but so many different terminologies. And however important to us is the tiny sliver of reality each of us has experienced firsthand, the whole overall "picture" is but a *construct* of our symbol systems. To meditate on this fact until one sees its full implications is much like peering over the edge of things into an ultimate abyss. And doubtless that's one reason why, though man is typically the symbol-using animal, he clings to a kind of naive verbal realism that refuses to realize the full extent of the role played by symbolicity in his notions of reality.   (DM 5, italics added; see also TS 48)

In *GM*, Burke's constructionism takes the form of a constitutionalism, the overlap between the two suggested by Jameson in his observation that "the concept of the 'text' . . . liberates us from the empirical object – whether institution, event, or individual work – by displacing our attention to its *constitution* as an object ..." (Jameson's italics).[13] *GM*'s dialectic of constitutions is the text that underwrites, in ways to be introduced in the present chapter, a rhetoric of the subject. From a bird's-eye viewpoint, our narrative of Burke's career charts his steps to this constitutional model and his later steps away from it, although a few years before his death in 1993 he may have contemplated returning to this model or a revised version of it.

In the constructionist theme in current theoretical discussion, one sees rhetoric transform itself upwards from the pejorative "mere rhetoric" into a discursive "worldview" with considerable power, one that a generation of theorists has put on the historical map. Even the sophists are today being rehabilitated.[14] Perhaps, however, the time has arrived to force constructionism to interrogate itself more rigorously. We take the constructionist argument for granted and will have occasion to reenact it. Discourse constructs, but what is the limit of its constructive power? Fish's "How to Recognize a Poem When You See One" seems to see none, but is that a defensible position? In short, on one level, we take the constructionist argument for granted and on another we ask it some questions: How can one determine the limits of constructive power? When do we encounter what can't be constructed and therefore what can't be reconstructed or transformed? Granted, we are always in some sense inside constructions, but how can we, however indirectly, determine their limits?

To sharpen the question, it may help to juxtapose two often-cited passages. First, Derrida: *"There is nothing outside of the text [il n'y a pas de hors-texte]."*[15] Second, Jameson: "history is *not* a text, not a narrative, master or otherwise, but ... it is inaccessible to us except in textual form, and ... our approach to it and to the Real itself necessarily passes through its prior textualization, its narrativization in the political unconscious."[16] Jameson makes a concession to Derrida insofar as he lets stand the premise of the primacy of language, but he insists that we are not dealing only with textual processes. He is in effect alerting us that as we focus our attention on the rhetorical processes of linguistic constructing – or constituting – we risk lapsing into absurdity if we forget that these processes have to be distinguished from God's verbal

---

13 *The Political Unconscious: Narrative as a Socially Symbolic Act* (Ithaca: Cornell University Press, 1981), p. 297.
14 See, for example, Susan C. Jarratt, *Rereading the Sophists: Classical Rhetoric Refigured* (Carbondale: Southern Illinois University Press, 1991).
15 *Of Grammatology*, trans. Gayatri Chakravorty Spivak (Baltimore: Johns Hopkins University Press, 1976), p. 158.   16 *Political Unconscious*, p. 35.

fiats in Genesis. We obviously don't construct quite in the way He does. In *PC*, Burke argues, "Stimuli do not possess an *absolute* meaning. Even a set of signs indicating the likelihood of death by torture has another meaning in the orientation of a comfort-loving skeptic than it would for the ascetic whose world-view promised eternal reward for martyrdom" (35). The point could even be made without the qualification of torture, since obviously death itself, in any form, is constructed one way in the skeptic's discourse, another in the ascetic's. But no construction can pencil out the materiality of death, not even constructions of immortality. However complex the problem of identifying the constraints that limit the constructive power of language, we avoid it at our peril. We have our differences with Jameson's solution.[17] But we applaud his foregrounding of the methodological problem.

Jameson's formulation, in sum, focuses our attention on the need for a distinction between rhetorical realism and rhetorical idealism. Rhetorical realism – which we'll find in Burke – is required to preserve the achievements of the constructionist argument.

It's necessary to add that while the customary reading of "there is nothing outside the text" exemplifies exactly what we mean by rhetorical idealism, Derrida is more complicated than this reading allows. He suffered in America the fate of being read through the eyes of a generation brought up by the New Criticism that saw only a textuality of words, filtering out a more complex textuality of existences. This latter textuality, we'll see in chapter 6, is compatible with rhetorical realism.[18]

Idealism is the temptation rhetoric must constantly guard against in protecting itself from the pejorative "mere rhetoric." Eagleton suggests as much in his brief narrative of the history of rhetoric, where at the hands of Nietzsche and deconstruction rhetoric suffers an "ultimate

---

17 See my "A New Hermeneutic in Old Clothes: Fredric Jameson's *The Political Unconscious: Narrative as a Socially Symbolic Act," Works and Days: Essays in the Socio-Historical Dimensions of Literature and the Arts* 2 (1984): 57–62; and the correction that puts paragraphs in the correct order: *Works and Days* 3 (1985): 94.

18 "What I call 'text,'" Derrida insists, "implies all the structures called 'real,' 'economic,' 'historical,' socio-institutional, in short: all possible referents. Another way of recalling once again that 'there is nothing outside the text.' That does not mean that all referents are suspended, denied, or enclosed in a book, as people have claimed, or have been naive enough to believe and to have accused me of believing. But it does mean that every referent, all reality has the structure of a differential trace, and that one cannot refer to this 'real' except in an interpretive experience" – *Limited Inc*, ed. Gerald Graff (Evanston: Northwestern University Press, 1988), p. 148.

reversal": "Born at the juncture of politics and discourse, rhetoric now had the Fool's function of unmasking all power as self-rationalization, all knowledge as a mere fumbling with metaphor."[19] Eagleton's narrative closes by proposing a restoration of the links between rhetoric and politics found in antiquity in order to enable contemporary theory to draw on rhetoric in analyzing ideological practices and their effects – in short, ideology as rhetoric.

"Ideology cannot be deduced from economic considerations alone. It also derives from man's nature as a 'symbol-using animal'" (*RM* 146) – so Burke wrote in 1950. Today, in the wake of post-Marxist texts such as Ernesto Laclau and Chantal Mouffe's *Hegemony and Socialist Strategy*, one would have to reverse Burke's formulation simply to repeat his point, so far have the scales tipped to the rhetorical side. The economistic Marxism that Burke writes against has largely disappeared, marginalized by contemporary Marxism itself. In the process, ideology has become rhetorical, a turn particularly apparent to rhetorically trained eyes, such as those in the field of speech. An example is an essay-review in the *Quarterly Journal of Speech* that exposes the rhetoricizing of ideology in a number of contemporary Marxist texts, including two that will receive attention here: Laclau's *Politics and Ideology in Marxist Theory*, which antedates his post-Marxism, and Göran Therborn's *The Ideology of Power and the Power of Ideology*.[20]

In Therborn, rhetoric is present as a conceptual structure, though the term "rhetoric" is absent, the word itself not appearing even in passing, if my memory is accurate. This structure is especially evident in his conceptualization of ideological struggle, as he simultaneously applies rhetorical principles blindly and writes insightfully within Althusser's conception of ideology as the interpellation of subjects (the principles are identified in the interpolations):

[Ethos – persuasion based on the character of the speaker:] First, the speaker or "agitator" has to establish his or her right to speak to, and to be given a hearing by the subjects addressed, as being one of them or as having a

19 *Walter Benjamin; or Towards a Revolutionary Criticism* (London: Verso, 1981), p. 108. See also Eagleton's *Literary Theory: An Introduction* (Minneapolis: University of Minnesota Press, 1983), pp. 205–07.
20 Ray E. McKerrow, "Marxism and a Rhetorical Conception of Ideology," *Quarterly Journal of Speech* 69 (1983): 192–205. See also (1) my "Ideology as Rhetoric," rev. of *On Law and Ideology*, by Paul Hirst, *Praxis* 6 (1982): 181–82; and (2) the 1988 conference sponsored by the Rhetoric Society of America: *Rhetoric and Ideology: Compositions and Criticisms of Power*, eds. Charles W. Kneupper (Arlington: Rhetoric Society of America, 1989).

position and a kind of knowledge that somehow fits into their conception of what should command respect. [Epideictic or ceremonial rhetoric – praise or blame aiming to display what is worthy of honor or the reverse:] Second, he or she must assert the overriding relevance of a particular kind of identity, say that of "workers" as opposed to "Christians," "Englishman," or "football fans." This mode of interpellation therefore implies the assertion that certain features of the world are more important than others ... Third, interpellations of what is good and bad must be situated in relation to elements of the prevailing normative conceptions ... [Deliberative rhetoric – urging one to do or not do something:] Finally, the call to some kind of action implies that the proposed course is the only or the best possible way to achieve the normative goals.[21]

These principles can all be found in chapters two and three in the first part of Aristotle's *Rhetoric*.

Therborn's rhetoric may be contrasted to Georg Lukács's epistemology in *History and Class Consciousness*. What is decisive for Lukács is always a relationship between subject and object, the subject being a class position in a system of production and the object being the teleological shape of history. The proletariat distinguishes itself in history as the first and only subject destined to comprehend this object. In this fashion, as Jameson suggests, Lukács locates the solution to the problem of knowledge in historical narrative.[22] In Therborn, Lukács's privileging of subject–object as determinative gives way to a rhetorical interaction that forms the subject as rhetoric advances from the wings to take over the stage.

Therborn's conception of ideological struggle can be applied to Burke's "Revolutionary Symbolism in America" (RSA), a paper delivered in the midst of the Great Depression to a pro-communist audience at a congress of writers. Calling it "perhaps the most unusual paper delivered at the congress – at least it provoked [the] most dissent," Daniel Aaron defines Burke's ethos at the congress in describing him as "a controversial figure to the Communists, welcomed during this period as an influential ally, yet distrusted because of his ideologically dangerous fondness for paradox."[23] Lentricchia gives extensive coverage to the paper and the dissent it provoked (21–38)[24];

---

21 *The Ideology of Power and the Power of Ideology* (London: Verso, 1980), pp. 80–81.
22 *Marxism and Form* (Princeton University Press, 1971), pp. 189–90.
23 *Writers on the Left: Episodes in American Literary Communism* (New York: Harcourt, Brace and World, 1961), p. 287.
24 Lentricchia's analysis, along with Burke's paper and the discussion of it at the congress, were reprinted together in 1989 (Simons 267–96). Lentricchia errs in placing the delivery of the paper at Madison Square Garden (21). The congress began with a plenary session at the

one can get the general picture if one imagines Therborn appearing before an audience that would prefer to hear Lukács. What provoked dissent was Burke's proposal that the left substitute "people" for "worker" as its revolutionary subject. Invoking epideictic criteria of prevailing norms, Burke contended that in America the worker is an object of sympathy, not an identity to which one aspires (89). Deliberating how best to achieve the goal of enlisting large numbers in the revolutionary movement, he insisted "that one cannot extend the doctrine of revolutionary thought among the lower middle class without using middle-class values" (89–90). His audience, in contrast, saw the worker as a revolutionary subject produced for its role by the process of history itself.

Laclau echoes Burke when, in *Politics and Ideology*, he adds "people" to the traditional Marxist picture of class struggle: "Every class struggles at the ideological level *simultaneously* as class and as the people, or rather, tries to give coherence to its ideological discourse by presenting its class objectives as the consummation of popular objectives."[25] Laclau thus identifies a rhetoric of the people that is relatively autonomous of the economic infrastructure.

Relative autonomy, as a principle in contemporary theory, derives from Althusser's seminal displacement of "expressive" in favor of "structural" causality. Economism is expressive, built on an economic base that is the centered cause of the superstructures that express it. Structural causality is centerless interaction among the different elements of a social formation, each of which is relatively autonomous in being both passive and active relative to the others.[26] This displacement produced, Jameson remarks, "powerful and challenging oppositional currents in a host of disciplines, from philosophy proper to political science, anthropology, legal studies, economics, and cultural studies."[27]

In Althusser's structural interaction, ideology's role is to transform bodies into relatively autonomous subjects. This ideological decentering of the subject dismantles not only the subjects of enlightenment certainty and romantic authenticity but also the Lukácsean proletarian subject of history, a narratively centered epistemological subject

Mecca Temple and held its subsequent sessions at the New School for Social Research (*The New Masses*, 7 May 1935, p. 7).

25 *Politics and Ideology in Marxist Theory* (London: Verso, 1979), p. 109.

26 See particularly "Marx's Immense Theoretical Revolution," *Reading 'Capital,'* trans. Ben Brewster (London: Verso, 1979), pp. 182–93.   27 *Political Unconscious*, p. 37.

destined to arise in history to step beyond ideology to comprehend the object of history. Althusser accentuates his innovation as he writes against the Lukácsean grain: "Human societies secrete ideology as the very element and atmosphere indispensable to their historical respiration and life ... And I am not going to steer clear of the crucial question: *historical materialism cannot conceive that even a communist society could ever do without ideology*, be it ethics, art or 'world outlook.'"[28]

Within the subject—object framework, ideology is always the other of truth on the one hand and authenticity on the other. Althusser displaces this framework as he makes ideology the process by which subjects are formed and transformed. He keeps the term "ideology" but uses it to speak rhetorically in conceiving it as the discursive construction of the subject:

ideology "acts" or "functions" in such a way that it "recruits" subjects among the individuals [i.e., bodies] ... or "transforms" the individuals into subjects (it transforms them all) by that very precise operation which I have called *interpellation* or hailing, and which can be imagined along the lines of the most commonplace everyday police (or other) hailing: "Hey, you there!"[29]

While Althusser invokes Lacan in using notions such as "imaginary" and "mirror-structure,"[30] he speaks rhetorically when he comes to his key concept of interpellation. As in Therborn, rhetoric is present and absent in Althusser.

In his Althusserian phase prior to his post-Marxism, Laclau subscribes to Althusser's thesis, qualifying structural causality, that the economic element in a social formation is determinate "in the last instance."[31] *Politics and Ideology*, which is from this phase, tries to conceive a subject that is relatively *autonomous* as a "people" independent of the economic and *relatively* autonomous as a "class" expressing the economic. This conception, however, proves incoherent.

28 *For Marx*, trans. Ben Brewster (New York: Pantheon, 1969), p. 232.
29 "Ideology and Ideological State Apparatuses," *Lenin and Philosophy and Other Essays*, trans. Ben Brewster (New York: Monthly Review Press, 1971), p. 174. Althusser's authoritarian rhetoric of police command stands in striking contrast to Therborn's courtship rhetoric of adaptation to one's audience. For a critique of the authoritarianism of Althusser's rhetoric, see my "Notes toward a Marxist Rhetoric," *Bucknell Review* 28 (1983): 126–48.
30 "Ideology," pp. 162, 180.
31 This thesis proved, of course, to make Althusser vulnerable to the charge that he kicks expressive causality out the front door but lets it return through the back. Norman Geras's "Post-Marxism?" (*New Left Review* 163 [1987]: 40–82) helps one to see the sense in which Laclau and Mouffe turn Althusser against Althusser. Subscribing to the "in the last instance" formula himself, Geras distinguishes two sides in Althusser, one upholding this formula, the other showing the way, which Laclau and Mouffe follow, to rejecting it.

In one passage he postulates: "the first contradiction – at the level of mode of production – is *expressed* [italics added] on the ideological level in the interpellation of the agents as a *class*"; but in another, he sees "classes as the poles of antagonistic production relations which have no *necessary* form of existence at the ideological and political levels."[32] In his post-Marxist phase, Laclau gets himself out of this contradiction when he writes with Mouffe that "there is no logical connection whatsoever between positions in the relations of production and the mentality of the producers."[33] The assumption of an expressive connection between production and ideology is the trademark of the expressive causality within which ideology has traditionally been conceived. When this causality is refused, ideology becomes rhetoric.

But it becomes, in Laclau and Mouffe, a rhetoric that is more idealist than realist. Their discourse's antagonist is the economistic privileging of class struggle in the workplace over all other struggles. Writing after the proletariat's failure to realize the destiny classical Marxism envisioned for it and in the midst of numerous contemporary struggles at multiple sites – e.g., gender, race, ecology, nuclear disarmament – Laclau and Mouffe speak to a receptive audience as they displace the privileging of the workplace in favor of a democratic logic of equivalency that conceives all contemporary social movements as equivalent to and independent of one another. There is, however, a sharp turn in their last few pages. The logic of democratic equivalency becomes

only a logic of the elimination of relations of subordination and inequalities. The logic of democracy is not a logic of the positivity of the social, and it is therefore incapable of founding a nodal point of any kind around which the social fabric can be reconstituted ... This being the case, no hegemonic project can be based exclusively on a democratic logic, but must also consist of a set of proposals for the positive organization of the social.[34]

In these qualifications, their idealism exposes itself.

Their post-Marxism is realist insofar as, in the end, it discovers the problem reality imposes, but it is fundamentally idealist because it constructs for us a utopian umbrella and then tells us we're on our own when we leave its shelter. Laclau and Mouffe discover the real in recognizing that any positive construction of the social necessitates setting priorities and thereby reintroducing what the logic of equivalency

32 *Politics and Ideology*, pp. 107, 159.
33 *Hegemony and Socialist Strategy: Towards a Radical Democratic Politics* (London: Verso, 1985), pp. 84–85.   34 *Hegemony*, pp. 188–89.

labors to refuse. Even this logic of equivalency, considered as a coalition strategy, is a privileging of one strategy against other possibilities that would privilege race, gender, ecology, or something else as the struggle of struggles in our time. In short, Laclau and Mouffe privilege even in their seeming refusal of privileging.

Our point is not to decide which of these or other privilegings is correct, only to insist that the real forces us to decide. The real appears not as an enlightenment representation or romantic expression of itself, but as the necessity of setting priorities in calculating the best course of action in a specific situation. Laclau and Mouffe's democratic equivalency of new social movements, no matter how good it sounds, isn't necessarily the best strategy for political action or analysis.[35] It may be best in one situation, but not in another.

The real is gauged in the act, a prioritizing of this rather than that. The necessity of prioritizing is the constraint that rhetorical realism recognizes. Burke's premise that language is action posits the act as the form in which language registers this constraint. As action, language inscribes rhetorical sayability rather than either enlightenment certainty or romantic authenticity. Charting that inscription is what Burke's dramatism is all about.

Language as action structures our lived relation to the real. This lived relation is ideology's domain, as Althusser defines it — "So ideology is a matter of the *lived* relation between men and their world" — but in charting this lived relation, we will substitute the Burkean act for Althusser's Lacanian imaginary: "In ideology men do indeed express... *the way* they live the relation between them and their conditions of existence: this presupposes both a real relation and an '*imaginary*,' '*lived*' relation... In ideology the real relation is inevitably invested in the imaginary relation, a relation that *expresses* a *will* (conservative, conformist, reformist or revolutionary), a hope or a nostalgia, rather than describing a reality."[36]

It's possible, as Laclau and Mouffe show, to refuse the Marxist privileging of the economic (though as we refuse it routinely these days, we might pause to reflect on the possible irony that as we do so the globalization of the productive base may be transforming the superstructures of the world before our eyes). But the final lesson of

---

35 See, for example, "Rereading Laclau and Mouffe," *Rethinking Marxism* 4 (1991): 54–55, where Donna Landry and Gerald MacLean discuss a real contemporary struggle and expose the inadequacy of the logic of equivalency as a method for understanding it.

36 *For Marx*, pp. 233–34. See also "Ideology," pp. 162–70.

Laclau and Mouffe's text, which it teaches in spite of itself, is that one can refuse only *a* specific act, not the necessity of the act. "In the last instance," the real is determinate in necessitating the act.

To conclude this section, we can turn to a *locus classicus* from the opening paragraphs of Marx's *The Eighteenth Brumaire*: "Men make their own history, but they do not make it just as they please; they do not make it under circumstances chosen by themselves, but under circumstances directly encountered, given, and transmitted from the past." The world is always already prioritized for us as we enter history *in medias res*, but history is constructed in a concrete that is always hardening, never hardened, so that reconstruction is always possible, however difficult. The real necessitates the possibility of the new.

Althusser's conceptualization of ideology as the interpellation of subjects has acquired a life of its own, living on even as Althusser's work generally stands in eclipse. Eagleton evidences this as he recounts in *The Function of Criticism* how after his foreign adventure with Althusser, he returned home to the steady beacon of Raymond Williams, yet one wonders if this book could have been written without the prior example of Althusser's theory of ideology. Eagleton is at his best in analyzing the institutional interpellations of such nineteenth-century subjects as the "sage" and the "man of letters."[37]

Despite the widespread use of the theory, however, one central feature of it has been largely ignored, namely, the thesis that ideology is transhistorical, which is the corollary of the claim that there is no step beyond ideology: "Ideology has no history ... [I]deology ... is endowed with a structure and a functioning such as to make it a non-historical reality, i.e. an *omni-historical* reality, in the sense in which that structure and functioning are immutable, present in the same form throughout what we can call history." To avoid a possible misunderstanding, Althusser then adds that ideology is "not transcendent to all (temporal) history, but omnipresent, trans-historical."[38] As a transhistorical structure within history, if history were to disappear, ideology would disappear with it.

Jameson's often-quoted maxim "always historicize" exemplifies a currently widespread trend among theorists to affirm the historical against not only the transcendent but also the transhistorical. Paul Smith provides an example:

37 See my review of this book in *the minnesota review*, n.s. 25 (1985): 139–41.
38 "Ideology," p. 159, 161.

If different social formations and differing means of production can be empirically verifiable throughout the course of history, then the "individual's" existence will have been materially altered in such a way that the appeal to a "real" existence will be as questionable as an appeal to an idea of the natural genus of the human. This is because such a "reality" could be posited only as a transhistorical notion, as a structural instance which itself could not be historicized.[39]

For Smith, in other words, a transcendental appeal to "natural genus" is as essentialistic as a transhistorical appeal, even though a natural genus would exist independently of history, whereas the transhistorical would not. By thus lumping together the transhistorical and the transcendental, one arrives at an oversimplifying binary opposition between essentializing and historicizing. The emergence of this opposition may be attributed to the historicizers and the heat of rhetorical battle. As they historicize to challenge oppressive discursive regimes such as patriarchy by exposing them as historical constructions that are authoritarian, even totalitarian, in their effects, they absolutize the historical to sharpen their attack. Any methodological move wavering however slightly from the straight-line commitment to historicizing becomes vulnerable to categorical dismissal.

But perhaps the rhetorical battle has by now cooled enough to consider legitimating the transhistorical as a category of theoretical inquiry. We align ourselves with the historicizers in current debates, breaking ranks only to add a word of caution that without the transhistorical they may defeat their own aims. For historicizing can also be totalitarian. Taken to an absolute extreme, historicizing assumes that everything is totally malleable, mere clay in the hands of constructions and deconstructions. One can get to the totalitarian from a transcendental essence, but one can also get there from the assumption that human beings, practices, and institutions can be made to fit any shape whatsoever. Althusser intervened in Marxist discourse, not only to war against the deterministic essentializing that spawned faith in the inevitable march toward utopia in the grand narrative of history, but also to war equally against the historicizing that stressed the "relative" to the exclusion of the "autonomous."

Consider "proletarian science," which historicized away the autonomy of science in assuming that by virtue of being proletarian it was better than bourgeois science, a historicizing project that Lysenko rode to the

---

39 *Discerning the Subject*, Theory and History of Literature 55 (Minneapolis: University of Minnesota Press, 1988), p. 9.

pinnacle of Soviet science.[40] Correcting Lysenko's theoretical error was one of the principal purposes of Althusser's intervention into Marxist discourse; Lysenkoism stands for him as a paradigmatic example of the error historicism makes in recognizing no limits to historicizing.[41] Science is relative to history insofar as history makes it possible and even influences its direction, but science also has an autonomy that cannot be reduced to history.[42] Roy Bhaskar usefully distinguishes two dimensions of science: the "transitive" — for example, the historical dimension of physics, such as its contemporary discourse — from the "intransitive," the physical world existing independently of this discourse.[43] We can only know the intransitive through the transitive, but the historical construction and reconstruction of the transitive doesn't extend, like the power of God, to the intransitive.

By analogy, one wonders if the recent collapse of communism in one country after another teaches another lesson, one about relative autonomy in the context of the state. Ellen Meiksins Wood anticipated the possibility of such a lesson when she revisited the traditional Marxist claim that the bourgeois state is merely the instrument of the bourgeois class and reached the untraditional conclusion that insofar as liberal forms of the capitalist state contain the most successful restraints on state power developed so far, "it is possible that socialists have something to learn from 'liberalism' in this regard." Insisting that it's naive to think that any advanced society, socialist or otherwise, could be administered by "simple forms of direct and spontaneous democracy," Wood concludes, "It is difficult to avoid the conviction that even classless society will require some form of *representation*, and hence *authority* and even *subordination* of some people to others."[44]

Wood here introduces the transhistorical. Our concern is with the

---

40 See Dominique Lecourt, *Proletarian Science? The Case of Lysenko,* intro. by Louis Althusser, trans. Ben Brewster (London: NLB, 1977), chapter 5, "The Theory of 'Two Sciences' and State Ideology," particularly pp. 111–16.

41 Gregory Elliott, *Althusser: The Detour of Theory* (London: Verso, 1987), p. 86. See also Althusser's "Unfinished History," the introduction he writes for *Proletarian Science?,* pp. 7–16.

42 To square Althusser's ideological decentering of the subject with his insistence that there is an autonomy in science that cannot be historicized away, one can begin with Karl Popper's "Epistemology without a Knowing Subject," *Objective Knowledge: An Evolutionary Approach* (Oxford: Clarendon Press, 1981), pp. 106–52. Descartes and Kant have penetrated our culture so deeply that it's difficult to divorce ourselves from the habit of conceiving knowledge as dependent on faculties in a "knowing subject." Popper's text is the simplest way I know to begin to break this habit.

43 *Reclaiming Reality: A Critical Introduction to Contemporary Philosophy* (London: Verso, 1989), pp. 149–51.

44 *The Retreat from Class: A New "True" Socialism* (London: Verso, 1986), pp. 160, 156.

value of the category, not with Wood's application of it. Her important claim is that in any society, no matter how ideal, a structure of power is necessary and inevitable. Historicity is not denied; the structure of power in any society will be relative to history. But the structure is also autonomous; it cannot be historicized away. Ways must be devised to keep it in check. Otherwise, one risks disaster. These examples from the areas of science and the state are not presented as a conclusive demonstration of the value of the transhistorical. That, by itself, would require a substantial study. The examples are intended mainly to forestall any immediate dismissal of the category.

The transhistorical should, moreover, be far from scandalous to historical method, since Marx himself introduces it in the principal outline of his historical method, "Introduction" to *A Critique of Political Economy*. He insists, at the very outset, that to avoid the bourgeois misconception of capitalism as "natural," one must paradoxically begin on the transhistorical level, with production in general. Using the sub-category "instrument of production" to illustrate, he shows how from it one can proceed to different historical modes, ranging from "hand" to "capital." The transhistorical renders visible the concrete historicity of capitalism. One must rise not from the concrete to the abstract, but from the abstract to the concrete; observation of the concrete can never be any better than the abstractions brought to it — imagine a geologist and a lay person looking at the same rock. Furthermore, Marx offers guidelines for keeping the transhistorical distinct from the transcendental. His category of production should not become a Platonic idea of production. In Marx's text, the antagonist is Hegel's idealism. Marx insists that "rising from the abstract to the concrete is only the way in which thought appropriates the concrete, reproduces it as the concrete in the mind. But this is by no means the process by which the concrete itself comes into being."[45] To deploy the transhistorical, in short, one must avoid confusing it with the transcendental.

Marx's basic message is that the transhistorical is the abstraction in history that makes it possible to identify the concreteness of historicity. Foucault tried to reverse Marx on this methodological point, but by the end of his *History of Sexuality*, as we'll see in the concluding section of the present chapter, he succeeded only in painting himself into a conceptual corner. One can say that the

45 *Grundrisse: Foundations of the Critique of Political Economy*, trans. Martin Nicolaus (New York: Random House, 1973), pp. 85–86, 101.

transhistorical essentializes if one is willing to distinguish transhistorical from transcendental essentializing. Now that historicizing has triumphed over essentializing, it may be time to recognize distinctions that the struggle obscured.[46] The constructionist claim that all cultures are historical constructs is itself a mode of essentializing – short of a construct that leads to the annihilation of the human race, constructing cannot construct away its own condition of possibility.

"Lukács invented the concept of the 'Subject of History'" – so observes Etienne Balibar, one of Althusser's collaborators in *Reading "Capital,"* adding that in Althusser and the early Lukács there is a remarkable symmetrical opposition: in the whole of twentieth-century Marxism "they lie on its edges, as intellectual signals of its complete cycle."[47] To Lukács's subject of history, Althusser counters, "History is a process, and a *process without a subject.*"[48]

> Marxist philosophy must break with the idealist category of the "Subject" as Origin, Essence and Cause, *responsible* in its internality for all the determinations of the external "Object," of which it is said to be the internal "Subject." ... One cannot ... *think* real history (the process of the reproduction of social formations and their revolutionary transformation) as if it could be reduced to *an* Origin, *an* Essence, or *a* Cause (even Man), which would be its Subject – a Subject ... thus capable of *accounting for* the whole of the "phenomena" of history.[49]

For Lukács, history is an effect of a narratively centered transcendental subject; for Althusser, the subject is a decentered effect of ideology, a transhistorical structure in history. Lukács gives us a subject of history; Althusser, a history of subjects.

Rhetorical realism pits the transhistorical against the transcendental, an opposition that structures Burke's career from the 1920s to the 1940s as he shifts from the transcendental to the transhistorical. Facilitating this shift, we'll see in chapter 5, is Burke's distinction between essentializing and proportionalizing, which appears in "Freud – and the Analysis of Poetry" (FAP) and reappears in *GM*. The

---

46 Evidence that such a reevaluation of essentializing is on the horizon is Diana Fuss's fine book, *Essentially Speaking: Feminism, Nature and Difference* (New York: Routledge, 1989).

47 "Non-Contemporaneity of Althusser," *The Althusserian Legacy,* eds. E. Ann Kaplan and Michael Sprinker (London: Verso, 1993), p. 6.

48 *Essays in Self-Criticism,* trans. Grahame Lock (London: NLB, 1976), p. 51. See also pp. 94–99, 195–207 in the same text as well as Althusser, *Politics and History: Montesquieu, Rousseau, Hegel and Marx,* trans. Ben Brewster (London: NLB, 1972), pp. 182–86.

49 *Essays in Self-Criticism,* pp. 96–97.

distinction can be illustrated by applying it to a hypothetical situation that Therborn imagines:

> when a strike is called, a worker may be addressed as a member of the working class, as a union member, as a mate of his fellow workers, as the long-faithful employee of a good employer, as a father or mother, as an honest worker, as a good citizen, as a Communist or an anti-communist, as a Catholic, and so on. The kind of address accepted − "Yes, that's how I am, that's me!" − has implications for how one acts in response to the strike call.[50]

Burke uses Freud as an example of essentializing that takes the sexual ingredient in a person's motivation to be primary and considers all others as sublimated variants; proportionalizing, which Burke prefers, considers instead the interrelations among the ingredients to determine their relative weights in a given situation (FAP 261–62). Applied to Therborn's example, essentializing would privilege in advance one of the multiple subject positions addressing the worker, whereas proportionalizing would examine the interrelations among the positions to see which gets privileged in the strike situation.

Such essentializing becomes transcendental when it not only crowns one subject position in the worker's situation and demands that all others defer to it, but also roots this position in a foundation prior to history, making its authority higher than anything in history, a higher law not a constructed law. The transcendental locates the real, in short, in a "human nature." The transcendental subject is divided in the sense that one foot is foundational, the other historically contingent. The overcoming of the division can be conceived as a lyrical epiphany, a momentary breakthrough that may make a permanent difference in one's experience, but that cannot sustain itself in reality; or as a linear narrative, where instead of an epiphany there is a utopia at the end of history. Both conceptions appear in Burke before he leaves the transcendental for the transhistorical.

Lukács exhibits the transcendental real in a fashion that Foucault sums up in the process of discrediting it:

> Continuous history is the indispensable correlative of the founding function of the subject . . . the certainty that time will disperse nothing without restoring it in a reconstituted unity . . . Making historical analysis the discourse of the continuous and making human consciousness the original subject of all historical development and all action are the two sides of the

---

50 *Ideology*, p. 78. Fish gives a comparable example in listing the various roles he plays (teacher, father, citizen, Jew, Democrat, etc.) and discussing how crises may arise that put them into conflict (*Doing*, pp. 29–32).

same system of thought. In this system, time is conceived in terms of totalization and revolutions are never more than moments of consciousness.[51]

Continuous history is "grand narrative," whose loss of credibility Jean-François Lyotard identifies as one dimension of our postmodern condition.[52] The beginning and end of history, Lukács's Hegelian meta-subject lives in a history that alienates it from its essence, but the essence transcends history, so restoration to it is inevitable. Alienation is a stretching of an unbreakable rubber-band – the revolutionary springing back is inexorable, occurring for Lukács in the proletariat's fulfillment of its historic destiny. The test demonstrating the transcendental real is the prediction of the uplifting experience that the restoration of unity will effect. This prediction is based on – to borrow from another Foucault sketch of the transcendental subject – "the idea that there does exist a nature or a human foundation ... [that entails] that man can be reconciled with himself, once again find his nature or renew contact with his roots and restore a full and positive relationship with himself."[53]

Therborn, in contrast, is postmodern in the sense that in post-modernism, as Jameson observes, "the alienation of the subject is displaced by the fragmentation of the subject."[54] Therborn's worker exemplifies this fragmentation, as for Therborn there is no transcendental basis for a priori privileging of any subject position. His worker is in the transhistorical real, which postulates that we live doubly, as bodies in a nature prior to history and as subjects in cultures constructed in history, and that the two together constitute the real. Lukács's alienated subject at least has a home to return to, however far off it may be. The home for Therborn's worker must be constructed from the subject positions at hand, with no transcendental guidance.

Rhetorical realism refuses the transcendental claim by rewriting it as a historical act, with the help of the somewhat different version of Burke's distinction appearing in *GM*, in its dialectic of constitutions: (1) "the essentializing strategy would be that of selecting some one clause or other in the Constitution, and judging a measure by reference to it"; (2) contrastingly, the "proportional strategy ... would test the

51 *The Archaeology of Knowledge*, trans. A. M. Sheridan Smith (New York: Harper & Row, 1976), p. 12.
52 *The Postmodern Condition: A Report on Knowledge*, trans. Geoff Bennington and Brian Massumi, Theory and History of Literature 10 (Minneapolis: University of Minnesota Press, 1984), pp. 37–41.
53 "The Ethic of Care for the Self as a Practice of Freedom," Interview, *The Final Foucault*, eds. James Bernauer and David Rasmussen (Cambridge: MIT Press, 1988), p. 2.
54 "Postmodernism, or the Cultural Logic of Late Capitalism," *New Left Review* 146 (1984): 63.

measure by reference to *all* the wishes in the Constitution...The proportional method would also require explicit reference to a *hierarchy* of wishes" (380). The term "hierarchy" adds a new dimension to Burke's analysis. One of the values Burke sees in the Constitution as an analytic model is that its clauses — its "wishes" — are not in a hierarchy fixed in advance but are hierarchized when the Supreme Court acts. The difference between essentializing and proportionalizing is that hierarchizing is implicit in one and explicit in the other, but there is hierarchizing in both, for both are equally acts, historical contingencies.

Applying Burkean constitutional analysis to Lukács, just as the Supreme Court may essentialistically test a legislature's law against a single constitutional clause, Lukács tests his law of human nature against the clause of the workplace: "one man during an hour is worth just as much as another man during an hour. Time is everything, man is nothing"; "in the proletariat...the process by which a man's achievement is split off from his total personality and becomes a commodity leads to a revolutionary consciousness."[55] The transcendental spark of humanity in the "total personality" is what commodification can never extinguish. Where alienation is greatest, there restoration begins — the unbreakable rubber-band springs back when it is stretched to the unreachable breaking-point. Other subject positions besides that of the worker are swept aside with a version of the opposition between truth and falsehood in which proletarian class consciousness comprehends history and all others are lost in the false consciousness of ideology — hierarchization by marginalization designed to conceal the act of hierarchization. Therborn, in contrast, is proportional. Just as the court proportionalizes when it tests a law from the standpoint of multiple clauses, Therborn's worker is addressed from the standpoint of multiple subject positions, no one of which is privileged transcendentally. Subject positions marginalized in Lukács have their day in court in Therborn. In responding to the strike call, whatever that response might be, Therborn's worker would hierarchize them, giving them different proportional weights.

Burke's use of the term "hierarchy" is a terminological gamble, since it has strong negative connotations. To read his use of the term properly, it's important first to dissociate "hierarchy" the noun from "hierarchize" the verb. The noun evokes something fixed and authoritarian, like an ecclesiastical hierarchy. With Burke, the emphasis

55 *History and Class Consciousness: Studies in Marxist Dialectics*, trans. Rodney Livingstone (Cambridge: MIT Press, 1971), pp. 89–90, 171.

is on the verb. The noun presents itself as eternally fixed, but the verb demystifies this fixity, exposing it as an effect of an act of hierarchizing. Conceiving the real as transcendental, Lukács fixes a hierarchy in which the subject position of the proletariat is privileged as the place of truth. Conceiving the real as transhistorical, Therborn destabilizes this hierarchy; if his worker strikes as a proletarian, that act will be a contingent hierarchization, not conformity to the truth of human nature.

As a verb, then, hierarchize has connotations that overlap with the positive connotations of terms such as "deciding" or "choosing," so that one might wonder why Burke doesn't simply dispense with "hierarchy" altogether in favor of one of these. The reason, as we'll see in chapter 6, is that Burke distinguishes voluntaristic choices from necessitarian ones. "Hierarchize" is used loosely when associated with the positive connotations of "voluntaristic," more precisely when associated with the negative connotations of "necessitarian." "Hierarchize" should have the connotations of "facing reality."

The example of Therborn's worker dramatizes the fashion in which the real appears in the form of the necessity of hierarchy. The multiple subject positions, with their different motivations, must be hierarchized. That will happen no matter what; something has to give way to something else. Hierarchizing is not an option we choose but a necessity we face.

The real is hierarchized for us by history, but never permanently. In the most fundamental sense, the real is not what is hierarchized, but what necessitates the act of hierarchizing. As the earlier example of Laclau and Mouffe suggests, one can refuse *a* hierarchy, such as the economistic, but one cannot refuse the necessity of hierarchy as such.

Behind Therborn's fragmented worker stands Althusser's concept of ideological state apparatuses (ISAs). In conceptualizing ISAs, Althusser offers a list that includes religion, education, family, law, politics, trade unions, media, culture (arts, sports, etc.).[56] This concept is a corollary of the thesis that history is a process without a subject. The subject is not, as in Lukács, the beginning and end of history, but a decentered effect of history, formed through such apparatuses. From these, the subject derives discourses articulating motivations that may conflict or reinforce one another in ways that the example of Therborn's fragmented worker suggests. An additional complication is that a

---

56 "Ideology," p. 143.

motivational discourse can itself be a site of struggle. There can be conflict within discourses as well as among them. One can, for example, imagine a debate about union discourse, one side ready to aggrandize one segment of the working class at the expense of others (the typical form of trade union discourse), the other side equally ready to subordinate the interests of different segments to the primacy of the interests of the class as a whole. One can strike for different reasons.

A society in which such conflict never arose, in which in every situation one knew automatically what should give way to what, would be a society that could be characterized as either utopian or the dream of totalitarianism – take your pick – but either way it would fall off the stage of history. Such a society would be homeostatic. Change could come only from without.

It's important to stress that Althusser's apparatuses constitute a list, not a systematic typology. This list is a cue for the kind of thing to look for in the formation of subjects in any historical situation, not a prescriptive table that tells you in advance what you will find. Constructing such a typology would be an extraordinarily difficult enterprise that would be worth undertaking only if there was the possibility of a big theoretical payoff at the end of the line. But in this case, there is more risk than payoff. The risk is that any such typology would be an ethnocentric projection. The notion of the transhistorical no doubt arouses suspicion precisely from the fear that it may simply be a device for disguising such a projection. That is why less is more in this case. The abstract is better than the concrete. Althusser's transhistorical claim that there is no society without ideology should be construed as positing only that there are always multiple motivational discourses. The possible forms these might take must be left to historical analysis. The claim simply stands as a point from which one can think the historicity of any set of discourses. Even the term "state" in ISA may be too concrete. To decide, one would have to determine if the term is conceived transhistorically, as a structure of authority necessary in any society; or narrowly, as the structure of the nation-state, which wasn't always here and which is now being subjected to pressures great enough to prompt predictions such as Perry Anderson's that "the future belongs to the set of forces that are overtaking the nation-state."[57]

In sum, the transhistorical model of the subject consists of a

57 *A Zone of Engagement* (London: Verso, 1992), p. 367.

conjuncture of conflicting motivational discourses in a single body. The term "body" merits underlining to avoid the ambiguity of "individual," which may refer to the body or the subject in the rhetoric of individualism. In an individualistic culture, it's difficult to think about the problem of the subject without lapsing into this rhetoric. Whether Therborn lapses into it, for instance, is not altogether clear. Since his worker is a recurrent example in the chapters ahead, it's important to clarify the present study's interpretation of his text. First, "worker" is understood as "worker-qua-body" to avoid the potential confusion of "a worker may be addressed . . .," which seems to privilege "worker" in advance. Only the body can be so privileged in advance insofar as being a body is a condition of being addressed discursively, as a worker or as anything else. Also potentially confusing are the "I" and "me" in the interpellative response to the strike call: "Yes, that's how I am, that's me." The danger here is to read this response as presupposing a classical individual standing apart from all the roles society offers and choosing among them.[58] The present study interprets this "me" as a cultural construct. "Me" refers to an individual only insofar as any culture presumably refers to the singularity of the body as an organism, even if only negatively, as in Burke's example of Plotinus, who, after determining that material existence is estrangement from God, "is said to have been unwilling to name either his parents or his birthplace" (*GM* 34), so that Plotinus' "me" excluded the bodily attributes of having been born of earthly parents at a singular time and place. The singularity of the body, then, is overlaid by the plurality of cultural constructions of what the body is. In reading Therborn's text, the present study accentuates such differences as those between a working-class "me" and a Catholic "me."

The conflict among the "me's" is the ingredient in this transhistorical model that insures its rhetorical realism. The risk of lapsing into rhetorical idealism arises from the postulation that the subject takes form in a field of motivational discourses. There is a sense in which the conflict is a function of the discourses. Simplifying Therborn's situation somewhat, imagine the worker-qua-body pulled one way by working-class discourse dictating a strike and another by Catholic discourse

---

58 Althusser's theory of interpellation, which stands behind Therborn's text, has been read along these lines by Paul Hirst in *On Law and Ideology* (Atlantic Highlands, NJ: Humanities Press, 1979), pp. 64–68. Eagleton enlists himself among those persuaded by this reading; see "Ideology, Fiction, Narrative," *Social Text* 2 (1979): 63. For further consideration of the issue, see my "Notes toward a Marxist Rhetoric," *Bucknell Review* 28 (1983): 143–44.

dictating deference to the authority of the employer. Without both discourses, there would be no conflict. But the conflict is a function not only of discourse but also of the material world. Rhetorical realism concedes that we can't get outside the constructions of discourse, but it insists that neither can we construct our way outside the materiality of living. Discourses participate in the creation of the conflict when they compete to put the worker-qua-body in different places, some having it join the strike, others putting it elsewhere. But no discourse can put this body in two places at the same time. Someone as ingenious as Fish might produce a text – "How to Recognize a Conflict When You See One" – in which it is *said* that the body is in different places at the same time, but the body could still not materially *be* in different places at the same time. That is a physical impossibility that, like death, cannot be constructed away.

There is thus in the struggle among competing discourses a material as well as a discursive level. The real encompasses both. As Burke puts it, an ideology makes a "body hop around in certain ways; and that same body would have hopped around in different ways had a different ideology happened to inhabit it" (*LSA* 6). To be in the real, simultaneously conditioned by material and discursive levels, is to be a cultural animal. Burke's term "act," as theorized in *GM*, is designed to encompass this double conditioning.

Laclau and Mouffe provide a useful retrospective review of the rhetorical struggle during the last few decades revolving around the opposition between the fragmented and transcendental subjects. Initially, "the rejection of the notion of subject as an originative and founding totality . . . [logically emphasized] dispersion, detotalization or decentring of certain positions with regard to others." In the process, all modes of relating the dispersed subject positions fell victim "to the suspicion of a retotalization which would surreptitiously reintroduce the category of subject as a unified and unifying essence." Eventually, the "*dispersion* of subject positions [hardened] into an effective *separation* among them."[59] It's this absolute separation that Laclau and Mouffe challenge because it stands in the way of any attempt to reunify the fragmented subject for political action on any ground whatsoever.

Perhaps this rhetorical battle is another that has cooled enough to

59 *Hegemony*, pp. 115–16.

make it easier for retotalization, rhetorically conceived, to get a fair hearing. Rhetorical retotalization is an alternative to the polar extremes of transcendental totalization on the one hand and fragmentation on the other. Transhistorical rather than transcendental, rhetorical retotalization is always a contingent hierarchizing, hence always subject to re-retotalization, re-re-retotalization, and so on to historical infinity. So conceived, retotalization is a form of totalizing that is not a mere front for an originary subject.

This rhetorical alternative is not simply a middle ground. It can also rewrite the extremes. As we've seen, rhetoric can rewrite Lukács's transcendental claim as a historically contingent hierarchizing. At the other extreme, the fragmented subject is the postmodern attempt to refuse hierarchy as absolutely as Lukács absolutizes his hierarchy. Derrida's "differance" exemplifies this refusal: "It commands nothing, rules over nothing, and nowhere does it exercise any authority."[60] In response to a question about where he is going, moreover, Derrida quips, "I was wondering myself if I know where I am going. So I would answer you by saying, first, that I am trying, precisely, to put myself at a point so that I do not know any longer where I am going."[61] This directionlessness is idealist in the sense that it cannot be lived, as Derrida's realist side seems to acknowledge in his wry tone. Only insofar as it's directional in spite of itself is it livable, a hierarchical privileging of going nowhere in particular against going somewhere definite.

Theorizing retotalization as relatively autonomous must resist the tendency to think of history and autonomy as a binary opposition in which autonomy is whatever escapes historical determinism. Conceiving autonomy this way makes the search for it a bit like the proverbial peeling of the onion and finding nothing at the core. What, after all, could escape history except something prior to history? As long as such priority is theoretically unacceptable, the search for autonomy within the framework of this binary will always result in an impasse. To get beyond this binary, one must get beyond the rhetoric of individualism in which it's inscribed. If we concede that the individual is a subject position historically invented like any other, then we must also concede that there must be some space for its invention. This space is the transhistorical scene for the rhetorical invention of

---

60 *Speech and Phenomena: And Other Essays on Husserl's Theory of Signs*, trans. David B. Allison (Evanston: Northwestern University Press, 1973), p. 153.
61 *Structuralist Controversy*, eds. Macksey and Donato, p. 267.

subjects, including the subject of individualism. That is where to find autonomy.

Relative autonomy and the transhistoricity of autonomy are two ways of saying the same thing. Autonomy is relative because it is always in history; there is no individualistic Lockean autonomy in a state of nature. History is the condition of autonomy, not a threat to it; autonomy is not apart from but a part of history. While history is the condition of autonomy, autonomy cannot be historicized away because it's a transhistorical structure in the historical process. With the help of a card-game metaphor, a sketch of this autonomous structure can be derived from the situation of Therborn's worker-qua-body. A normal card game is enough to get started, although not enough to complete the sketch.

The subject positions competing for this body's commitment are in effect cards dealt by history in a game from which there is no exit. The body cannot leave the table for a state of nature. But history, in dealing the cards, is also giving the body a hand to play – different hierarchies are possible – so that there is autonomy in the game. Totalitarianism might try to historicize away the autonomy by standing behind the body to make sure the hand is played the authorized way, but that would only drive the autonomy underground, not historicize it away.

A shortcoming in this game is that as it stands it is too synchronic. Presupposing a fixed number of cards and rules, it is in effect a totalizing set of structuralist combinations in which all possibilities are determined in advance. The game must be revised to accommodate the diachrony of history. The game must be abnormal, one in which the rules can be changed in the middle of play – a card game with a rule by which after play starts cards can be added or dropped and the rules for playing them changed – a game, in short, where rhetorical invention can transform the game. Burke's act is designed to theorize such transformations. This act is a constitutional act, the US Constitution serving as Burke's principal model. The Constitution serves his purposes because cards can be added or dropped through its amendment procedure, and new rules for playing the cards, old and new, can be put in place by the Court any time it acts. The Constitution says what the Court reads it as saying. The Constitution is the rule, but the Court is repeatedly transforming the rule. The Constitution is thus a game in which transforming the rules of the game is a central part of the game.

Therborn's worker-qua-body, in the references to it in later chapters, should always be understood to be in this constitutional game of changing the rules of the game. The rule of rules in this game — the unchanging rule by which rules can be changed — is the agon of history. "Constitutions," Burke emphasizes, "are agonistic intruments" (*GM* 357). The autonomy of rhetorical invention in this agon is always relative, limited by material conditions and configurations of power, but rhetorical invention can never be reduced to these conditions, as their mere epiphenomenon. The subject positions invented in history are not an afterthought, but forces that galvanize bodies for the role they play in making history. Reading Therborn's text in the context of this game, the present study understands the act it depicts — "Yes, that's how I am, that's me!" — as occurring in the agon of history. Only this agon, later chapters argue, can theorize this act. The normal card game structurally decenters the individual in one sense, while in another it leaves to the individual the playing of the hand, as we are free to speak sentences in the language that speaks us. The abnormal game that displaces it continues this decentering but makes the agon the ultimate arbiter of play. This agon decides whether the subject that is sayable — "that's how I am, that's me" — is this one or that. In this game, it's not language that speaks us, but history.

Instead of positioning autonomy in the individual, then, rhetorical realism positions it in history, at the heart of agonistic struggle. Burke remarks in *RM* that a subject can be defined narratively either by a beginning (he's a bastard) or an end (he was born to be hung) (13–15). Rhetorical autonomy is beginning and end, both origination and re-origination, a molten liquidity that can harden but that can always be agonistically melted down and transformed. Autonomy is a potentiality that history creates and that is actualized in the rhetorical invention of new subject positions, often at great risk to the inventors. Opportunities for such invention are greater at some times than at others; not everyone lives at moments of epochal transformation.

The agonistic space of rhetorical invention is humanistic in a traditional sense insofar as it is a space of creation. But the subject positions created in this space are not necessarily themselves humanistic. The subject of fascism is a subject position too. This consideration thus raises the age-old issue of whether there is in rhetoric an ethical principle that can at least moralize rhetoric if not prevent immorality. Rhetoric has always been haunted by the suspicion that when all is said and done it's just a hired gun. *RM* addresses this issue, on which hangs the determination of whether a rhetoric of the subject is a new humanism, that is, a basis for a new humanistic critique of social formations.

In sum, action entails hierarchy, either implicit or explicit, conscious or unconscious. This hierarchizing can become a complicated affair when discursively rationalized. One could respond to a strike call as a Catholic, complete with a principled account of a Catholic ordering of subject positions. Further, the invention of a new subject position entails re-hierarchizing insofar as it involves new relations among old positions. For example, the tension in the opening pages of *Robinson Crusoe* is between father and son. At issue is whether Crusoe is to be the obedient son or the individual author of his destiny. Changing the rules of the game, Defoe gives Crusoe the new trump card of individualism, allowing him to disobey his father to launch a career in which he becomes wealthy and even acquires a colony, an entrepreneurial form of landed wealth in a culture that values landed wealth above all other kinds. Not, however, without considerable rhetorical struggle, for Crusoe carries the burden of guilt for disobeying his father – calling it his "original sin" – even as he becomes the hero in, as Ian Watt puts it, "an epic of individual enterprise."[62] This new individual needed a new constitutional rationalization, which Defoe found in God, to Whom Crusoe turns on the island, where he eventually persuades himself that his deepest individualistic desires are promptings from God. When he finally overcomes his uncertainty about whether to make war against the cannibals, it is such a prompting that settles the issue. In short, Crusoe's disobedience introduces at the inception of his career the re-hierarchizing that the new subject of individualism entails, and this new hierarchy is constitutionally legitimated when God sanctions it.

Having identified the agon of history as the site of the invention of subject positions, we must now scrutinize this agon at the transhistorical level. The transhistorical agon need be only concrete enough to distinguish the form of the agonistic resistance involved in historical transformation. The problem, in other words, is to determine when an agon is historically transformative, at least potentially, and when it is not. We'll address this problem through a consideration of Foucault,

---

62 "*Robinson Crusoe* as a Myth," in *Robinson Crusoe*, ed. Michael Shinagel, Norton Critical Edition (New York: W. W. Norton & Co., 1975), p. 321. Reprinted from *Essays in Criticism* 1 (1951): 95–119.

particularly *The History of Sexuality (HS)*,[63] whose deliberation about resistance is instructive for our purposes. But first we must consider Foucault's conception of power, which makes power more visible than ever before, but paradoxically seems thereby to make resistance to it more difficult rather than less.

The power that interests Foucault least is physical constraint. Even in his *Discipline and Punish*, prison is more a metaphor than a building. Power presupposes the freedom to resist, however limited the options: "At the very heart of the power relationship, and constantly provoking it, are the recalcitrance of the will and the intransigence of freedom. Rather than speaking of an essential freedom, it would be better to speak of an 'agonism' − of a relationship..."[64] The agon is thus in Foucault's text, there for us to interrogate.

Foucault even inscribes his analytic method within an agon. As he puts it, "I would like to suggest another way to go further toward a new economy of power relations... It consists of taking the forms of resistance against different forms of power as a starting point... For example, to find out what our society means by sanity, perhaps we should investigate what is happening in the field of insanity. And what we mean by legality in the field of illegality."[65] With this methodological starting-point, Foucault portrays any orthodoxy not as it sees itself in the self-portrait of its own rationality, but as an imposition of power.[66] In its self-portrait, orthodoxy is empowerment in the fully positive sense. In Foucault's portrait, empowerment is orthodoxy's most insidious instrument of control. Prohibition falls within the scope of power, as Foucault conceives it, but the power that interests him most is not such negative power but the positive, productive power of empowerment. In teaching the postmodern world that power and knowledge are inseparable, Foucault qualifies the Baconian idea that knowledge is power in the sense of empowerment with the proviso that knowledge is also an effect and instrument of power. Knowledge is still knowledge, but in its effects it is also a mode of control. To be empowered through knowledge is also to be controlled by it.

---

63 *History of Sexuality: An Introduction*, trans. Robert Hurley (New York: Pantheon, 1978). *HS* is used in the text and, when necessary, in parenthetical page references.

64 "The Subject and Power," *Critical Inquiry* 8 (1982): 790.   65 Ibid., p. 780.

66 We have no great investment in the term "orthodoxy." Readers may wish to substitute another that works better for them. "Orthodoxy" is for us close to Foucault's "normalization," but using his term would imply that we are limiting ourselves to peculiar features of modern society, which is not our intention. Our choice is also partly influenced by Burke's occasional use of this term for a similar purpose.

Conceived in this positive sense, power is more visible, penetrating areas such as sexuality previously thought to be outside power, and even dismantling traditional humanistic discourses of liberation, such as those, like Lukács's, that take the form of "continuous history." These discourses, seeing power as oppressive when it starves human interests rooted in our nature and as productively empowering when it helps them to blossom, offer a perspective from which liberation is at least thinkable. But for Foucault, power forms the subject. Whatever interests the subject has are posterior to power, not prior to it. One cannot start with interests, rooted in nature or anywhere else, and then determine whether a power serves or frustrates them. One must start with power. Because there are no prior interests, there is seemingly no basis from which to prescribe a remedy for the ills of power. Throwing out these discourses, in short, seems to throw the baby of liberation out with the bath-water of the discourse of liberation. By producing interests, power seems to be above their judgmental eye, and by coming anonymously from everywhere, it seems to be nowhere. The tail that wags the dog, power produces us and always stays just beyond our grasp. Power is a process without a subject (Foucault's retort to Althusser's "history is a process without a subject"?). Power is exercised with purpose but it doesn't derive from a somewhere. It's not locatable – a Bastille one could storm. One can't find the "headquarters" of power because power is in "comprehensive systems" that are "anonymous" (*HS* 95). As it becomes more visible, power thus also becomes more difficult to resist.

In its transindividuality, power also displaces individualism.[67] Individualism portrays itself, of course, as outside all orthodoxies, but it is an orthodoxy still. It remains so, moreover, no matter how deeply one roots individualism, as Foucault's analytic of power is equipped to demonstrate. Consider automatic writing. Some twenty years ago I heard a poet lecture on how he uses it to tap into what he conceives to be his authentic self. He relies, necessarily, on his conscious self to produce a finished poem, but he always selects his most important images from words that arise spontaneously from within during automatic writing. He thus conforms to an orthodoxy based on a knowledge of the condition of authentic self-expression. This knowledge is an effect of a power that emerged in history and a hub around which are clustered multiple practices that continue to reproduce this knowledge, including techniques like automatic writing for producing poetry, pedagogies for teaching such techniques, and strategies for the

---

67 See, for example, Foucault, *Power/Knowledge*, trans. Colin Gordon *et al.* (New York: Pantheon, 1980), p. 98.

valorization of the poetry produced. Left to its own devices, such a circle of knowledge and power could perpetuate itself forever.

In this example, orthodoxy sees itself in the truth of romantic authenticity. A Foucauldian demystification exposes this truth as a power that empowers. The deep human and personal interests expressed in the images rising from within in automatic writing are exposed as posterior to power, not prior. They arise posterior to the knowledge that is the incentive to search for them and to distinguish the authentic from the inauthentic. A Foucauldian analysis reveals this truth of authenticity not as the eternal truth it sees in itself, but as a rhetorical sayability relative to a time and place, a sayability that was more acceptable when I heard it twenty years ago than it is today. I couldn't hear now what I heard then. This example of sayability demonstrates that we cannot engage in rhetorical interaction without assumptions about the truth of motivation, our own and our audience's. Any regime of orthodoxy is rhetorical in the sense that it consists of authorized motivations that have predictable rhetorical force among the orthodox. Such predictability makes cultural life navigable.

Foucault's originality resides, in part, in his reconstruction of what is commonly called the socializing process. To give his reconstruction a name, one might term it the "powerizing process." Becoming a cultural animal is a long travail of seemingly endless rituals, pervading all areas of life, that inscribe dependable orthodox behavior. Foucault reconstructs the relations in these rituals as powerizing rather than socializing relations: "I don't believe," he remarks, "there can be a society without relations of power, if you understand them as means by which individuals try to conduct, to determine the behavior of others."[68] All

---

68 "Ethic of Care for the Self," p. 18. Strictly speaking, the relations can only be constructed and reconstructed, not described. Foucault speaks as a rhetorical realist in remarking that an anthropological description of a society "is a construct in relationship to another description," because he adds, "That does not mean that there is nothing there and that everything comes out of somebody's head" (p. 17). Recognizing a relationship of competition among constructs presupposes recognition that they are competing over the same "thing," best conceived not as an entity but as a problem: for example, how are bodies transformed into cultural animals? Recognition of the problem makes it possible to debate the competing constructions: socializing vs. powerizing. Without the common problem we wouldn't see the competition; without the competition we wouldn't see the problem (one construction would stand for reality until a challenger came along). Even "the transformation of bodies into cultural animals" is a construction, so that one could debate it too, but that would simply force a reformulation of the common problem. Debate presupposes sharing a problem; one is not possible without the other. This example involves a general rhetorical principle to be introduced in a later chapter, with the help of Derrida, to demonstrate that the rhetoric of competing constructions displaces philosophy. There is something beyond rhetoric, but it can be detected only indirectly, through such competition, as rhetoric realizes.

the distinguishing features of Foucault's exposure of power are designed to uncover this powerizing process. There is the focus on local contexts of power, a choice that is Foucault's methodological wager against Marx that one can uncover more about power by beginning with concrete, micro-level operations than with an abstraction at the macro-level like production. Within these contexts, in turn, power is examined not as a point of concentration, such as state power, but as a relation where the persons occupying the positions in the relationship may even change places. Power is relationality rather than concentration, a conception that reaches its logical conclusion in the discovery that "power is everywhere" (*HS* 93). Power "is a total structure of actions brought to bear upon possible actions; it incites, it induces, it seduces."[69] In a word, it's rhetoric. The negative power of prohibition and the threat of physical constraint are necessary sticks in any social formation, but they are secondary to the carrot of positive rhetoric of empowerment. Becoming a cultural animal – that is, a rhetorical animal – is becoming empowered to behave in a way distinctive of a cultural orthodoxy.

Turning to *HS*'s deliberation about resistance, one may divide it into two stages. The first is summed up in Foucault's critique of Wilhelm Reich:

The fact that so many things were able to change in the sexual behavior of Western societies without any of the promises or political conditions predicted by Reich being realized is sufficient proof that this whole sexual "revolution," this whole "antirepressive" struggle, represented nothing more, but nothing less – and its importance is undeniable – than a tactical shift and reversal in the great deployment of sexuality. But it is also apparent why one could not expect this critique to be the grid for a history of that very deployment. Nor the basis for a movement to dismantle it. (*HS* 131)

In other words, Reich saw himself resisting the orthodoxy of sexuality, but he simply reaffirmed it in a different way. Its resistance historically going nowhere, Reich's agon is not a historical agon. Reich entrapped himself in the logic that ties resistance as deviance to the orthodoxy it struggles against. An orthodoxy is a rule that by definition is breakable, so that deviance is a condition of orthodoxy, and in more than just a theoretical sense. Deviance functions to enforce orthodoxy. Deviants who end up in prison or other horrific places stand as negative examples to keep the orthodox in line, and by virtue of the positivity of power, orthodoxy is implanted so deeply that deviance

---

69 "Subject and Power," p. 789.

brings with it the internal check of guilt, such as Crusoe's "original sin," which must finally be displaced for individualism to become a new orthodoxy. Reich's sexual liberation is deviance at its outer limit, since it is a call for deviance without guilt, but even so radical a deviance, Foucault recognizes, could not dismantle the orthodoxy. After all was said and done, Reich did nothing more than reaffirm the identification, at the core of the orthodoxy, of the subject with sexuality. The disciplinary agon between orthodoxy and deviance, in short, is not the agon of history.

This critique of Reich is most instructive, however, when it is read as an autocritique. For the agon within which Foucault inscribes his method, while it's innovative in examining orthodoxy from the standpoint of resistance, is like Reich's, a disciplinary agon: the resistance it privileges – e.g., insanity, illegality – is mere deviance. By exposing the socializing process as a powerizing process, the disciplinary agon makes power visible in new places, but it does so at the price of making power more difficult to resist rather than less because it theorizes only the resistance of deviance. Even Foucault's placement of this critique suggests that it is an autocritique: it concludes the book's penultimate chapter and is followed by a search in the last chapter – the second stage in *HS*'s deliberation about resistance – for an alternative to the disciplinary agon.

This search takes the form of a narrative that reduces history to two huge epochs, the line between them being the eighteenth century, which saw "the entry of life into history" (141): "the fact of living was no longer an inaccessible substrate that only emerged from time to time ... Power would no longer be dealing simply with legal subjects over whom the ultimate dominion was death, but with living beings, and the mastery it would be able to exercise over them would have to be applied at the level of life itself" (142–43). New techniques of discipline and surveillance were required. In the panopticon Foucault found a brilliant metaphor for this new disciplinary power.[70] One might view the panopticon as simply the secularization of God, a new technique of constant surveillance, but such a view would undermine the design of Foucault's narrative, since it would mean that life entered history long before the eighteenth century. The point of the narrative is to establish that life once eluded power to make it conceivable that it might do so once again. This narrative logic prepares for the

---

70 See "Panopticism," in *Discipline and Punish: The Birth of the Prison*, trans. Alan Sheridan (New York: Pantheon Books, 1977), pp. 195–228.

prescription for change that Foucault introduces as his climax: "We must not think that by saying yes to sex, one says no to power [Reich's mistake]... [T]o counter the grips of power with the claims of bodies... [t]he rallying point for the counterattack against the deployment of sexuality ought not to be sex desire, but bodies and pleasures" (157). Contextualized by Foucault's historical narrative, bodies and pleasures are in a realm of "living" outside power, a realm to be recovered to serve as a basis for a resistance that, unlike Reich's, is more than a mere reflex of orthodoxy.

As an alternative to the disciplinary agon between orthodoxy and deviance, Foucault thus turns to an agon between orthodoxies served up by history and a set of permanent interests in the body, interests that are prior to power, not posterior to it. The difficulty with this new agon is that it is inscribed within the discourse of humanism, which is premised on a foundation outside history. James Miller records that when Foucault started his 1978 lectures, after spending a year on sabbatical, everyone expected a continuation of the "bio-politics" sketched in *HS*'s last chapter. Foucault started in this vein but then stopped abruptly: "He could not go on. And it was clear that this problematic, of bio-politics, was over for him – it was *finished*."[71] The price for the humanistic premise with which *HS* concludes – nothing less than the unraveling of Foucault's whole achievement – was too high. Additional evidence that *HS* left Foucault at an impasse is the eight-year hiatus between *HS* and the final two books, which continue the history of sexuality in one sense but give us a new Foucault in another.[72] The ultimate source of this impasse appears to be *HS*'s thesis that "power is everywhere" (93), since it seems to have prompted Foucault, in searching for an alternative to the disciplinary agon, to look for a point outside power from which to resist power, a point that he more than anyone has taught us does not exist. This thesis need not, however, lead to this impasse if it is modified.

HS investigates the historical invention of the subject of sexuality, which was at the center of a new orthodoxy that emerged to rival an

---

71 *The Passion of Michel Foucault* (New York: Simon & Schuster, 1993), p. 299. Perhaps more than anything else, Miller's narrative indicates that Foucault was never far from slipping into this impasse. We share Lynn Hunt's reading: "He [Miller] has shown that despite Foucault's own protestations at various points in his career, the philosopher had never entirely emancipated himself from the grip of the transcendental subject and its experiences" ("The Revenge of the Subject/The Return of Experience," *Salmagundi* 97 [1993]: 51).

72 One should ask if in these final books there is a reversal in method in which Foucault analyzes orthodoxy from the standpoint of its own self-portrait rather than from that of resistance to it.

old one. Foucault sees this empirically without seeing it theoretically when he compares the bourgeoisie to the aristocracy:

> for the aristocracy had also asserted the special character of its body, but this was in the form of *blood*, that is, in the form of the antiquity of its ancestry and of the value of its alliances; the bourgeoisie on the contrary looked to its progeny and the health of its organism when it laid claim to a specific body. The bourgeoisie's "blood" was its sex. (*HS* 124)

A new subject, we should expect, is agonistically introduced to change the rules of the cultural game. Aristocratic blood identifies the rule that stood in the way of the bourgeoisie's cultural legitimation. As long as the hierarchical privileging of ancestral blood was the cultural standard of standards, any aristocrat, no matter how impoverished, towered over any merchant, no matter how wealthy. This rule of blood shows that while power may come from everywhere, it comes in different forms, producing different effects. Some modes of power benefit some at the expense of others. Foucault sometimes speaks of how, in complex systems of power, persons can shift places, someone in the strong position one time can be in the weak another — see, for example, his rule of "continual variations" (*HS* 99). Such shifts support his thesis that power is relational, not concentrated — everywhere rather than somewhere. But as the rule of blood shows, power can also produce subjects with interests that permanently pit some persons (those with ancestral blood) against others (those without it) as long as the rule is in place. Aristocratic blood was a concentration of power that was somewhere, as was the concentration that rose against it.

By thus analyzing the power coming from everywhere to identify the modes of power that are somewhere, one can theorize a resistance to orthodoxy that comes from neither mere deviancy nor a humanistic point outside history but from a rival orthodoxy in an agon of history. Foucault's contrast of aristocratic blood to bourgeois sex functions in his narrative — "Periodization" is the chapter in which it appears — to motivate the invention of the subject of sexuality. At this crucial point in his narrative, Foucault deploys neither a disciplinary nor a humanistic agon but a historical agon between rival orthodoxies because only it makes this invention historically intelligible. The agon of history informs his narrative even as his "power is everywhere" thesis blocks its theorization.

The agon of history is an abstraction that allows one to rise to the historical concrete. Consider Daniel Defoe's *The True-Born Englishman*, whose enormous popularity indicates that it struck a chord that an emergent bourgeois culture was ready to hear. Its last two lines laid out a strategy of resistance that proved to have a future:

> For fame of families is all a cheat,
> *'Tis personal virtue only makes us great.*[73]

This goes beyond deviancy, such as an insolent refusal to defer to an aristocrat in the expected manner, because it defies aristocratic "fame of families" from the standpoint of a rival orthodoxy of "personal virtue." Virtue, unlike blood, was within the grasp of the bourgeoisie. With this new standard, the way to the top of the cultural ladder would be open, as evidenced by the mythic status Crusoe achieved in the new bourgeois culture. Crusoe ceased to be a wayward deviant burdened by his "original sin" when his personal virtue, sanctioned by God, became the cornerstone for a new orthodoxy of individual enterprise.

The chasteness of the new subject of sexuality exploited a rhetorical opportunity that the aristocracy delivered on a silver platter in glamorizing the sexual immorality of the aristocratic rake. With Richardson's Pamela, lowly virginity brought the aristocratic predator to his knees in deference to a new constitutional rule of the cultural game.[74] It's not surprising, as Foucault shows, that the more the bourgeoisie talked about repressing sexuality in the name of virtue, the more they seemed unable to take their mind off it. One cannot be done, after all, without the other, as *Pamela* confirms on nearly every page. *Shamela*, part of Fielding's last-ditch defense of the aristocratic rake (what else is *Tom Jones*?), tries to outflank *Pamela* with laughter directed at this bourgeois preoccupation, beginning with Parson Tickletext's first letter to Parson Oliver: "Oh! I feel an emotion even while I am relating this: methinks I see Pamela at this instant, with all the pride of ornament cast off."

The transhistorical abstraction missing in Foucault directs attention to the powers that are somewhere in the agon of history. Whether these powers will stay where they are is precisely what is at stake in such an agon. Burke theorizes this transhistorical structure via the constitutional game in which the changing of the rules of the game is at its heart. The game positions the subject not outside history as its

---

73 *Daniel Defoe*, ed. J. T. Boulton (New York: Schocken, 1965), p. 81.
74 For a powerful analysis of *Pamela*'s role in constitutionalizing this new rule, see Nancy Armstrong, *Desire and Domestic Fiction: A Political History of the Novel* (New York: Oxford University Press, 1987). She draws on Foucault, but seeing that his analysis is "partial" in deflecting attention from the agon of history, she supplies the necessary corrective (p. 22).

beginning and end, but *in medias res*, as an effect of power on two levels: first, the power that is everywhere in the powerizing process; second, and more importantly, the power that is somewhere in the rules that pit subject against subject in struggles over these rules, not over their disciplinary enforcement, but over their constitutionality.

Rhetorical realism proposes a method for the discovery of power that is somewhere. Try to change some rules, not as a deviant but as the bringer of a new orthodoxy. If you meet no resistance, you're cold; your new orthodoxy doesn't change any rules that matter. If you meet stiff resistance, you're hot. This is a method that is easy to test; try it in your academic department. Rhetorical realism, in short, measures the magnitude of the antagonist not by the inflationary "power is everywhere" formula, but by the reality of the opposition that actually galvanizes itself to beat down a new orthodoxy.

Rhetorical realism also reverses Lukács, who begins with subject and object to predict when and where revolutionary transformation will occur. Rhetorical realism begins at the other end, with revolutionary assertion. The assertion may be analogized to the jar Wallace Stevens places upon a hill in Tennessee. In one sense, the jar changes little; in another, it changes everything. Similarly, revolutionary assertion may change little, especially initially, but in galvanizing opposition to it, it changes everything as it forces power to declare its locations.

Furthermore, in the complexities of modern society, where the agon of history assumes forms much more complex than a struggle at a barricade in the street, such assertion may smoke out oppositional power in unsuspected locations. Consider the opposition forming in the US to beat down the emergent subject of multiculturalism that challenges the traditional monocultural constitutional rules of the game. To the surprise of no one, the oppositional coalition includes the likes of Pat Buchanan, who declared multiculturalism a "landfill" in announcing his candidacy for President in the 1992 race; but the coalition also includes some traditional liberals (e.g., Arthur Schlesinger, *The Disuniting of America*), for whom there is somehow an important difference between marching with blacks in a civil rights demonstration in a monoculture, and being on equal terms with African-Americans in a rainbow multiculture.

This transhistorical structure is anonymous in the sense that it is not an object of a negative hermeneutics of suspicion.[75] In its transhistoricity,

---

75 Jameson faults Burke's dramatism for lacking a negative hermeneutic (521–22). But if dramatism is transhistorical, he is looking for such a hermeneutic in the wrong place.

it is beyond suspicion. Exposing it simply exposes history. Even if history is a nightmare from which we all wish to awake, pointing the finger of suspicion at it is pointless.

But though it is anonymous in a transhistorical sense, it is anything but anonymous in a historical sense. We can analyze it in the abstract but we always encounter it in the concrete. Rhetorical realism does not theorize in advance where to expect the lines in the sand to be drawn — race, gender, the economy, whatever. Instead, rhetorical realism prepares us to be ready for anything.

Perhaps someday there will be a world with rules by which everyone can function materially, and with no rule that benefits anyone at the expense of anyone else. The world might then be ready for the utopian game of ideal communication that Habermas envisions. Meanwhile, the game of changing the rules of the game is the only game in town.

❖❖

2

Counter-Statement: aesthetic humanism

❖❖

As for our set-piece, the "Lexicon Rhetoricæ"... [It] would look upon literature as the thing added – the little white houses in a valley that was once a wilderness.   Burke, *CS*

A college dropout, Burke quit Columbia University in 1918 and settled in Greenwich Village to become a writer (*SCBC* 5). He took his inspiration from Flaubert, as he wrote in a letter that year a few months before his twenty-first birthday. "I shall get a room," he writes,

and begin my existence as a Flaubert. Flaubert is to be my Talmud, my Homer, my beacon... Already I have begun going through his letters... I am going to nourish myself with *Madame Bovary*, learn how every character is brought in, tabulate every incident. I am sure there is a triumph in every sentence of Flaubert, and I am going to find it.   (*SCBC* 56)

Broom, Secession, The Little Review, S4N, Manuscripts – these experimental "little magazines," usually short-lived, are among the places where Burke first published stories later collected in *WO*, which appeared in 1924. In 1916, he had published a poem, "Adam's Song, and Mine," in *Others: a Magazine of the New Verse*, which included William Carlos Williams among its associate editors and Marianne Moore, Ezra Pound, Wallace Stevens, and T. S. Eliot among the poets it featured during its four years of existence, from 1915 to 1919.[1]

During the 1920s, while his friends Malcolm Cowley and Matthew Josephson expatriated to Paris, Burke became closely associated with *The Dial*, generally considered the decade's "most important aesthetic journal."[2] Burke worked as an editorial assistant, contributed reviews and essays regularly, and served as music critic from 1927 to 1929.

1 Frederick J. Hoffman, Charles Allen, and Carolyn F. Ulrich, *The Little Magazine: A History and a Bibliography*, 2nd ed. (Princeton University Press, 1947), pp. 247–48.

2 Morton D. Zabel, "Summary in Criticism," *Literary History of the United States*, ed. Robert E. Spiller *et al.*, 3rd ed. rev. (London: Macmillan Company, 1963), p. 1359.

This association, he once remarked retrospectively, "was almost as momentous a moment as the act, or accident, of being born" (*WO* xi).[3] The capstone was the Dial Award, which he received in 1929, "the first recognition on a major scale he received."[4] Earlier recipients included Moore, Eliot, Pound, Williams, and E. E. Cummings.

Eliot won in 1922, the year that *The Dial* and Eliot's *Criterion* cooperated in the transatlantic publication of "The Waste Land." In announcing the award that year, *The Dial* issued a critical manifesto:

The journalists who wish critics to be for ever concerned with social laws, economic fundamentals, and the science of psychoanalysis, and never by any chance with the erection into laws of those personal impressions which are the great pleasure of appreciation, would do well to destroy Mr. Eliot first; for it is from him that new critics are learning "that the 'historical' and the 'philosophical' critics had better be called historians and philosophers quite simply" and that criticism has other functions, and other pleasures to give.

With the benefit of hindsight, we can see these "new critics" as precursors of the New Criticism. *The Dial*, reports one historian, was the first American journal to establish "the critical habit of looking at the work of art rather than at the artist and his milieu."[5] An irony in Burke's career is that he used, in the 1920s, arguments that the New Criticism later used against him. In a review of Van Wyck Brooks's *The Ordeal of Mark Twain*, for example, he faults "extrinsic criticism" for "neglect[ing] to smell the rose because it is so busy explaining how the rose came to be there," concluding "that it furthers our knowledge but offers no clear guide to the formation of tastes and standards" (AHC 59, 102).

Burke seems to have been a theorist virtually from the beginning, not only in essays and reviews, but even in early stories that seem to have a theoretical principle as their premise. His first substantial work of theory appeared appropriately enough in *The Dial*. In a 1924 letter to Alyse Gregory, then its managing editor, Burke begins,

You once, in a moment of generosity, suggested that I write on aesthetics — and now, for better or worse, I have begun to do precisely that. Herewith is the first of a series of three or four essays in which I hope to round out an

3 Burke remembers *The Dial*, over a decade after its demise, in dedicating *PLF* to J. S. Watson, Jr., one of the patrons who kept *The Dial* afloat in the 1920s. Watson was also Burke's patron for many years, beginning in 1922 with the money Burke used that year to buy the place in Andover, New Jersey, where he lived until his death in 1993 (BCC 188).
4 Nicholas Joost, *Scofield Thayer and "The Dial": An Illustrated History* (Carbondale: Southern Illinois University Press, 1964), p. 149.   5 Ibid., p. 257.

attitude towards art, primarily indicating the elements which make for *permanency* in art. (L1; italics added)

The essay included "herewith" is not identified by title, but it must be "Psychology and Form," since of the two theoretical essays that Burke published in 1925, that is the one that appeared in *The Dial*. The other is "The Poetic Process." These constitute Burke's early aesthetic, the "series" projected in the letter stopping with these two. A few years later, these appear in *CS* with "Lexicon Rhetoricæ," ("LR"), which Burke introduces as "a Codification, Amplification, and *Correction* of the Two Essays, 'Psychology and Form' and 'The Poetic Process'" (123; italics added). *CS* is thus a text that in effect corrects itself. This correction includes, as we'll see, a reconsideration of the early aesthetic's principle of permanency.

It's useful to contextualize these two essays by considering, from the years immediately preceding them, a few additional texts, beginning with "The Correspondence of Flaubert" (CF), which appeared in *The Dial* in 1922; parts of it are later combined with portions of essays on Pater and De Gourmont to form *CS*'s first chapter, "Three Adepts of 'Pure' Literature." No longer simply a source of inspiration, Flaubert appears in "Correspondence" as a site of contradiction. On the one hand, he elevated pure form above everything else, a point Burke illustrates by quoting Flaubert's famous declaration, "What seems beautiful to me, the thing that I should like to do, would be a book about nothing"; on the other hand, he enslaved himself to realism, "devot[ing] years on end to the patient accumulation of detail, of matter ... [of] those minute fixations which his disciples look upon as the basis of his intentions (and which he himself, at a moment of faith in them, called of secondary importance)" (CF 154). As a result of this contradiction, Flaubert "finished each successive book with a sense of revulsion, of frustration" (154). "The anomaly of the situation," Burke observes wryly, "would have wearied any one but this ox of art" (154).

Burke's diagnosis of this malaise is framed by an opposition between "art-to-conceal-art" and "art-to-display-art" (153). In his wish to write a book about nothing, Flaubert aspired to art-to-display-art; in his accumulation of the minute details of his realism, he practiced art-to-conceal-art. Art-to-display-art is where art in the fullest sense lies. As Burke puts it in diagnosing Flaubert, "matter is incidental to movement and form — which are the artist's essential interest — and therefore detracts from the pure beauty of those forms" (154). Flaubert the realist frustrated Flaubert the artist. His problem, Burke suggests, is that he never quite addressed the right artistic problem. Wishing to write about nothing – pure form – is too abstract a formulation because it doesn't recognize the different realities of the different artistic media. Only music, Burke observes in "Psychology and Form," is suited to be about nothing (36). The literary medium forces literature to be about something. The artistic problem is to accommodate this something to the ends of art.

One can see Burke addressing this problem himself in his early stories, which he characterizes in the "Author's Note" in the first edition of *WO* as collectively representing "a gradual shifting of stress away from the realistically convincing and true to life; while there is a corresponding increase of stress upon the more rhetorical properties of letters." Of particular interest is "A Progression" (*WO* 177–87), which seems designed to take the literary medium as close to nothing as possible. It begins in an office filled with people working busily, who divide to form an aisle for their boss, Mr. Daugherty, as he exits. Once outside, he is submerged in a mass of pedestrians and forced to fight his way to the subway. The narrative continues on this realistic level until the train rises from its underground tunnel to a stretch of elevated tracks, at which point it is suddenly surrounded with airplanes filled with Indians screaming war-whoops. A window near Mr. Daugherty breaks, and he is promptly lassoed, hauled into one of the airplanes, and flown to a deserted island in the South Seas, where he is killed and eaten. Shortly afterwards, the narrator mutates into an essayist to reflect on the Idea of Progress, argue that ghosts don't exist, and insist that the devil's tongue is dart-like, not rounded. In the conclusion, the essayist mutates back into a narrator to entertain us with a romantic tale about King Argubot, which ends when the king dies and his soul ascends to his Angel-Wife in heaven. Parts of "A Progression" are thus about something – which is unavoidable in the literary medium – but the parts are designed to add up to nothing as they are discontinuous on all levels: plot, character, theme, imagery, even genre, insofar as there is a break from narrative to essay and back to narrative.

In adding up to nothing, however, "A Progression" arrives at the "pure" form of "pure" literature. By refusing so absolutely all normal modes of continuity, "A Progression" arrives at the artistic functions of beginning, middle, and end constitutive of "a progression" in a form purified of content. The contrast between the beginning level of mundane reality and the concluding level of romantic fantasy displays beginning and ending as functionally interdependent formal principles, each formed through its distance from the other. The workers in the opening scene, moreover, are busily moving about *in medias res*, bringing the story into conformity with Horace's maxim. In the tale of King Argubot, in contrast, the king's ascent to his wife in heaven effects a strong sense of finality: "O glory of their re-union in that gentle land above the sky!" (*WO 187*). It's worth noting, in passing, that Burke faulted one novel about two lovers that he reviewed in the 1920s for lacking sufficient contrast between beginning and ending. The relation of the lovers at the end is too similiar, he charged, to their relation at the beginning — the "decay of their affection, that final embarrassment between the lovers which it was [the novelist's] program to disclose progressively, has been too apparent to the reader from the start" (LAR 7). What Burke here identifies as a problem of progression is equivalent to what Aristotle conceptualized as a problem of magnitude (*Poetics* 1450b35–1451a15).

A beginning and an ending, in turn, because of the sharp contrast required between them, pose the formal problem of constructing a middle to get from one to the other. The formal function of a middle is set in relief in "A Progression" by the shift in its middle section to an essayistic posture. This section performs its function by modulating from the ordinary reality of the office routine to the romantic level of the King Argubot tale. The essayistic middle takes as its point of departure the fantastic conclusion of the opening realistic section, moving from it to the concluding romantic fantasy. All told, "A Progression" throws into extraordinarily clear relief the functional interdependence of beginnings, middles, and endings — "art-to-display-art" — precisely because the only connections between its beginning, middle, and end are formal in nature.

In 1923, in a review of Gertrude Stein, Burke proposes a "fallacy of subtraction." Unlike the New Criticism's intentional and affective fallacies, Burke's fallacy is concerned, not with the author or the audience, but with the function of content. The fallacy of subtraction, which Burke faults Stein for committing, consists of subtracting the content inherent in the literary medium to an excessive degree: Stein "ignore[s] the inherent property of words: that quality in the literary man's medium which makes him start out with a definiteness that the other arts do not possess. That is, if the musician plays G-sharp he has prescribed no definitions; but if the literary man writes 'boy' he has already laid down certain demarcations" (EW 409). "A Progression" avoids this fallacy because it always moves from word to word and sentence to sentence with the definiteness of semantic intelligibility, but it seems to define a borderline, for in no other story does Burke subtract content quite as radically as in this one.

Cowley, writing in 1921, groups Burke with young writers preoccupied with literary form. He singles Burke out as going to "geometrical extremes," but he writes approvingly, predicting that these writers will produce work "at least as well composed as a good landscape; it may even attain to the logical organization of music."[6] Burke participated in modernism's differentiation of itself from romanticism, as one can see in his complaint in 1922 that "the emphasis on emotion and pure, immediate expression...dominates art at the present time," an emphasis he labels an "aesthetic of adolescence" (LWE 897–98). One should not displace genuine aesthetic values of "poise, balance, restraint, technique," Burke insists, in favor of "the immediate, blind, instinctive expression of a virulent and fluid emotion" (897). Burke's earliest writings translate his commitment to these aesthetic values into artistic and critical practices. In "Psychology and Form" and "The Poetic Process," he turns to the problem of theorizing the values themselves.

Not surprisingly in a decade punctuated by I. A. Richards's landmark "Science and Poetry," Burke's "Psychology and Form" takes the form of an apology for aesthetic value in a scientific age.[7] While Burke starts with the same concerns as Richards, it needs to be added, he explicitly takes issue with him in *PC*, as we'll see in the next chapter, in ways that anticipate the later differences between himself and the New Criticism, which Richards helped to invent.[8]

Burke frames his apology as a contest between two psychologies: "The hypertrophy of the psychology of information is accompanied by the corresponding atrophy of the psychology of form" (*CS* 33). In other words, the prestige of science valorizes "information" against

6 "The Youngest Generation," *Literary Review of the New York Evening Post*, 15 October 1921, p. 82.
7 In a letter, Burke takes umbrage at the suggestion that he derived his defense directly from Richards, noting that "Psychology and Form" appeared in 1925, the year before "Science and Poetry" (*SCBC* 233).
8 Burke's relation to Richards in these years might well repay careful study, since Richards is evidently the reason that the series of essays on aesthetics that Burke envisioned stopped after only two. Burke remarks retrospectively that he started a third, but then read Richards and Ogden's *The Meaning of Meaning* "and was so knocked over that I was unable to write the third essay" (*SCBC* 233).

"form," even to the extent of "scientific criteria being unconsciously introduced into matters of purely aesthetic judgment" (31), a point Burke substantiates by reference to a critic left unnamed: "a contemporary writer has objected to Joyce's *Ulysses* on the ground that there are more psychoanalytic data available in Freud. (How much more drastically he might, by the same system, have destroyed Homer's *Odyssey!*)" (32). Contrastingly, the psychology of form seeks eloquence rather than information:

> The contemporary audience hears the lines of a play or novel with the same equipment as it brings to reading the lines of its daily paper. It is content to have facts placed before it in some more or less adequate sequence. Eloquence is the minimizing of this interest in fact, *per se*... [E]lements of surprise and suspense are subtilized, carried down into the writing of a line or a sentence, until in all its smallest details the work bristles with disclosures, contrasts, restatements with a difference, ellipses, images, aphorism, volume, sound-values, in short all that complex wealth of minutiæ which in their line-for-line aspect we call style and in their broader outlines we call form.   (37–38)

The aesthetic value of information is limited to its value as "surprise," a value so transitory that it is ironically lost in the moment of its realization. As Burke puts it, "the aesthetic value of information is lost once that information is imparted. If one returns to such a work again it is purely because, in the chaos of modern life, he has been able to forget it ... We cannot take a recurrent pleasure in the new (in information) but we can in the natural (in form)" (35). In form, because of the recurrent pleasure that it provides, Burke finds "the elements which make for the permanency in art," to repeat the phrase he uses in his letter to Gregory. His aesthetic humanism appears in the equation of form to the natural: to take pleasure in form is to be human in the fullest sense.

   In Burke's aesthetic, as noted earlier, music is the ideal artistic medium, the one in which the elements making for permanence display themselves most readily: "Music, then, fitted less than any other art for imparting information, deals minutely in frustrations and fulfillments of desire, and for that reason more often gives us those curves of emotion which, because they are natural, can bear repetition without loss" (36). This insistence on the naturalness of the experience of form is crucial to Burke's project. Any aesthetic must establish the self-sufficiency of art, such that art can stand on its own as an end in itself rather than as a mere means to some other end, whether it be moral, political, theological, or whatever. For Burke, the naturalness of the experience of form makes this experience its own end. For an aesthetic humanist, moreover, art is not only its own end, it is also superior to any other end.[9]

A theoretical difficulty arises, however, when one considers that if aesthetic experience is as natural as Burke says, we should take to it like a fish to water. There should be no need for an apology such as "Psychology and Form." Burke's solution to this difficulty is evident in the diagnostic posture he assumes: "The flourishing of science has been so vigorous that we have not yet had time to make a spiritual readjustment adequate to the changes in our resources of material and knowledge"; lacking this readjustment, we suffer from "disorders of culture and taste" (31). Burke's aesthetic humanism, in other words, presupposes a transcendental subject for whom the experience of form is natural but who is trapped within a culture that tends to alienate it from this experience. This dialectic of alienation from and restoration to one's nature allows Burke both to claim that aesthetic experience is natural and to explain why the natural seems unnatural in the current cultural configuration.

Within the framework of this dialectic, the focus is on the vehicle by which restoration is effected. In the example of Lukács examined in chapter 1, restoration is envisioned in a narrative of revolutionary transformation. In Burke's aesthetic, restoration occurs in a leap of aesthetic transcendence.

"Psychology and Form" incorporates in its conception of form a rhetorical ingredient that rises to a position of ascendency in the later "LR." "If," Burke explains, "in a work of art, the poet says something, let us say, about a meeting, writes in such a way that we desire to observe that meeting, and then, if he places that meeting before us — that is form. While obviously, that is also the psychology of the audience, since it involves desires and their appeasements" (*CS* 31). But not just any audience, as is evident when Burke emphasizes, "Eloquence is not showiness; it is, rather, the result of that desire in the artist to make a work perfect by adapting it in every minute detail to the racial appetites" (41). Rooted in the human race, the audience's appetite for form is the transcendental condition of perfection in art as well as

9 Remembering these premises helps one to avoid mistaking the particular form aestheticism assumed in the New Criticism for aestheticism in general, so that one fails, as sometimes happens, to see Burke's early aesthetic for what it is because it doesn't square with all the tenets of the New Criticism.

permanence and universality – a triumvirate Burke reevaluates in "LR."

In "The Poetic Process," Burke shifts from the standpoint of audience to that of the artist. The process that Burke charts begins with the untrammeled emotion of the artist and ends with the artistic construct that evokes emotion in an audience: "the self-expression of the artist, *qua* artist, is not distinguished by the uttering of emotion, but by the evocation of emotion" (*CS* 53). Burke uses Mark Twain as his principal example, arguing that Twain, "before setting pen to paper, again and again transformed the bitterness that he *wanted* to utter into the humor that he *could* evoke" (53). Burke here draws on his review of *The Ordeal of Mark Twain*, noted above, where he argues, against Brooks, that Twain actually disproves the doctrine of art as self-expression because the letters and posthumous writings, which supposedly express what Twain actually felt, are altogether without the artistic distinction of his humorist writings (AHC 59). Burke thus sees in the artist a shift in attention from the raw material to the formal techniques of art: "*the artist's means are always tending to become ends in themselves. The artist begins with his emotion, he translates this emotion into a mechanism for arousing emotion in others, and thus his interest in his own emotion transcends into his interest in the treatment*" (*CS* 55). In this transcendence, personal appetite defers to the racial appetite for form.

The emotion a work of art evokes, Burke argues, may depend on either the work's content or its form. Content is the basis when the emotion is evoked because the experience of the artist and the audience overlap enough to give the content a significance for the audience that is comparable to its significance for the artist. Hence, "mute Byrons" will respond to Byron strongly (58). Form is the basis when the emotion evoked depends on the technique of the content's artistic presentation. Shakespeare's Falstaff, Burke suggests, is "an almost perfect symbol from the standpoint of ... workmanship, for nearly all readers are led to Falstaff solely through the brilliancy of his presentation" (59). The more a work's appeal depends on its form, therefore, the more it appeals across differences among readers. The more "perfect" it is, the more "permanent" it becomes:

[T]hroughout the permutations of history, art has always appealed, by the changing individuations of changing subject-matter, to certain potentialities of appreciation which would seem to be inherent in the very germ-plasm of man, and which, since they are constant, we might call *innate forms of the mind*. These forms are the "potentiality for being interested by certain processes or arrangements," or the "feeling for such arrangements of subject-matter as produce cresendo, contrast, comparison, balance, repetition, disclosure, reversal, contraction, expansion, magnification, series, and so on."

(46; italics added)

"Innate forms of the mind" thus underwrite the perfection, permanence, and universality of art, empowering its appeal across historical differences.

Burke conceives emotions as mediating between the concrete experiences of individuals and these innate forms. Burke underlines this point when he stresses that we can discuss the forms intellectually but that "to experience them emotionally, we must have them singularized into an example, an example which will be chosen by the artist from among his emotional and environmental experiences" (49). Our access to the innate forms is thus indirect, through concrete experiences. But access is possible through art, where the artist-qua-artist elevates form above content, thereby making form available for aesthetic experience. Paradoxically, then, through works of art – "the little white houses in a valley that was once a wilderness" (*CS* x) – we are restored to what we always already possess innately.

Burke analogizes his aesthetic to Platonic doctrine, concluding that nominalism went too far in its critique of Plato: "For we need but take his universals out of heaven and situate them in the human mind (a process begun by Kant), making them not metaphysical, but psychological" (48). Prior to history, Burke's innate forms thus constitute a subject of aesthetic humanism. The eloquence of art-to-display-art effects the aesthetic transcendence that restores us to what we are, an experience we can repeat with pleasure to infinity.

Near the end of "LR," written during the turn to a new decade, Burke seems to look back to distance himself from his earlier self:

As a kind of hypothetical norm, we might divide our readers into the "hysteric" and the "connoisseur." The hysteric will demand in art a Symbol which is "medicinal" to his situation. He will require one very specific kind of art. In so far as the reader approaches the hypothetical state of the connoisseur, he is open to the appeal of all Symbols, but is overwhelmed by none. He will approach art *as art*, thus requiring the maximum of ritualization, verbalization ... The actual reader is obviously an indeterminate and fluctuant mixture of these two extremes. An art might be said to approach "perfection" in proportion as its appeal is made to the second kind of reader – but in all purity he could not possibly exist. (180)

In thus refusing to privilege the "connoisseur," Burke revises his early aesthetic in the direction of the "hysteric" without, obviously, going all the way over to this opposite extreme, exemplified in the "mute Byron" who finds a voice in the real Byron.

"LR" delivers its promised "correction" of the early aesthetic in its fifth and last section: "Universality, Permanence, Perfection" (171). A reevaluation of this triumvirate, this concluding section includes one short paragraph that concisely dismantles all three in a single stroke: "Perfection could exist only if the entire range of the reader's and writer's experience were identical down to the last detail. Universal and permanent perfection could exist only if this entire range of experiences were identical for all men forever" (179). The reorientation in Burke's thought that "LR" signals appears dramatically on the last page of "The Status of Art," which, like "LR," appears for the first time in *CS*:

[A] work may be popular and good, popular and bad, unpopular and good, unpopular and bad. It may be widely read and ineffectual, widely read and influential, little read and ineffectual, little read and influential. It may usher in something of great value; it may "keep something alive"; it may represent the concerns of a few people living under exceptional conditions. *It may, in fact, do all of these things at different times in its history, or in its action upon different kinds of readers.* (91; italics added)

What a work does, in short, is a function of a situation. It may do one thing in one situation, something else in another. Instead of uncovering the formal basis of appeal across historical differences, "LR" theorizes the differences that render perfection, permanence, and universality empty abstractions — or so it appears.

Burke's title "Lexicon Rhetoricæ" introduces in its reference to rhetoric the principle that Burke uses to privilege such differences. He begins by indicating that his analysis "will be diagnostic rather than hortatory: it will be more concerned with *how* effects are produced than with *what effects should be produced*" (123). In other words, he seems to stake out a position of rhetorical neutrality, one that considers whatever effect comes along in its own terms to focus on the "how" of its production.

The term "eloquence" provides a bird's-eye perspective from which to see that "LR" reevaluates Burke's triumvirate mainly by equalizing content and form rather than subordinating the former to the latter. In his book on Burke, Armin Paul Frank astutely identifies a number of textual signs of this shift in emphasis (67–68). The most important of these is a revised conception of eloquence. In the early aesthetic, it is

49

conceived as a minimizing of content and a maximizing of form, whereas in "LR," it is a maximization of both form and content: "eloquence is a frequency of Symbolic and formal effects. One work is more eloquent than another if it contains Symbolic and formal charges in greater profusion. That work would be most eloquent in which each line had some image or statement relying strongly upon our experience outside the work of art, and in which each image or statement had a pronounced formal saliency" (165). The capitalization in "Symbolic" but not in "formal" may even signal a tilt in favor of content.

The lexicon in "LR" consists of a plethora of categories that function together as a terminology to analyze symbolic and formal effects. The principal strategy on both sides, the symbolic and the formal, is to show that what contributes to eloquence in one situation may retard it in another. On the symbolic side, Burke argues, even if "a pattern of experience could be proved universal (common to all men) or permanent (common to some men in every age), the work of art in which it is symbolized would not be thereby proved universal or permanent" (172). No matter how universal or permanent the pattern, it has to be individuated symbolically; no symbol can function the same way in all situations. "What Dickens considered the height of female virtue," Burke notes, "the reader may consider exceptional unimaginativeness" (172). Differences that make all the difference in a symbol's "intensity" are examined in categories such as (1) "variations in ideology," (2) "remoteness of patterns," (3) "divergence of modes" (172). On the formal side, the story is more complicated.

"Psychology and Form" introduces form as a sequential process in which one part of a work is so designed that a later part gratifies the audience. "LR" codifies different ways of doing this, including (1) "syllogistic progression" – one part is a premise for a subsequent one; (2) "qualitative progression" – the rightness of a step is recognized after its occurrence rather than anticipated beforehand; (3) "repetitive form" – the repetition of a principle in different guises (124–25); (4) "minor or incidental forms" – sequencing at the level of smaller units, even the sentence or phrase, including "metaphor, paradox, disclosure, reversal, contraction, expansion, bathos, apostrophe, series, chiasmus" (127). Most notable, however, is the inclusion of "conventional form" (126), which is categorically worlds away from the innate forms of the early aesthetic. The reason for its inclusion is evident from Burke's analytic strategy, since it is easy to show that a convention that contributes to eloquence in one situation may get in the way in another. A section entitled "Formal Obstacles" illustrates the point: "Our analysis . . . equips us to consider the possible alienation of readers through conventional form, or 'categorical expectancy.' Elizabethan audiences, through expecting the bluster of the proscenium speech, found it readily acceptable — but a modern audience not schooled in this expectation will object to it as 'unreal'" (173).

While Burke's analytic strategy works well when the form under consideration is conventional, it encounters difficulties in other cases. For example, in the case of progressive and repetitive form, Burke offers no examples where these forms, like conventional form, work in one situation but not another. Instead, he offers examples where ideology, which is on the symbolic side, interferes with their functioning, such that what works for one audience doesn't work for another (147, 178). But in these cases, the individuation works differently for different audiences because of the ideology rather than the form. Form doesn't interfere with itself as does the conventional form of the Elizabethan "bluster." Forms that seem to appeal across differences could be paraded as innate in the early aesthetic, but they become a problem in "LR," which tries to foreground differences.

Part of Burke's solution is the revised conception of eloquence noted above. By virtue of this revision, Burke can effectively dismantle his triumvirate. In the early aesthetic, as noted above, perfection is a function of adapting to "racial appetites" (41), whereas in "LR," because eloquence is a function of adapting to all the appetites, not just the innate forms constitutive of racial appetites, perfection is subjected to a *reductio ad absurdum*:

we can only preserve "perfection" in this sense: "a perfect work for girls of seventeen who are living in small provincial towns in 1931 . . . and dream of a career in Hollywood," or "a perfect work for people with six toes, this spring." We can save the concept of perfection only by making it of no critical value. If a work of art were perfectly adapted to one situation, by this very fact its chances of subsequent perfection would be eliminated, as the identical situation will not recur.   (180–81)

Hence, even if Burke is forced to concede that the forms the early aesthetic conceived as innate do indeed contribute to eloquence equally well in all situations, he can counter that they are at best only a part of eloquence and perhaps a small part at that.

Burke tries, however, not to concede even this much. This attempt is evident in passages where "LR" is most uncertain theoretically and of greatest interest from the standpoint of the present study. In a section entitled "'Priority' of forms," priority is placed within quotation marks to call into question the Kantian priority that the early aesthetic embraced. Here, Burke suggests that even "such basic forms [contrast, comparison, etc.] may, for all that concerns us, be wholly conventional" (142). The "for all that concerns us" betrays a theoretical uncertainty great enough to prompt Burke to table the whole issue: "Psychology and philosophy may decide whether they [the forms] are innate or resultant" (141–42). By thus entertaining the possibility that conventional form may extend all the way down to the level conceived earlier as innate, Burke stakes out the outermost point of his theorizing in "LR," especially as it bears on the present study's interest in the question of the subject, since to get to this point, he has to glimpse at the possibility of a historical decentering of the subject.

This point, more dramatically than any other, exhibits the reorientation that "LR" effects from an aesthetic to a historical approach to the subject. We will consider in the next and following chapters, as their titles suggest, Burke's reliance on history as a theoretical framework. Burke turns to history and then revises and revises again his conceptionalization of it. From the standpoint of this later work, "LR" marks a beginning.

In "LR" itself, however, the ultimate framework for analysis remains closer to aesthetic transcendence than to history. On the historicizing side, "LR" dismantles the literary monument insofar as its rhetorical analysis discloses that no work can be equally eloquent for the same reasons in all historical situations. Eloquence is not a property a work possesses for all time, but a conjuncture of a work and a historical situation. A work that is eloquent today may be less so in the next century, more in the century after that. But the historicizing of Burke's rhetorical analysis stops at the door of eloquence itself. The eloquence of particular works is historicized, but not eloquence itself.

Burke's criterion of eloquence is quantitative: one instance is more eloquent than another by virtue of possessing a greater quantity of symbolic and formal effects. "Intensity" is Burke's term for measuring this quantity (163). The danger Burke cites is that any instance of eloquence can be reified, such that it becomes a standard of measurement that closes off new forms of eloquence that may have as much or even more "intensity."[10]

10 Heath's "Kenneth Burke's Break with Formalism" offers an insightful examination of one example of qualitative reification, deriving from metaphysical idealism, that Burke rejected — see especially 133.

The great danger in eloquence resides in the fact that it tends to become not a *quantitative* but a *qualitative* thing ... Eloquence thus comes to be allied with strict doctrines of inclusion and exclusion. It utilizes the traditionally dignified, overlooking the fact that any traditionally dignified word or image or "thought" is dignified not through an intrinsic quality but because earlier artists made it so. (169–70; italics added).

The virtue of Burke's quantitative criterion is that it opens the door to new possibilities of eloquence. But this criterion can open this door only by closing it on itself, putting itself beyond historicizing as it functions qualitatively. "LR" intends, as noted earlier, to be diagnostic rather than hortatory, analyzing "how" effects are produced rather than preaching what effects "should" be produced. Against the text's will, however, a "should" appears with its quantitative criterion of intensity.

In this criterion, the early aesthetic survives on one level even as it is displaced on another. The early aesthetic's innate forms are a collection of diverse structures, none of which is privileged in particular, all of which are privileged in general insofar as what matters most is appealing quantitatively to as many as possible, at every level, ranging from plot down to the sentence and the phrase. Intensity is the overall effect, the privileging of which presupposes a subject for whom it is a supreme value because the experience of it is "natural." "LR" broadens intensity to encompass symbolic as well as formal effects, but it retains intensity, itself still a formal criterion even if it encompasses symbolic effects. The ultimate measurement of aesthetic value is not the quality of this symbolic effect as opposed to that one, but the formalism of quantity. Intensity is aesthetic value: "the thing added – the little white houses in a valley that was once a wilderness" (*CS* x).

In "LR," intensity becomes a platform on which Burke explicitly dismantles permanence, perfection, and universality, even as this triumvirate, albeit in a new form, holds up the platform. The privileging of quantity over any particular quality is itself a qualitative privileging of newness – a variant of the modernist "make it new" – a privileging that presupposes a subject for whom making it new is a supreme value: universal, permanent, and perfect in the sense in which origination is a moment of perfection. What is distinctive about Burke's variant of making it new is that, instead of theorizing it by looking back to imagination (even though Coleridge would interest him greatly), he looked to rhetoric, which was looking forward, as we can see from our standpoint at the end of the century.

In "LR" Burke turns against the subject of his early aesthetic humanism in one sense by not turning against it in another. His fence-straddling is evident when, as noted earlier, he leaves to others the job of deciding whether forms are "innate or resultant." "LR" leaves us with an aesthetic subject but one that is homeless, or at least not sure about which way to turn to find a home. At its peak, intensity is still a transcendent moment, but whether it transcends history is left theoretically uncertain. It turns out, as we shall see in the next chapter, that Burke does eventually find a new home for his commitment to art, not in ethereal innate forms, but in the body in the material world, where the commitment takes a new form, less aesthetic in particular, more cultural in general.

In *CS*, in sum, there is a tension between aesthetics and rhetoric that perhaps has less to do with Burke than with aesthetics and rhetoric themselves. Historically, the rise of aesthetics in the romantic period seems to have entailed the fall of rhetoric, a functional interdependency that in our time seems to be headed in the opposite direction. Burke's beginning as an aesthetic humanist leaves its mark on his later work insofar as he habitually returns to aesthetic activity, even as he repeatedly reconceives it, to find a humanist center in some sense ultimately apart from history, where one can purge oneself of history's messiness. Whether he ever breaks this habit once and for all is a tough question – the answer appearing in the chapters ahead is yes and no. Burke's beginning as a rhetorician equally leaves its mark, as he repeatedly moves away from this aesthetic center toward the agon of history, where the aesthetic subject was constituted in the first place.[11]

11 For a concise account of A. G. Baumgarten's landmark *Aesthetica*, which appeared in two volumes, the first in 1750 and the second in 1758, see Richard McKeon, *Thought, Action and Passion* (University of Chicago Press, 1954), pp. 147–49.

3

Permanence and Change: a biological subject of history

> And if one wishes to convince me that a concern with pure literature is inapposite to the season, I should at least point out to him that there are two deductions possible from this premise, since one may either say, "So much the worse for pure literature" or "So much the worse for the season."
>
> Burke, "Spring during Crisis"

Imagining the situation in which Burke found himself as he wrote *PC* should be easy for Americans who matured as New Critics during the 1950s only later to find themselves forced to revisit, in the 1960s, convictions that once seemed settled for good. Richard Ohmann, for example, recounts the invigoration he experienced internalizing the values of New Critical "close reading – exactness, sensitivity to shades of feeling, the need to see pattern and order, the effort to shut out from consciousness one's own life-situation while reading the poem, and to pry the words loose from their social origins" – as well as the divorce he later experienced between working in this literary culture and living through the upheavals of the 1960s.[1] What Vietnam did to Ohmann's generation, the Great Depression did to Burke's.

For *PC*'s second edition, Burke wrote a "Prologue" (xlvii–lix) that begins, "This book was written in the early days of the Great Depression, at a time when there was a general feeling that our traditional ways were headed for a tremendous change, maybe even a permanent collapse. It is such a book as authors in those days sometimes put together, to keep themselves from falling apart." In another retrospective self-portrait he remembers himself before writing *PC* as a "wayward son (whom the Great Depression compelled to

---

1 *English in America: A Radical View of the Profession* (New York: Oxford University Press, 1976), pp. 70–71, 20–21.

laugh on the other side of his face)" (*CS* 213).[2] *PC* stands as a watershed in Burke's career, marking the first step of a shift roughly analogous to the one from literary to cultural studies that the academic field of English is presently undergoing.

Burke's leftist politics during the 1930s were enough to work against him in the 1950s[3] – demonstrating in the process how little could prove to be enough during the McCarthy era.[4] Burke isn't even mentioned in David Caute's *The Fellow-Travellers*, while his close friends Cowley and Josephson are, Cowley frequently. Nor did Burke join the intellectuals who endorsed *Culture and Crisis*, a pamphlet Cowley and Josephson helped to write in support of William Foster, the 1932 candidate for President put forward by the Communist Party of the United States (CPUSA).[5] Josephson's biographer contrasts Burke to his friends:

Kenneth Burke was also attracted to Marxism and communism, but in a much more esoteric sense than either Cowley or Josephson. He was always the independent theorist of language and literary form, persistently withholding his complete allegiance from all political organizations. "Marxism does," he wrote Josephson in 1935, "provide some necessary admonitions as to our faulty institutions – but as I understand it, it is exactly 180 degrees short of being a completely rounded philosophy of human motivation." He admitted that socialism was a necessary first step toward solving the material problems facing the West, but it did nothing to alleviate the spiritual crisis. For his own part he felt more comfortable in Andover, chopping wood and studying literature.[6]

2 The early 1930s will merit an important chapter in any future Burke biography, not only because of the effects of the Great Depression, but also because 1932 saw his one novel, *Towards a Better Life*, an ironically entitled, allusively autobiographical tale about a mental breakdown, ending in a stream of mental fragments. Even while writing it, Burke saw it as the agency of his self-transformation, remarking in an August 1931 letter, "I rely upon...[it] to burn away certain very uncomfortable parts of me" (*SCBC* 195). He elaborates further on this interpretation in retrospective comments: see *TBL* vii–viii, *LSA* 338–39, OSIS 37–38.

3 In 1952, the English Department at the University of Washington voted to appoint Burke to be a visiting professor, but the university administration refused to approve the appointment after deciding Burke's activities in the 1930s made him too subversive. Burke and Cowley discuss the politics of the episode in a number of letters between August 1952 and January 1953 (*SCBC* 306–15). For a detailed chronology, see Heilman. The episode is also chronicled in Jane Sanders, *Cold War on the Campus: Academic Freedom at the University of Washington* (Seattle: University of Washington, 1979), pp. 105–14; and in Ellen W. Schrecker, *No Ivory Tower: McCarthyism and the Universities* (New York: Oxford University Press, 1986), p. 267.

4 In a poem written partly in response to what the University of Washington did – "An Old Liberal Looks to the New Year, 1953" – Burke captures through black humor how '53 reverses '35, turning "social conscience" into "treason" (*CP* 18–19).

5 Alexander Bloom, *Prodigal Sons: The New York Intellectuals and Their World* (New York: Oxford University Press, 1986), p. 45; David Caute, *The Fellow-Travellers: A Postscript to the Enlightenment* (New York: Macmillan, 1973), pp. 215–16; David Shi, *Matthew Josephson, Bourgeois Bohemian* (New Haven: Yale University Press, 1981), p. 144. 6 Shi, p. 174.

In a June 1932 letter to Burke, Cowley seems to give up hope of ever involving him more actively in the communist cause (*SCBC* 201–02).

Burke did give papers – "Revolutionary Symbolism in America" in 1935, "The Relation between Literature and Science" in 1937 – at the first and second American Writers' Congresses, two major cultural events organized by the CPUSA (TYL 497).[7] But these were olive branches, part of the communist effort, formally declared in August 1935, to lead a coalitional Popular Front against fascism. A historian of the CPUSA indicates that it saw the first congress as an opportunity to show "that cultural activities should be less sectarian, and that sympathetic writers should not be confronted with either joining the Party or being perceived as outcasts."[8] Cowley remembers this policy as "something new."[9]

Part of the same policy shift saw the disbanding of the John Reed Clubs and their replacement at the first congress with a new League of American Writers. "The League . . . would be broadly based, a united front manoeuvre, with only fascists and 'out-and-out' reactionaries excluded. Membership in it will not imply acceptance of the Communist political position."[10] The League also magnified its visibility by seeking more established writers than had the Clubs.[11] It was formally organized at the concluding session of the congress, at which Burke was elected to the League's executive committee – a sign of his stature, since the committee consisted of only 17 among the more than 200 writers at the congress, whose opening session drew an audience of over 4,000.[12]

As chapter 1 noted, the nub of Burke's 1935 paper – its proposal to substitute "people" for "worker" in revolutionary rhetoric – provoked dissent. The irony is that later in the year – in August, with the

7 A "call" for the first congress appeared in the *New Masses*, 22 January 1935, p. 20. Burke was one of the 64 signers. The first congress was virtually unprecedented, the only previous comparable gathering of writers in American history occurring in 1893 (TYL 512).

8 Lawrence H. Schwartz, *Marxism and Culture: The CPUSA and Aesthetics* (Port Washington, NY: Kennikat Press, 1980), p. 45.

9 *The Dream of the Golden Mountains: Remembering the 1930s* (New York: Viking Press, 1980), p. 272.

10 John Chamberlain, "The First American Writers' Congress," *The Saturday Review*, 4 May 1935, p. 4.

11 Cowley observes that a major failing of this League policy was that it alienated radical writers from the bottom of the social ladder who, with the encouragement of the John Reed Clubs, had been entering the American literary tradition for the first time (TYL 512–13).

12 "The League of American Writers," *New Masses*, 7 May 1935, p. 7. Burke also participated in the John Reed Club of New York. The *Partisan Review*, at that time the club's publication, lists Burke in its April–May 1934 issue as offering a course on "English Prose." Burke, in addition, appeared on a panel at a January 1934 event sponsored by the New York Club – see Eric Homberger, *American Writers and Radical Politics, 1900–39: Equivocal Commitments* (New York: St. Martin's Press, 1986), p. 130.

formation of the Popular Front — Burke's proposal became official policy, a new masthead even appearing on the *Daily Worker*: "People's Champion of Liberty, Progress, Peace and Prosperity."[13] But at the congress in April, the proposal provoked some heavy hitting, none heavier than the charge that "people" was Hitler's symbol (*das Volk*).[14]

Burke alludes to the dissent — in a passage notable for its definition of the contours of his relationship with communism — in his report on the congress for *The Nation*:

While attempting to enlist cultural allies on the basis of the widest possible latitude, this congress was unquestionably made possible only by the vitality and organizational ability of the Communist Party. As one who is not a member of the Communist Party, and indeed whose theories of propaganda, expressed at one session, even called down upon him the wrath of the party's most demonic orators, I can state with some claim to "impartiality" my belief that no other organization in the country could have assembled and carried through a congress of this sort. The results justify the assertion that those who approach the issues of today from the standpoint of cultural survival must have sympathy at least with communism as a historical direction. (WC 571)

Burke explicitly advocates communism in the first edition of *PC*. The advocacy, however, is pitched at the level of culture and value rather than economics and power. When it first appears at the end of part 1, what motivates it in the immediately preceding chapters is not the account of economic injustice under capitalism that one would expect, but an analysis of the cultural disorders that have created difficulties for literary artists. Communism, in other words, is depicted as necessary to make things better for literature.

Burke narrated his turn to communism as an evolution from his aestheticism. He makes the connection exceptionally explicit in publishing a periodical version of part 1 (in a statement supplied for the periodical's biographical blurb): "Beginning as an esthete who distrusted

13 Schwartz, *Marxism and Culture*, p. 70.
14 *American Writers' Congress*, ed. Henry Hart (New York: International Publishers, 1935), p. 168; Simons 276. Three decades later, in a symposium that takes a retrospective look at the congress, Burke returns to the attack on his paper (TYL 506–08). It left him emotionally devastated, he recalls, even occasioning a nightmarish image, "Of a sudden I experienced a fantasy, a feeling that excrement was dripping from my tongue... I felt absolutely lost" (507). Despite the attack, Burke was elected to the executive committee in the congress's closing session. He construes the election as a reconciliation of sorts, making the point with an Aesopian fable of two frogs, one large (the chief attacker), one small (Burke), in which the large frog almost swallows the small one before a peaceful conclusion is reached (508).

the superstructure of values arising from the intensities of economic combat, I have come to the conclusion that this attitude requires for its completion the championing of Communistic ideals, as the only ideals which can adapt the modern productive plant to humanistic ends" (OI 2).[15] "So far as I can see," Burke remarks in *PC*, "the only coherent and organized movement making for the subjection of the technological genius to humane ends is that of Communism, by whatever name it may finally prevail" (*PC*1 93; see also 213, 344–45). One possible alternative name, he suggests, is "'cooperative' (as distinct from the 'competitive' which flourished when the acquisitions of science were backed by the stimuli of business enterprise)" (*PC*1 94). Burke thus revised the convictions he formed during the 1920s by expanding from an aesthetic to a cultural humanism.

This advocacy of communism is deleted in the book's second edition, published in 1954. One should not be too quick to conclude that this deletion represents a simple about-face. Burke suggests that the deletion is actually a "restoration" of the first edition, since in 1954 his discussion of communism could not possibly be read as it was in 1935 (*PC* xlix) – an indisputable point. In one instance, by substituting "cooperative" (*PC* 268) for "Communistic" (*PC*1 345), he does manage to make the 1954 text repeat the 1935 text exactly. One should recall, moreover, a statement Burke makes in *RM*, another Cold War text:

We consider it a sign of flimsy thinking, indeed, to let anti-Communist hysteria bulldoze one into neglect of Marx. (We say "bulldoze," but we are aware that the typical pedagogue today is not "bulldozed" into such speculative crudity; he welcomes it, and even feels positively edified by it. If he cannot grace his country with any bright thoughts of his own, he can at least persuade himself that he is being a patriot in closing his mind to the bright thoughts of his opponents. No wonder the tendency is so widespread. It is a negative kind of accomplishment for which many can qualify.) (105)

Burke didn't become an orthodox Marxist during the 1930s when doing so was easy – even *de rigueur* in some circles in which he traveled – nor did he later jump on the anti-Marxist bandwagon. He took Marx seriously without taking him as gospel.

---

15 A contemporary reviewer of this periodical version of part 1 noted how Burke's argument "turn[ed] upside down the usual notions of the role of art under Communism" (Johnson 110).

Just how seriously appears dramatically in *ACR*, written in 1932.[16] That text and *PC* are first and second drafts of Burke's initial response to the Marxist challenge to his aesthetic convictions. *ACR* is especially revealing because in it Burke's quarrel with the Marxists of his day is more direct and sustained than in *PC* – or anywhere else.

A June 1932 letter to Cowley suggests the rhetorical pressures and strategies running through Burke's mind during the writing of *ACR*:

> I look forward to tomorrow's opening battle. "Just what do you have against Communism?" Bob [Robert Cantwell] asked me last night – and I had never thought of it so bluntly, but my answer was as blunt: "Absolutely nothing." And then, in the night, I awoke and asked myself the same question and discovered the following qualifications: "I am not a joiner of societies, I am a literary man. I can only welcome Communism by converting it into my own vocabulary...My book[17] will have the communist objectives, and the communist tenor, but the approach will be the approach that seems significant to me.
> (*SCBC* 202)

ACR displays Burke simultaneously resisting Marxism because of the mature aesthetic convictions with which he comes to it and modifying those convictions in the process. It's instructive to contrast *ACR* with the earlier "The Status of Art," where Burke discusses economic determinism alongside psychoanalyis, pairing them as "causation" theories of art (*CS* 72–81). Both are depicted as threats to art, but threats that Burke confidently dismisses with dispatch. The situation is quite different in *ACR*. The Great Depression has enhanced the credibility of Marxism enormously. The case against psychoanalysis in "The Status of Art" can remain at rest, but not the case against Marxism.

In reopening the case, Burke develops both constructionist and essentialist arguments. These serve diverse purposes and sometimes even shift their polemical function in different contexts. We will observe how they arise in *ACR*, but our main interest will be the form they finally take in *PC*.

The contradiction between them is apparent to Burke when he looks back at *PC* in his retrospective "Prologue." He fears, moreover, that the

---

16 *ACR* went unpublished until 1993; after it was rejected by the first editor to whom Burke sent it, he let it sit (*ACR* 44–45). He refers to it by title, misremembering a few details, in a review of his career added to *CS* for its second edition (213–14).

17 Jay's editorial note says the referent is *PC* (*SCBC* 203), but other letters later in the summer and early fall of 1932 argue that it's *ACR*. By September Burke has settled on the title "Auscultation, Creation, and Revision" (L2, L3); by October he has sent the essay to a publisher (L4). Jay's selection omits these letters, skipping a year from 4 June 1932 to 4 June 1933. It's disappointing that his selection includes relatively few letters from the 1930–35 period, despite its importance for both Cowley and Burke.

essentialist side outweighs the constructionist. He reluctantly concedes that the book often seems to be saying that "all 'higher manifestations' of human culture are to be explained as 'projections' of the body in its sheerly physiological nature" (l). Asking that the "references to animal experiments and the like . . . be interpreted not as 'scientific proof' of anything, but merely as a scientific-seeming kind of Aesop's fable," he adds a firm rule: "an experiment with organisms that do not use language cannot tell us anything essential about the distinctive motives of a species that does use language" (li). The formation of this rule in Burke's thought is an important event. But in *PC*, Burke violates it routinely. Its formation lies in the future.

Burke uses the "Prologue" to revise the book's essentialism in a constructionist direction. Biology, he insists, "needs the corrective of a concern with *social motives as such*. Thus, human kinds of domination and subjection must decidedly never be reduced to the strictly 'natural' or 'biological'" (li). The constructionist "discount" needed to offset the essentialist biologism is, Burke insists, "implicit . . . at many points," but he admits, "it is not as explicit as the author would now have it" (li).

Resisting the essentialist reading that Burke fears requires considerable strain. Two examples illustrate the point. In one, "Outlines of a 'Metabiology,'" Burke poses the question of the ultimate biological purpose. Is it a Nietzschean will to power asserted even at the risk of cruelty? Or is it more beneficent? A desire to communicate, to cooperate, to act as a participant in a collective endeavor? Burke opts for the more charitable view and then underlines its significance in his thought by stepping back in a gesture of disarming honesty – "Here, in all its nudity, is the Jamesian 'will to believe.' It amounts in the end to the assumption that good, rather than evil, lies at the roots of human purpose" (236). One additional argument is added that could be construed as a constructionist "discount": "And as for those who would suggest that this is merely a verbal solution, I would answer that by no other fiction can men truly cooperate in historic processes, hence the fiction itself is universally gounded" (236). This one-sentence argument, however, gives the constructionist reader little more than a small oar with which to row upstream against a strong essentialist current.

In the second example, Burke addresses a problem like the one emerging in current debates that take their cue from Jameson's maxim, "always historicize." The historicizing line of argument against essentializing has effectively revised our view of practices that in the past have been seen as "natural." The problem arises when one turns from this denaturalizing operation to proposing alternatives. At this point, we may wish we could take back the now discredited category of the natural. Exhortation in the name of something natural has obvious rhetorical advantages. The role of "permanence" in *PC* addresses this problem:

> In closing, we might add a few remarks on the relation between the permanent and the historic ... In subscribing to a philosophy of being, as here conceived, one may hold that certain historically conditioned institutions interfere with the establishment of decent social or communicative relationships, and thereby affront permanent biologic norms ... And since we insist a point of view requires, as its material counterpart, adequate embodiment in the architecture of the State, a philosophy of being may commit one to open conflict with any persons or class of persons who would use their power to uphold institutions serving an anti-social function. (271–72)

The essentialist current thus runs strong to the end.

The *bête noire* throughout *ACR* is the principle of antithesis in the class struggle between the bourgeoisie and the proletariat. The constructionist and essentialist arguments first emerge in Burke's polemic with various aspects and effects of this principle. The arguments reappear in *PC*, sometimes functioning in different ways. What disappears is the direct polemic with the bourgeois–proletariat antithesis. Compared to one another, *ACR* dismantles this antithesis and *PC* shifts from the negativity of attack to the affirmation of a theoretical alternative.

His alternative includes a history. There is also a history in *ACR*, but it's limited to placing the situation created by the Great Depression against a backdrop extending back a little more than a century. In the past, *ACR* argues, the aesthetic tradition resisted the way of life fostered by the capitalist market and industrial organization, creating a deep cultural opposition between the aesthetic and the practical; but in the present, with the collapse of capitalism, the old practicalities are impractical and the aesthetic alternative is the new practicality (151–65). Burke thus depicts his personal evolution as riding the wave of history. He continues to ride that wave in *PC*, but in a new historical narrative with sufficient scope to rival the classic Marxist dialectic of history. Pitched at an extraordinarily abstract level, however, Burke's narrative flies over the trench warfare in Marxist class struggle like a jet airliner at 30,000 feet. An example of what Lyotard calls "grand narrative,"[18] Burke's history moves through three periods – distinguished

---

18 Jean-François Lyotard, *The Postmodern Condition: A Report on Knowledge*, trans. Geoff Bennington and Brian Massumi (Minneapolis: University of Minnesota Press, 1984), p. 37.

as magic, religion, and science – and concludes with an emergent fourth, the new practicality that communism promises to advance (*PC* 59–66; *PC1* 82–94).

But even at this abstract level – and despite all Burke's efforts to transcend antithesis to the biological level of oneness – antithesis returns, imposing itself on his history to render it intelligible. It does so silently, without benefit of acknowledgment, but it nonetheless does its necessary work. As we'll see, antithesis leaves the body politic to reappear in the body biologic.

In *ACR* itself, antithesis reappears even after Burke offers an alternative model of historical change, one that substitutes "difference" for "antithesis": a society is "integrated" when everyone wants to do what it requires of them; "disintegrated" when people begin acting more out of necessity than desire; and "reintegrated" through a process of incremental "differences" (99–104). This model offers "an explanation of history which can ... say that thinking becomes *different* from what it was, rather than *antithetical* to what it was" (104). The model appeals to Burke because it is more spacious, making it easier to accommodate discourses remote from the terms of a privileged antithetical opposition. With this model, he argues, one wouldn't valorize a "trivial party-member on a Communistic committee" while marginalizing a great writer as remote (100). Yet when Burke turns from this theoretical model to construct a narrative explanation of actual historical data, antithesis returns: throughout the nineteenth century, when the practicality of capitalism appeared unimpeachable, at least when compared to the way it appeared in the 1930s, "intellectuals ... fortified themselves against this authority of the practical frame by formulating a directly antithetical esthetic frame" (161). Further, in surveying the work of these intellectuals, while Burke finds many differences among them, these are all subsumed under the antithetical function they share together (156). With the collapse of capitalism and the emergence of the aesthetic as the new practicality, it would appear that thinking is becoming antithetical rather than merely different. Burke says as much in *PC* by proposing "cooperative" as the word that may antithetically displace "competitive."[19]

In the later *PLF*, Burke equates "dramatic" with "dialectic" to produce a "perspective for the analysis of history, which is a 'dramatic' process, involving dialectical oppositions" (109). The equation transforms

---

19 For alternative views of the relation in *ACR* of difference to antithesis, see Crusius, "*Auscultation*"; and Henderson, "Aesthetic."

the Hegelian antithesis into the Burkean agon. In *GM*, constitutions are defined as "agonistic instruments" (357). Not until the final phase of his career, as we'll see in our final chapter, does Burke once again seek to marginalize the agon, albeit in a very different way.

It's true that *PC*'s concluding chapter introduces "the poetic or dramatic metaphor" (263). But when one scrutinizes this chapter, one finds nothing about the dramatic agon. The chapter draws, instead, on the model of the cooperative relation of artist to audience constructed in "The Poetic Process," where, as noted in chapter 2, what defines an artist is the capacity not to express emotion but to craft a structure that evokes emotion. "The ultimate goal of the poetic metaphor would be a society in which the participant aspect of action attained its maximum expression ... Meanwhile, alas! we are forced to live by economic patterns which reduce the cooperative aspects of action to a minimum" (269–71). Later, whether a discourse incorporates the agonistic becomes a test of whether it is dramatistic (*PLF* 290–91).

One effect of the Marxist antithesis, in Burke's account in *ACR*, was to label art works as bourgeois or proletarian and to judge their value accordingly. *ACR*'s subtitle – "the Rout of the Esthetes" – sums up Burke's depiction of his generation. The esthetes "cleared out," Burke remonstrates, portraying himself as the one left behind to stand alone in defense of art (61–62). Brought up to appreciate monuments of art, his generation now ostracized them as bourgeois, cultivating instead proletarian substitutes. Burke scoffs at such efforts to find "the proletarian opposite of a sonnet, or the antithesis of a tone-poem by Debussy," dismissing them as a cultural politics of "proletarian denudation" (103–04). In an "Addendum" added an unspecified time after the completion of the main text, Burke quips that defending art became a bit easier only when the news got around that "Marx read Shakespeare with enjoyment" (166).

It's easy to imagine how Burke might have entertained himself by compiling a long list of invidious comparisons of classics to the proletarian literature of the day. But he refused such Arnoldian one-upmanship, searching instead for a new aesthetic that would be compatible with Marxist economics but authorize an alternative cultural politics.

He begins *ACR*, after a few introductory preliminaries, by taking on the charge of escapism that became commonplace as the deepening economic crisis made the antithesis between bourgeoisie and proletariat seem to be the only reality, attention to anything else mere escapism (63–84). Burke distinguishes three realities – primary, secondary, and tertiary – to change the issue. Primary reality is the body as it matures, forms habits, and finally decays; secondary, the "natural society, in which tools are hand-shaped and appeasements are doglike" (64) – in line with Burke's "will to believe," it's the tail-wagging dog that turns up in natural society, not the Nietzschean pit bull. The natural society is the face-to-face community where relations are human, not mediated through abstractions of the market, and where one labors in control of one's tools, not as a cog in an industrial machine. Both primary and secondary realities are necessary. Tertiary reality is contingent; the Great Depression is an example (66). However real the effects of the economic crisis, human life is imaginable without modern industrial society. The real issue is whether one may, Burke argues, "recognize the menaces of the tertiary world as menaces, without being forced to conclude that concerns with anything else are proved, once and for all, chimerical" (65). Burke anticipates his typology of realities in "Spring during Crisis," the foreword to *ACR*, as he narrates a train ride in early spring away from the tertiary world of the metropolis back to his farm in New Jersey.[20]

Burke reaffirms the primacy of biological reality in an argument that turns the Marxist category of "production" against Marxism. Describing *ACR* as he was completing it, he remarks, "My big number, however, is in taking the Marxian concept of 'productive forces,' and showing how this concept can be manipulated to obtain quite different kinds of critical exhortation than are customarily circulated among the joiners and committeemen" (L2). Burke's argument is synopsized in an introductory title: "Wherein We Play the Permanent 'Organic Productive Forces' against the Contemporary 'Social Productive Forces' Thus Restoring in Part the 'Human Substrate'" (119). Burke's premise is that if changes in production can change ideology, then by the same token constancy in one should produce constancy in the other: "the organic productive forces, the weapons integral to the body, have remained unchanged, so we might expect some vestiges of an ideological

---

20 Purchased in 1922, the farm has been Burke's home ever since, and for many decades he was content with a nineteenth-century standard of creature comforts: an outhouse, water from a well, no electricity (Rueckert, "Field," 4, 35). In "Spring during Crisis," Burke dreams, more as a "mood" than a "project," of a society of small agrarian landowners restored to a barter economy (51).

'constant' in keeping with this constancy on the part of the organic productive forces themselves" (120). Biological essentialism thus empowered Burke to hear – auscultation – a primary oneness beneath the temporary noise of tertiary divisions: "Such a thought would suggest that we could not simplify our esthetic canons by envisaging the literary problem in terms of a strictly bourgeois–proletarian dichotomy, as there should be some ideological overlap of the groups corresponding to this identity in the organic productive forces of both groups" (120).

In the body, then, Burke locates a primal level of identification that makes possible a corresponding level of aesthetic communication cutting across bourgeois and proletarian differences. In his early aesthetic, as we saw in the last chapter, Burke sought permanence and found it in innate forms in the mind. In the 1930s, he seeks it again, this time finding it in the body, as his concerns become less purely aesthetic and more broadly cultural. In *PC*, furthermore, as we'll see later, he roots in the body a will to eloquence, one designed to counter the Nietzschean will to power.

The constructionist argument in *ACR* functions in resistance to the principle of economic determinism. Burke's resistance distinguished him among leftists; one report on the first Writers' Congress depicted him as a "revolutionary 'free-willer.'"[21] Burke forges the argument in a context where he reconceives the aesthetic as a process of naming that encompasses science, art, philosophy, and criticism (146). An economic situation, Burke concedes, may occasion a new name, but it doesn't determine it. The situation is determinative only in the sense that it presents a problem demanding a solution: "The 'solution,' however, would be something unpredictably added, a re-adaptation of past meanings to the new situation, requiring a new 'combination' so extrinsic to the situation itself that it need never be found at all" (148). Burke thus steps toward a view of language as playing a constitutive role in the construction of reality. *PC* takes additional steps, those portions of the book proving in time to anticipate the direction Burke takes in subsequent books. But these steps coexist with the biological essentialism that ultimately makes the book about permanence more than change.

In the beginning of *PC*, Burke addresses once again the escapist charge.

21 John Chamberlain, "The Literary Left Grows Up," *The Saturday Review of Literature*, 11 May 1935: 17.

The argument against it, however, no longer relies on the typology of primary, secondary, and tertiary realities. Instead it relies on the concept of "trained incapacity," which Burke borrows from Thorstein Veblen (7): "The concept of trained incapacity has the great advantage of avoiding the contemporary tendency to discuss matters of orientation by reference to 'avoidance' and 'escape'" (8).

ACR responds to the escapist charge by simply reversing it, keeping the form of the argument but changing its terms to turn it against his polemical antagonist. For the implication of his typology of realities is that to preoccupy oneself with tertiary reality is to escape the more fundamental primary and secondary realities. Given the effects of the economic crisis on the tertiary level, however, Burke couldn't say that attending to them was escapist. But he could say that the crisis, however severe, was temporary. And he does in fact quote a passage from John Maynard Keynes to the effect that it will take twenty-five years or so to resolve the crisis but that one day it can indeed be resolved once and for all. "It is no insult to a burning issue," Burke adds, "to hope that it will someday cease to be burning" (82).

ACR's response works, in other words, by positing a different foundational reality. With trained incapacity, Burke deploys an altogether different form of argument — a constructionist argument. Any orientation, Burke argues, is a training, a way of interpreting experience and thereby constructing a reality: "Reality is *what things will do to us or for us*. It is the expectation of comfort or discomfort, prosperity or risk" (*PC* 22). The irony is that training is also always an incapacity, because situations inevitably arise where one's training leads to precisely the wrong action. Training is necessary, but sometimes it's an incapacity. Orientations are constructed realities. One is always dealing with reality one constructionist move away from it. Orientation is another word for ideology, one less charged, especially in the context of the Great Depression. In a retrospective comment added for *PC*'s third edition, Burke indicates that he preferred orientation because it was not tied to the base-superstructure model (304–05).

With trained incapacity, Burke thus devises an argument that can work against the postulation of any reality as foundational and the categorization of everyone as either facing or avoiding it. The difficulty with the escapist charge, Burke contends in *PC*, is that it "suggested that the people to whom it was applied tended to orientate themselves in a totally different way from the people to whom it was not applied, the former always trying to escape from life or avoid realities, while the latter faced realities ... In this way ... they were free to accuse many writers and thinkers of escape" (8). The customary form of the escapist charge, in other words, presupposes that the question of reality is settled. Burke reopens the question by revising it: ask not, "is reality being faced?" but "which reality are we talking about?" Rather than distinguishing and ranking realities – primary, secondary, and tertiary – the concept of trained incapacity defines realities as constructions that are equal as trained incapacities. The concept marginalizes the issue of escape to direct attention to the issue of determining which reality to construct. No construction is foolproof, but one may be preferable to others in a given situation.

The implication of trained incapacity is that history is open-ended, moving from orientation to orientation with no final orientation. There is no place of truth in which to rest. It's a history without a telos, change without permanence. This implication, however, is ultimately curtailed by biological essentialism, which delays Burke's pursuit of it to another day.

Before turning to that curtailment, however, it's necessary to see how the constructionist side of *PC* is further developed in the concept of "perspective by incongruity," which Burke invented as he reflected on Nietzsche's perspectivism (88). This concept anticipates Burke's later work even more than trained incapacity. *Perspectives by Incongruity* is the title Stanley Edgar Hyman used in the 1960s for one of the two volumes of Burke texts that he collected to make Burke more familiar to a wider audience (*Terms for Order* is the other). It would be difficult to imagine using "trained incapacities" for such a purpose. The reason is that the theoretical basis for perspective by incongruity is linguistic, whereas for trained incapacity it's behavioristic. After Burke becomes anti-behaviorist, the combination of "blindness and insight" in trained incapacity is rebuilt on a linguistic basis in the notion of "terministic screens" (see TS).

The opening of *PC* is one of the many places in the book where Burke moves back and forth between human and animal worlds. He begins, "All Living Things Are Critics," explaining that they are all interpreters. Chickens conditioned to respond to a bell to receive food have a training, an interpretive orientation. The training may, of course, become an incapacity. One day they may respond to the bell and receive not food but a chop severing their heads. "Chickens not so well educated would have acted more wisely" (6). This is the kind of example – and there are many of them – that Burke asks us, in his retrospective "Prologue," to read as an Aesopian fable. It can be read this way. It is an invention; Burke doesn't assemble data used in actual behavioristic research. Nonetheless, what such examples substantiate is a theoretical model limited to stimulus and response on the level that Burke later routinely identifies as "motion" to distinguish it from "action." The limits of the model are escaped in part simply by not observing them rigorously. For example, Burke contrasts humans to the chickens by citing the greater complexity of human orientations, which fact doesn't, however, make them any less immune to disaster. "No slight critical ability is required," Burke gibes, "for one to hate as his deepest enemy a people thousands of miles away" (6). But hatred across great distance suggests that language introduces a level of motivation not reducible to the motion in the immediacies of behavioristic stimulus and response. Later, Burke makes this point over and over, as one standard way he introduces dramatism places it in polemical opposition to behaviorism. But in *PC*, he isn't ready to draw this line. Just as the bell derives its meaning for the chickens from the past contexts in which it rings, "words . . . [derive] their meanings out of past contexts" (7). There is no break in going from one to the other.[22]

Perspective by incongruity, by contrast, is based on a theory of language as metaphor. One can reconstruct reality by changing metaphors. Words customarily construed as literal are really dead metaphors. What can revive them is perspective by incongruity. Orientation is trained incapacity; reorientation is perspective by incongruity. Burke illustrates perspective by incongruity with a veritable constructionist saturnalia, offering strategies, amply illustrated, for melting down common sense into total verbal liquidity (118–24).[23] When he was writing about perspective by incongruity, he reports in the "Prologue," he had a dream in which he played a card game in

22 In 1976, Burke wrote for *Behaviorism* a review of B. F. Skinner's autobiography. While he concerns himself mainly with his differences with behaviorism, he does note its early appeal, looking to *PC* to recall it. In *PC*, he credits Pavlov with giving the vagueness of "speculative psychology a precise empirical grounding" (11). It's this step away from reliance on introspection that interested Burke initially and that remains an area of methodological overlap (SPP 264–65). Incidentally, *Behaviorism* also published a review, written by a behaviorist, of Burke's review, thus offering a rare opportunity to see what behaviorists say in response to what Burke has been saying about them all these years (see Baer).

23 The saturnalia takes to its ultimate conclusion the side of *PC* that Jay, in "Modernism," privileges in his astute depiction of Burke as a forerunner of Derrida. See Murray for a reading of Burke's work that privileges this saturnalia on the ground that in it Burke faces verbal "dissonance" instead of trying, as elsewhere, to displace it (156).

which all the cards were wild (lv). The saturnalia, isolated and read out of context, amounts to a *reductio ad absurdum* of rhetorical idealism. Here, Burke says, "Let us say with [D. H.] Lawrence that the earth's crops make the sun shine," a perspective by incongruity that seemingly turns things upside down (122). This example reappears, as we'll see later, in Burke's debate with I. A. Richards at the end of *PC*, where Burke defends Lawrence once again, though there the defense is qualified to keep his constructionism on the side of realism rather than idealism. This debate exhibits in emergent form, as suggested in the last chapter, differences between the high road to the New Criticism that Richards helped to pave and the different path that Burke cleared in the 1930s and 1940s.

Burke forges his theory of perspective by incongruity in the context of the classic presupposition that language can represent reality transparently. This presupposition makes it possible to distinguish uses of language in which such representation occurs from uses in which it doesn't, a distinction that can be made in various terms such as literal vs. metaphor, and statement vs. pseudo-statement. So firmly was the distinction put into place by logical positivism that the New Critics challenged not the distinction but the conclusions positivists derived from it. A classic example of this challenge is I. A. Richards's "Science and Poetry," the text Burke cites in debating Richards.

Positivism admonished, "What we cannot speak about we must pass over in silence."[24] Troubled that words may look like a statement of sense when they are really a pseudo-statement of nonsense, positivism envisioned a logical syntax that would make pseudo-statements ungrammatical and therefore unsayable.[25] This distinction between statements and pseudo-statements continues in place until mid-century. It appears in the first lecture in *How to Do Things with Words*, as Austin invokes the discursive regime he is about to displace altogether, a displacement that has, as we'll see in a later chapter, its analogue in Burke's dramatism.

Richards used the distinction between pseudo-statement and statement – the language of his antagonist – challenging not the distinction but the positivist devaluation of poetry that threatened to reduce it to silence, along with all other pseudo-statements. He

---

24 Ludwig Wittgenstein, *Tractatus Logico-Philosophicus*, trans. D. F. Pears and B. F. McGuinness (London: Routledge & Kegan Paul, 1961), p. 151.
25 Rudolf Carnap, "The Elimination of Metaphysics through Logical Analysis of Language," *Logical Positivism*, ed. A. J. Ayer (New York: Free Press, 1959), p. 68.

conceded that science gives us statements not to be confused with the pseudo-statements of poetry. He objected to Lawrence's line, "the earth's crops make the sun shine," because it is a pseudo-statement parading as a statement. His strategy was to defend the pseudo-statements of great poetry as expressing attitudes that must be preserved for civilization to survive. He warns that the positivist dismissal of all pseudo-statements is effecting a change in the cultural landscape that will leave nothing for "more finely developed individuals . . . Such people cannot live by warmth, food, fighting, drink and sex alone. Those who are least affected by the change are those who are emotionally least removed from the animals."[26] Less willing than Richards to speak in defense of pseudo-statements, later New Critics changed his terminology and with the changes came revisions, but they adopted his fundamental strategy. Leaving the distinction between scientific and poetic language intact, they concentrated on valorizing the complexity of the language of poetry.

In *PC*, by contrast, Burke attacks the distinction by deconstructing *avant la lettre* the presupposition on which it rests. His polemical antagonist presupposes that analogizing, such as that in metaphor, can be put aside to represent reality in literal statements — statements of sense rather than the nonsense of pseudo-statement. Instead of following the Richards strategy — leave this presupposition intact but defend the value of pseudo-statement — Burke dismantles the presupposition, demonstrating that it's not possible to put analogizing aside: "all abstract general notions are, indeed, nothing but marks of analogies between a given fact and all the other facts belonging to the same class: [at most] they may mark rather closer analogies than those brought out by an ordinary metaphor" (95). One can see Burke's point with an example like "living human beings breathe." Obviously a statement rather than a pseudo-statement, it is an inductive generalization that could serve as a premise in a syllogism. Burke's argument is that in going from one factual instance of breathing to the next to arrive at this generalization, one must overlook the differences dividing instance from instance: differences in lung tissue, in the quality and amount of air taken in, and so on. Even in an individual life, each breath occurs at a different time; we all have a first breath and a last. The

---

26 "Science and Poetry," *Criticism: The Foundations of Modern Literary Judgment*, revised ed., ed. Mark Schorer *et al.* (New York: Harcourt, Brace and Company, 1958), pp. 519, 522. Richards was doubly troubled by Lawrence, whom he saw not only confusing a pseudo-statement with a statement, but also reverting in the process to a "primitive mentality."

generalization is built on an analogizing that brushes such differences aside. In deconstructive fashion, Burke thus demonstrates that his antagonist excludes and subordinates the very analogizing on which it depends. The point is not to question the generalization "living human beings breathe," but to identify the constructivity in the analogizing that makes it possible.

The demonstration disrupts the classic opposition between essential and accidental attributes – an opposition that, Derrida remarks, "is precisely what all deconstruction has from the start called into question."[27] In its classic deployment, one could relegate to the realm of the accidental all the differences subtracted in arriving at an inductive generalization and enshrine the core analogy as an essence. Such familiar confidence is shaken by exposing the constructivity that it ignores. The essences and the accidents are constructed, not given. No system of classification is foundational. Such systems are constructions that routinely displace one another: "When a philosopher invents a new approach to reality, he promptly finds that his predecessors saw something as a unit which he can subdivide, or that they accepted distinctions which his system can name as unities" (*PC* 103). Classification is inevitable, but not any single classification, because all classifications are dictated by "interest" (102). Classifications are always positional in the sense that they are constructions erected from the standpoint of an interest that can be located and dated.

Classification is "accomplished by the two processes of over-simplication and analogical extension. We over-simplify a given event when we characterize it from the standpoint of a given interest – and we attempt to invent a similar characterization for other events by analogy" (107). Perspectival incongruities arise as a new mode of analogical extension disrupts previous classifications that have come to seem "natural." At the core of the over-simplification, one finds a metaphor. "Over-simplification" is sometimes alternatively called the "basis of simplification," the phrase used to entitle the third and last part of the book, where Burke concludes by contrasting his "humans are poets" metaphor to the mechanistic metaphor of science (261).

---

27 "Afterword: Toward an Ethic of Discussion," *Limited Inc*, ed. Gerald Graff (Evanston: Northwestern University Press, 1988), p. 141. For a shrewd study of Derrida from the standpoint of deconstruction's challenge to this classic opposition, see Henry Staten, *Wittgenstein and Derrida* (Lincoln: University of Nebraska Press, 1984).

Perspective by incongruity serves as the title for part two. Trained incapacity is the key concept in part one. Both point toward the complexity of open-ended change that could be summed up in an image of constructions and reconstructions succeeding one another indefinitely. This open-ended image, however, is not allowed to get too far off the ground. Burke's historical narrative reduces change to three periods, plus the emergent fourth Burke midwives into the verbal form of *PC*.

These four are designated "rationalizations." In introducing this term, Burke takes pains to dissociate his use of it from its use to name a process of self-deception. In his use, rationalization is the verbalization of an orientation (18). All living organisms have orientations; humans have, in addition, rationalizations subject to the formal transformations of perspective by incongruity.

In the historical narrative of these successive rationalizations, as noted earlier, the agonistic appears. The first agon is between magic and religion. Burke questions the depiction of magic in Frazer's *The Golden Bough* as collapsing from the weight of its errors. It's too easy, he suggests, to imagine ways that a magician could blame counter-spells whenever things didn't turn out as anticipated.

It would seem to me that a system so self-sustaining could be attacked only *from without*. And I would suggest that the attack arose as a new point of view arose. This point of view emphasized, not the dominance of natural power, but the stressing of *human* cooperation. We may call this rising point of view the *philosophic corrective* to magic, with its brutal indifference to the sufferings of the victims it required for its success... This corrective philosophy gradually becomes metamorphosed into a new rationalization, religion. (61)

One glimpses here, however sketchily, competing groups locked in ideological struggle. On one side, there is religion, calling for an end to the brutality magic requires; on the other, there is magic, proud in its dominance of nature, warning that turning to religion is as foolhardy as sailing a ship without a rudder.

The agon between religion and science is even more sketchy (62); Burke not only assumes greater familiarity with it but also is principally interested in hurrying forward to the agon between science and his poetic alternative, the agon in which he is a participant. He enters it to contend that a "corrective rationalization must certainly move in the direction of the anthropomorphic or humanistic or poetic, since this is the aspect of culture which the scientific criteria, with their emphasis

73

upon dominance rather than upon inducement, have tended to eliminate or minimize" (65).

Science, then, however different from magic, returns to magic's emphasis on "dominance" of nature. Further, while science doesn't entail the sacrifice of human life that magic demanded, its great achievement, technology, is willing to subordinate human needs to technological demands, precisely the tendency Burke looks to communism to reverse. Hence, rationalizations radically different on one level, perform functions that are very much alike. Similarly, the poetic rationalization returns to religion's emphasis on cooperation. Again, difference on one level, similarity on a functional level.

In sum, the historical narrative, when scrutinized, appears less linear than cyclical, alternating on the foundational level between two functions, whatever the differences among the verbal rationalizations performing each function at different points in history. Burke's history, in short, ironically puts us on the track of permanence rather than change: "the fact that man's neurological structure has remained pretty much of a constant through all the shifts of his environment would justify us in looking for permanencies beneath the differences" (159). The search is the burden of the book's concluding part. These permanencies explain the cycle of history in general and, more particularly and importantly, the motivations behind science and poetry in the agon that pits them against one another.

The agon Burke stages between science and poetry explains his interest in Richards. Despite their differences they both center their attention on the same crisis, one located at a site distant from the opposition between bourgeoisie and proletariat. Together at this site, Richards and Burke go in opposite directions: Richards, toward a view of poetry as an oasis apart from reality; Burke, toward a view of culture as a constructionist part of reality.

The debate with Richards unfolds in an epistemological context as Burke addresses the epistemological anxiety produced by his constructionist collapse of the distinction between statements and pseudo-statements. In allaying this anxiety, Burke draws on both the biological and the linguistic. The biological serves to make the Nietzschean point that there is no alternative to perspectivism, even on a biological level, as Burke again moves back and forth between animal and human worlds to argue that the human being and the grasshopper are alike in that "each approaches the universe from a different 'point of view,' and the difference in point of view will reveal

a corresponding difference in the discovery of relevant 'facts'"
(256).[28] The linguistic returns Burke once again to the Lawrence
claim, troubling to Richards, that "the earth's crops make the sun
shine." Burke defends the claim, but qualifies his defense by introducing
a realist principle he calls "recalcitrance" (255). Language, in constructing
a world, can guide the performance of tests by which one can first
discern whether a statement encounters nonverbal recalcitrance and
then revise it accordingly. "I am a bird" can be tested and revised to "I
am an aviator" (255). The revising of a seminal perspective, moreover,
involves additional orders of recalcitrance that enter the process as
others participate in the revising. By the time these revisions finish
fitting the perspective "to the recalcitrance of social relationships,
political exigencies, economic procedures, etc., transferring it from the
private architecture of a poem into the public architecture of a social
order, those who dealt with it in its incipient or emergent stages could
hardly recognize it as having stemmed from them" (258). Lawrence's
claim, by making the end the cause of the beginning, reintroduces an
Aristotelian final cause that in the twentieth century is a radical
perspective by incongruity. Its shortcoming is not that it's a
pseudo-statement, but that it stands unrevised by the recalcitrance
principle (256). Burke suggests some possible lines of revision to
conclude his debate with Richards (258–61).

Science concerns Burke because of the permanency he discerns in
his history behind its will to dominate. He even personalizes this
permanency in his characterization of science, surprising us moreover
with the person he chooses for this role.

Science is the threat for both Richards and Burke, but it's a different
threat for each. For Richards, it's science's lock on the representation of
reality which forces him to find a way to make do with pseudo-statements.
But Burke deconstructs that lock; Richards's problem is not his
problem. For Burke, behind any construction of reality there is always
an interest, a standpoint from which the classificatory analogizing that
erects the construction is carried out. His characterization of science
portrays the interest that he finds threatening.

28 One place Nietzsche makes the argument is in "On Truth and Lying in an Extra-Moral
    Sense," a text that has received considerable attention of late: "the insect or the bird perceives
    a completely different world than man does ... the question which of the two world-perceptions
    is more right is a completely senseless one, since it could be decided only by the criterion of
    the *right perception*, i.e., by a standard *which does not exist*"; *Friedrich Nietzsche on Rhetoric and
    Language*, ed. and trans. Sander L. Gilman, Carole Blair, and David J. Parent (New York:
    Oxford University Press, 1989), p. 252.

The portrayal narrows from science to its child, technology. Like magic, science is a rationalization designed to dominate nature, but it does so at one remove, through the agency of technology: "We are now concerned with a third great rationalization, science, the attempt to control for our purposes the forces of technology, or machinery" (44). When he designates the antagonistic threat to poetry, he calls it the "technological psychosis," not the scientific (44).

Technology, it should be noted in passing, continues as the antagonist in Burke's politics decades after the 1930s. Eventually, the hope that a communist system could tame technology gives way to an ecological politics in which the late USSR and the US, whatever their differences, are partners in foisting onto the world a technological imperialism that threatens the planet.[29] This picture of the world is emergent in the 1940s (e.g., *GM* 442) and becomes increasingly prominent in later work, as evidenced, for example, by the afterwords Burke added to *PC* and *ATH* for their third editions, in 1984.[30] Looking back at these books across nearly half a century, Burke offers radical rereadings to assimilate them to his later depiction of his agon with technology, in which technology is sometimes called "counter-nature" (*PC* 306–08, *ATH* 377–79).

From the standpoint of technology, *PC* rewrites the history of science, giving less emphasis to pioneers like Galileo and Bacon, and more to the later maturation of technology in the time of Bentham and utilitarianism. In utilitarianism Burke finds the informing principle of the technological psychosis (44–45). Utilitarian valuation proved to be essentially transvaluation, since it fostered the rewriting from the standpoint of a narrow conception of utility all traditional religious, ethical, and aesthetic judgments (45).

Casting the antagonist in the agon, then, is a matter of selecting the figure who, more radically than anyone else, transvalued every traditional piety. Burke's choice is Nietzsche:

---

29 In an article that merits attention, Wolfe uses *PC* to incorporate ecology within a radical politics. Essential to Wolfe's analysis is his correlation, which confirms Burke's, of the dominance of nature with the dominance of human subjects (78–85). Wolfe's reading of *PC* complements readings that ignore altogether its biological essentialism in favor of its verbal constructionism.

30 There is also evidence in *ATH*'s second edition (350). In the first edition, Burke prophesies, "Among the sciences, there is one little fellow named Ecology, and in time we shall pay him more attention." Decades later, a report on surging interest in ecology credits Burke with being "exceedingly perspicacious." See William Bowen, "Our New Awareness of the Great Web," *Fortune*, Feb. 1970, p. 198.

He was questioning, down to the very last value, every pious linkage which man had derived from his cultural past . . . His magnificent equipment as an artist opened him constantly to the processes of piety; yet his sharply aphoristic intellect was turned upon the doubting of these processes.

The result is perhaps the fullest, most self-contradictory symbolization of the transition from the pre-technological to the technological psychosis which mankind will ever possess. Zarathustra, coming down to us from among the severities and strangenesses of lonely, snow-capped mountains, to hint of dangerous earthly and unearthy revels, and then piously to ritualize a kind of skepticism, of irreligious shrewdness, which is the very essence of the metropolis.   (46)

Nietzsche plays a double role in *PC*. Burke is heavily indebted to his perspectivism, yet the Nietzschean will to power is a threat, as Burke makes explicit when he prepares for the assertion of his "will to believe" in a charitable biological purpose: "Since war and action are both parts of a graded series, having cruelty and vengeance at one end and the highest manifestations of thought and sympathy at the other, I see no logical necessity for selecting the dyslogistic choice of the Nietzscheans as descriptive of the series' essence" (235).

Nietzsche returns in Burke's retrospective afterwords to *PC* and *ATH*, where he is identified even more closely with technology. The identification is capsulated in Burke's use of brackets to interpolate his interpretation of Nietzsche's trademark phrase: "a will to [technological, instrumental, manmade] power" (*ATH* 379). Through identification with technological power, Burke suggests, a new mode of self-magnification became available that found its most enduring voice in the Nietzschean *Übermensch* (385).[31]

No person appears to serve as the protagonist to the Nietzschean antagonist, but the poetic metaphor comes close. Behind the metaphor, as already noted, is the earlier aestheticism and its artist, defined not by self-expression, but by the eloquence that evokes emotion.

Since social life, like art, is a *problem of appeal*, the poetic metaphor would give us invaluable hints for describing modes of practical action which are too often measured by simple tests of utility . . . Is not the relation between individual and group greatly illumined by reference to the corresponding relation between writer and audience? . . . The metaphor also has the advantage of emphasizing the *participant* aspect of action rather than its *competitive*

31 See Desilet for a reading of Nietzsche, based on a positive interpretation of the "will to power" (74–75), that sides with him against Burke.

77

aspect, hence offering a prompt basis of objection when the contingencies of our economic structure force us to overstress competitive attitudes.

(*PC* 264–65, 266)

The agon: the will to power as the antagonist; the will to eloquence as the protagonist.

These contrary motivations, localized in bodies, are rooted in biology. In other words, they are rooted not in the body politic – as are the competing motivations surrounding Therborn's worker-qua-body, examined in chapter 1 – but in the body biologic. The issue of which is subordinated to which is decided transcendentally, by biology, and registered in Burke's "will to believe," though perhaps not without irony. As Burke steps back to spotlight his belief, he may be saying that he believes while unwittingly showing to skeptical readers that he is having a hard time believing it. In any case, the resolution of the agon is "essentialist" rather than "proportional," to return to the terms, discussed in chapter 1, that Burke later uses to refuse essentialism. The subject that *PC* theorizes is not rhetorical but a subject of history.

It's easy to assimilate to the Nietzschean will to power Burke's view that all classifications derive from an informing interest. To keep Nietzsche at arm's length, therefore, Burke needs in *PC* to identify a higher interest. He locates one in ideal poetic communication – the will to eloquence – holding it up as a beacon for the culture, and generalizing it to everyday life, so that all human relations have the potential to approximate the ideal. Cultural humanism thus displaces his early aesthetic humanism.

The science–poetry and the bourgeoisie–proletariat agons are distant from one another, but it's possible to speculate on affinities Burke may have discerned between the Marxist approach to the latter and his to the former. The workplace is the standard site for the bourgeois–proletarian agon, as we saw earlier in the Lukács narrative. The alienation theme in that narrative is an effect of the separation in the capitalist workplace of the manual side of work from the mental or purposive. Assembly-line workers are alienated cogs in a machine designed by others. A classic study of the spread of this alienating pattern is Harry Braverman's *Labor and Monopoly Capital: The Degradation of Work in the Twentieth Century*.[32] Burke glances at this workplace alienation in his references to the subordination of human

32 *Labor and Monopoly Capital: The Degradation of Work in the Twentieth Century* (New York: Monthly Review Press, 1974).

needs to technological demands that he looks to communism to reverse. But his main interest is the poet rather than the worker.

In relation to the alienation theme, two things may be said about the poet. On the one hand, the poet's work is relatively, if not completely, unalienated. Literary culture, in modern industrial society, stands out as one of the rare places holding out the promise of work where the manual and the mental are indissolubly one. This promise, given the paucity of financial rewards that literary culture has had to offer, no doubt has played a crucial role in sustaining what little there is of it. Burke, then, instead of focusing on the site of maximum alienation, turned his attention in the opposite direction, to a site where one might conceivably uncover the conditions of human fulfillment. On the other hand, scrutiny of these conditions also uncovers ways that the larger culture limits fulfillment. Unalienated in one sense, the modern poet is alienated in another. If the alienated proletariat is the place from which to revolutionize the economic base, the alienated poet may be the place from which to revolutionize the cultural superstructure.

Hence, in Burke's historical narrative, instead of a proletariat struggling against becoming a cog in a machine, one finds a poet struggling against a culture that makes it difficult to be a poet: "A sound system of communication, such as lies at the roots of civilization, cannot be built upon a structure of economic warfare. It must be economically, as well as spiritually, Communistic – otherwise the wells of sociality are poisoned" (*PC1* 213). As Burke turns from aesthetic to cultural theory, he thus shifts his primary attention from the technical rhetorical operations involved in aesthetic communication to the cultural conditions that foster or retard such communication. These conditions were not altogether ignored in the 1920s, but Burke's attention to them did not get much beyond the deleterious effects, analyzed in "Psychology and Form," of the "psychology of information" fostered by the prestige of science.

"The Nature of Art under Capitalism" (NAC), a 1933 essay, examines ways that the texture of the historical environment shapes the options available to artists. Ideally a productive system should valorize cooperative values by making them pay. When a productive system is morally sound, artists can practice "pure art." Humans can communicate most fully, in idealized poetic communication, when "pure art" devises ways for humans to come together in accepting contradictions that no human construction can eliminate. Burke offers the example of the family, which is built on the incest taboo, itself paradoxically the condition for incestful desires. But because "pure art makes for acceptance, it tends to become a social menace in so far as it assists us in tolerating the intolerable" (321). It is an ideal that must be put on hold under capitalism, which "leaves man's capacities for 'force and fraud' too purely capacities for force and fraud" (317). In this context, "there must necessarily be a large *corrective* or *propaganda* element in art. Art cannot safely confine itself to merely *using* the values which arise out of a given social texture and integrating their conflicts, as the soundest, 'purest' art will do" (321). The argument in this essay suggests why, as Burke turns from aesthetic to cultural theory, the framework for his analysis shifts from aesthetic transcendence, which is still the framework in "LR," to historical transformation. If even "pure art" can become a "social menace," then transcendent leaps beyond culture are not enough. Only a cultural transformation of historical proportions will do.

"My Approach to Communism" (MAC), a 1934 essay, shows Burke contrasting his aesthetic approach to rational, ethical, and historical approaches. Burke hoped for a social formation that not only would promote cooperation but also would institute stabilities in place of the instabilities characteristic of industrial societies. Instabilities breed insecurity, and people who are insecure are forced to overvalue the primitive values clustered around the desperation tactics of survival: "In sum, great instability both interferes with the firm establishment of the moral-esthetic superstructure which the artist draws upon, and often imparts an inferior cultural quality to whatever fragments of such a superstructure are established" (20).

Furthermore, Burke argues in *PC*, instability affects the linguistic medium of communication itself. Style is "ingratiation," a process that depends on agreement about what the right thing to say is (50). The will to eloquence depends on linkages connecting verbal expressions to circumstances in which they are appropriate, linkages that take form in contexts of social stability. Instability breaks down these linkages, leaving fewer and fewer in place. Burke uses another animal example to illustrate his analysis: imagine a flock of birds, first living and working cooperatively together, then fragmenting, smaller groups going in diverse directions. Communication would break down: "A cry of danger among those feeding on the shore might no longer indicate similar danger for those in the water or in the trees" (55). Conditions of modern instability have left the will to eloquence with two options, both unsatisfactory: to appeal widely, it has to rely on the handful of superficial linkages still in place; to be profound, it has to rely on linkages whose appeal is restricted (58).

Instabilities, moreover, enhance the prestige of vocabulary that is neutral rather than weighted stylistically, since it cuts across the differences that the instabilities produce; Burke analogizes the cultural function of this vocabulary to the function of Latin in the Middle Ages as the one universal language atop multiple vernaculars (54–57). The newspaper, he suggests, best represents the neutral ideal, reminding us of his earlier invidious distinction, in "Psychology and Form," between the psychologies of information and form. A neutral vocabulary, by prompting a utilitarian rather than a poetic attitude toward what it names, asks for "the suppression of those very overtones to which the earnest poet most resolutely exposes himself" (72). To measure the magnitude of this suppression, Burke returns to Nietzsche: "And we may see why a writer of so deeply poetic a nature as Nietzsche felt that the purely rationalistic, utilitarian ideal required the perfection of a different breed, a superman who would be hard and brutal in the performance of his acts" (72).

In varying ways, then, the existing historical environment alienates the will to eloquence. Despite its importance in Burke's analysis in *PC*, however, this environment remains theoretically secondary. A foundational subject of history presupposes that a historical trend may depart from or return to the subject's transcendental essence, but the essence itself is prior to history, not something constituted in the historical process. In the ideal historical environment, history no longer stands in the way but simply allows the essence to realize itself fully. The ultimate agon in *PC* is in the body rather than history, because that is where the question of the essence of the subject of history is answered.

It should be added, in passing, that there is an ambiguity in part three arising from the core contradiction between the essentialist and constructionist sides of the book: on the one hand, the poetic metaphor appears in the concluding chapter, so it appears to be compelled by the evidence about the subject compiled in the preceding chapters; on the other hand, it's possible to see the poetic metaphor as the source of this evidence. One can even draw on the book to justify reading part three this way (see especially 98–99). In contrast, there is no such ambiguity in *GM*, where its terminological instrument of discovery – the pentad – is introduced on the very first page.

Two chapters in succession, "The Ethical Confusion" and "The

Search for Motives," establish Burke's subject of history. The nature of the various arguments deployed merits attention. First, to establish the "confusion," considerable evidence is amassed to conclude that egoism is unable to function independently of altruism (211). In the argument, the notion of altruism is stretched to encompass any "extra" rather than "self" regarding behavior (202). In one example, a kind of frontier aestheticism, Burke imagines someone living alone in the woods, relying on his gun for food and practicing "a cult of 'Gun for Gun's Sake'" in his attentions to the gun, extending even to a willingness to risk danger to rescue it if it were in danger, say, of falling over a cliff (206). Later, in connection with the poetic metaphor, an analogous egoistic–altruistic continuity is found in the relation of poets to their material (264–65). In many examples, the altruism appears in an appeal to an audience. A general who ruthlessly pursues military glory is nonetheless trying "to excel by the criteria of his group" (203). The most arresting example of appealing to an audience appears in the "recommending by tragedy" argument that nothing appeals more powerfully than people willing to die for a cause (195–97). Burke here builds on a 1933 essay in which he countered the view that magnifying the horror of war always acts as a deterrent with the argument that such magnification also magnifies the opportunity for heroic sacrifice (WRC).

Is egoism really altruism? Or is altruism disguised egoism? Which side is transcendentally primary? Burke links one with the other without initially answering such questions: "I do not see how the establishment of a continuity between one extreme and the other forces us to select either as primary. *Some other judgment* must enter before we can make this choice" (211). The other judgment – the "will to believe" – awaits the next chapter, "The Search for Motives." The argument supporting Burke's "will to believe" consists not of additional evidence supporting the primacy of egoism or altruism but of the egoistic–altruistic continuity itself. Since the continuity doesn't *dictate* that one select either end as primary, one is free to *choose* the more beneficent interpretation of human purpose (235). The subsequent self-conscious foregrounding of the "will to believe" seems to function as compensation for the paucity of evidence supporting the transcendental essence of *PC*'s subject of history.

An alternative would have been to make no judgment at all, letting the continuity stand and using it to explain cyclical shifts from one extreme to the other. The cycles in Burke's history point toward that possibility, and at one point in "The Search for Motives" Burke seems ready to embrace it. He speculates that different historical constructs could be effects of different biological needs, each construct ultimately self-destructing as it fulfilled one need by frustrating another. The final point of the speculation, however, is to subordinate history to transcendental biological motivation rather than to establish such a cyclical pattern (226–28). The "will to believe," by positing a transcendental essence, promises the possibility of fulfillment without frustration, or at least maximizing one and minimizing the other.

This biological essentialism produces a standpoint from which it's possible to judge as wayward those instances of the egoistic–altruistic continuity that are destructive not only to the group but also to the individual. An example would be the businessman whose devotion to capitalist accumulation becomes self-destructive to his family and even his health (205). In this self-destructive behavior, the will to eloquence appears in a perverse form of recommending capitalism by tragically dying for it. The will to power side cannot be eliminated, but it can be subordinated to the will to eloquence in forms of virtuous behavior (212). The artist who egoistically seeks to stand above all other artists can do so altruistically, through offerings to audiences. If to produce these offerings the artist engages in self-destructive behavior, the artist is only ennobled even more. Whatever minimal frustration remains to limit absolutely complete biological fulfillment can be attributed to limitations in the human condition – the proper subject of "pure art." Such fulfillment, with whatever minimal limitations attending it, is the restoration of full being that *PC* promises in its version of the "guarantee" that Foucault, as noted in chapter 1, defines as the characteristic of history based on a foundational subject.

PC, convinced that the "essentials of purpose and gratification will not change" (162), leads ultimately "back to a concern with 'the Way,' the old notion of Tao, the conviction that there is one fundamental course of human satisfaction, forever being glimpsed and lost again, and forever being restated in the changing terms of reference that corresponds with the changes of historic texture" (183–84). *PC*'s history is ultimately a cycle of alternating human waywardness and return to the normative cooperative ways where the will to eloquence is most at home. It turns out that there is after all "a way" that is all training, no incapacity, except perhaps the incapacity inherent in human limitations. These would be the appropriate subject of "pure art" in an ideal historical environment.

❖❖

4

Attitudes toward History: the agon of history

❖❖

...*peace* is something we must *fight* for...   Burke, *GM*

The so-called "I" is merely a unique combination of partially conflicting "corporate we's."   Burke, "Dictionary of Pivotal Terms"

In later commentary on *PC*, Burke twice disavows its history — magic, religion, science — first in the second edition (lix) and again in the third (307). He also implicitly disavows it in *ATH*, only two years after *PC*, as he offers a new historical narrative, one that is much longer, constituting the second of the book's three parts, and altogether different in conception and theoretical importance.[1]

Burke remarks retrospectively "that *P&C* is to *ATH* as Plato's *Republic* is to his *Laws*. That is, just as the *Republic* deals with an ideal state, and the *Laws* deals with a real one, so *P&C* thinks of communication in terms of ideal cooperation, whereas *ATH* would characterize tactics and patterns of conflict typical of actual human associations" (*CS* 216). This characterization is accurate as far as it goes, though it can mislead: *ATH* is not an application of an ideal to reality but a theoretical reorientation in which the tension between *PC*'s constructionist and essentialist sides is resolved in favor of the constructionist.

In the historical narratives in both *PC* and *ATH* there is an agonistic process in which cultural orthodoxies displace one another. But *PC*'s narrative is simple and abstract because it conceives this process as a projection of motivations rooted in a biological subject of history. In

---

1 In a June 1934 letter, with *PC* about done, Burke asks "what next?" and envisions a project that he soon dropped: "a kind of research-work epic, attempting to establish in four parts and a fifth, the specific imagery, in customs and aims, behind my schema of the 'four rationalizations, magic, religion, science, and communism'" (*SCBC* 209).

ATH, in contrast, in the absence of this foundational subject, the succession of orthodoxies becomes a history of the cultural construction and reconstruction of subjects. The "I" becomes a "combination of partially conflicting 'corporate we's'" (264). Burke elaborates on this point in responding to a review of *ATH*: "For instance, one may have a job in some large financial corporation, while at the same time being a member of a party opposed to its policies" (TP 307). As a conjunction of disparate subject positions, this subject anticipates the postmodern fragmentation of the subject considered earlier in the example of Therborn's worker-qua-body. This fragmented subject is a turn toward the transhistorical, since the hierarchization of the fragments is a historical contingency rather than a transcendental necessity.

Burke adds to *ATH*'s historical narrative a chapter called "Comic Correctives," which capsulates his "propagandistic (didactic) strategy": "it must be employed as an essentially *comic* notion, containing two-way attributes lacking in polemical, one-way approaches ... It is neither wholly euphemistic, nor wholly debunking – hence it provides the *charitable* attitude towards people that is required for purposes of persuasion and co-operation, but at the same time maintains our shrewdness concerning the simplicities of 'cashing in'" (166). This comic strategy of interpretation is the critical posture that Burke stakes out for himself in *ATH* – see also "The Virtues and Limitations of Debunking" (VLD).[2] Its premise is constructionist in the sense that it presupposes that in attributing motives "to the actions of ourselves and our neighbors, there is implicit a program of socialization. In deciding *why* people do as they do, we get the cues that place us with relation to them" (*ATH* 170). Comedy's smile demystifies without the corrosive effects of demystification that is socially disintegrative, even diminishing the demystifier along with everyone else – "in lowering human dignity so greatly, it lowers us all" (*ATH* 166). Comic interpretation is doubly motivated: "willingness to suspect, willingness to listen."[3]

The foundational subject toward which *PC*'s narrative points needs a utopian future to fulfill itself. *ATH*'s narrative, in contrast, points toward a subject that can realize itself among the comic realities of the way of the world. *ATH*'s historical narrative, in the absence of a

---

2 Biographical investigation may add another perspective on Burke's comic subject. Burke construes signs in the closing pages of *TBL* of an emergent comic attitude as evidence that his novel was the agency of his own "rebirth" as a comic subject (*TBL* viii, *LSA* 339, OSIS 38).

3 The phrases are from Paul Ricoeur's often cited definition of contrasting positive and negative hermeneutics. *Freud and Philosophy: An Essay on Interpretation*, trans. Denis Savage (New Haven: Yale University Press, 1970), p. 27.

transcendental foundation, is itself a constructionist act in its contemporary context. Organizing his narrative act as a five-act drama, Burke pauses at the beginning of its last act:

> Act V of one's historical drama should be left partly unfinished, that readers may be induced to participate in the writing of it. And one tries to arrange his scenario of the first four acts in such a way, so "weighting" his material and "pointing" his arrows, that the reader will continue in the same spirit. A history of the past is worthless except as a documented way of talking about the future. (159–60)

At the end of this history, there is no foundational fullness of being to transcend to. Rather, there is the invitation to join Burke in continuing the narrative from the subject position of comic demystification.

Transcendence itself, as an analytic category, is historicized. Burke conceives it as a shift in perspective rather than a leap to a foundation beyond perspectives: "When approached from a certain point of view, A and B are 'opposites.' We mean by 'transcendence' the adoption of another point of view from which they cease to be opposites" (336). One of Burke's examples, by coordinating one episode in *ATH*'s historical narrative with another, shows why this conception of transcendence is framed transhistorically.

In the first episode, Calvinism acts as a "transcendence" of a historically antecedent contradiction (136). Prior to it, there were proscriptions against usury on one hand, and legal fictions invented to allow it in some situations on the other (133). Burke terms such inventions "casuistic stretching" to identify the demoralizing process by which an orthodoxy sustains itself through blatant opportunism — opportunism, Burke stresses, forestalls transcendence (306). Following Weber's well-known correlation of Protestantism to the rise of capitalism, Burke portrays Calvinism as a historical act "whereby the spiritual futurism of 'providence' could be equated with the worldly futurism of 'investment'" (137). This transcendence displaced the previously demoralizing casuistic stretching with a new perspective in which "material prosperity . . . [became] the visible sign of God's favor" (137).

An analogue to this transcendence appears later in Burke's history, which concludes with signs of an emergent collectivism. One of these is the "socialization of losses," a tendency that "begins with the largest financial interests, as in times of adversity they call upon the government to protect their private holdings by drawing upon the collective medium of exchange, the national credit" (160–61). Such a collective bailout in a system supposed to work through competition is casuistic stretching, analogous, Burke suggests, to finding a room for usury in a spiritual house built to exclude it (163). In each case, an orthodoxy keeps itself going opportunistically. What is needed is an analogue to Calvinism, a new transcendence: "Socialism would scrap all these covert, casuistically engendered processes of socialization-via-the-back-door, and put a positive rationale of socialization in their place" (163).

Transcendence, so conceived, is rhetorical, always relative to historically engendered tensions. A perspective that is transcendent in one situation is not necessarily transcendent in others. Transcendental motivation is not essentialistic, grounded outside history, as in *PC*'s biological essentialism. Transcendental motivation, rather, is a function in the historical process. If history disappeared, transcendence would disappear with it. Thus conceived, transcendence is transhistorical.

ATH's historical narrative bears a family resemblance to the familiar "grand narrative" bequeathed by classical Marxism. Concluding with an emergent collectivism struggling against capitalism, it recounts capitalism's earlier struggle with feudalism, and begins with the laying of the foundations for this mediaeval formation in the late Roman empire. In the first chapter of *ATH*'s history, Burke remarks, "When beginning this book, we tended to resist the purely 'economic' interpretation of history ... But as we proceeded, we found the economic emphasis inescapable" (115).

While there is enough economic interpretation in this history to give it its family resemblance to Marxist "grand narrative," this resemblance ironically proves just enough to make Burke's history a black sheep in the 1930s economistic family. Reviewing *ATH* from inside this family, Margaret Schlauch fears that despite its good intentions the book ends up subordinating the economic. She concludes, "It must be said in justice to Mr. Burke that this is obviously not his intent; but his literary preoccuptions at the expense of economic factors give this impression all too readily" ("Review" 109).[4] Her review prompted Burke to write "Twelve Propositions on the Relation between Economics and Psychology" (TP), an important companion text to *ATH*, which in turn prompted a reply from

4 The review appeared in *Science and Society*, a new journal at the time. For valuable commentary on its orthodox Marxist position, see Feehan, "Discovery," pp. 406–07.

Schlauch, itself notable for largely ignoring the propositions – a sign of the extent to which Burke's concerns seemed beside the point to a more orthodox Marxist.[5]

Economistic vocabulary, moreover, is not only sparse but also overshadowed by Burke's own portmanteau vocabulary. Always terminologically venturesome, Burke sets in *ATH* a kind of record that even he is never quite able to match again. "Being driven into a corner," "bureaucratization of the imaginative," "casuistic stretching," "neo-Malthusian principle," "secular prayer," "stealing back and forth of symbols," "symbols of authority" – these are only a sampling of the many terms in quotation marks that dot this text, which concludes with a long "Dictionary of Pivotal Terms." The deeper one gets into this terminological bazaar, the more removed one feels from the Marxist factory.[6]

Even when Burke is close to economism, he introduces important qualifications. He doubts "whether all heresies can be explained 'economically'... But when a heresy recruits a large group, and leads to active resistance, and even the use of force, on the part of the orthodoxy, *here* we may look for economic factors" (131).[7] In other words, as the critique of Foucault in chapter 1 argues, when a power with a stake in an orthodoxy sees its vital interests threatened, it declares its location, even using force if necessary. Burke's reasoning in this passage is continuous and discontinuous with *ACR*. It continues *ACR*'s resistance to the expressive causality of economism, which conceives the economic as an essence from which everything else radiates in the form of a consistent totalized expression. This resistance is the subtext of his doubt that all "heresies can be explained 'economically'" as well as his interest in *ACR* in "difference" as a term

---

5 "Twelve Propositions" is included in *PLF* but in shortened form. There are no additional propositions in the original, but there is some additional discussion that isn't cast in propositional form. References to this text will be to the more accessible version in *PLF* except when the passage appears only in the original. Feehan, in "Discovery," provides a first-rate analysis of the rhetorical strategy Burke uses in the text to address an orthodox Marxist audience.

6 Rueckert describes Burke's style as an "underbrush" and advises recognizing "this underbrush for what it is – an irritation, a distraction, the rank growth of a fecund mind" (*Drama* 5). Decades later, Rueckert's description continues to be quoted (Allen, 10–11; Jay, "Modernism," p. 347). Having started his career as a creative writer, Burke always seems to have looked for ways to stretch the meanings of words; his terminological innovations can distract but they can also illuminate.

7 We agree with Crusius who, in "Case," refers to this passage (citing *ATH1* 1: 167–68) as evidence that Burke refuses "to reduce symbol-using to a mere epiphenomenon of physical and economic forces."

to accommodate discourses not readily assimilable to the terms of the bourgeois–proletarian antithesis. The difficulty in *ACR*, as we saw in the last chapter, is that when Burke writes his historical narrative he turns seemingly against his will from difference to antithesis. *ATH* eliminates this inconsistency. Difference appears in the full range of "heresies," whereas antithesis emerges when high stakes – "economic factors" – prompt different groups to square off in an agon of history. The discourses deployed agonistically are not expressions of an economic essence, but opportunistic selections from the full range available.

While *ATH*, contrasted to *PC*, represents a far greater accommodation to Marxism on Burke's part, it's difficult to discern the exact point of convergence. Essential to Marxism is the notion of a "mode of production." In capitalism, it's the mode of production itself that pits the owners of the means of production against those who have only their labor power to sell. Burke displays little interest in these and related conceptions, despite what he says about becoming convinced about the inescapability of the "economic emphasis." To see the point of compatibility that Burke found between himself and Marx, it is necessary to turn to "The Relation between Literature and Science," the paper Burke gave at the second Writers' Congress in the same year that *ATH* appeared. Considerable attention has been directed at his appearance at the first; perhaps more should be directed toward his encore.

In this paper, Burke proposes that Marxism may be positioned as a shift from nominalism to realism in which realism is equated to "a stressing of man as a *political being*, a context of definition whereby his individual role is defined by his membership in a group" (RLS 164–65). As Burke accentuates in another formulation of his preference for the realist emphasis, *"realism considered individuals as members of a group ... nominalism considered groups as aggregates of individuals"* (PLF 126; see also *GM* 129). Realism, so conceived, offers an alternative to the bourgeois individual, as exemplified perhaps most dramatically in enlightenment "state of nature" theorizing, such as the Lockean social contract theory of sovereignty. From the standpoint of realism, individualism is simply another form of group behavior that paradoxically valorizes competitions designed to pit individuals against one another.

Burke makes this same point about Marx by positioning him in another way. Augustine defined "man as citizen of a *super*-natural city";

Darwin countered supernaturalism with an antithetical naturalism, fostering "purely biological vocabularies of human motivation"; and Marx "corrected this naturalistic oversimplification. He restored the Aristotelian notion of man *in society* as the basic approach to the study of human motives. Like Aristotle, he considers men as members of politico-economic corporations" (RLS 161). In *ATH*, Burke similarly positions his "comic attitude" as a social middle ground between the supernatural and the natural:

The Church thought of man as a prospective citizen of heaven ... Against man as a citizen of heaven, thinkers opposed man in nature; and with the progress of efficiency in reasoning, we got simply to *man in the jungle*. A comic synthesis of these antithetical emphases would "transcend" them by stressing *man in society*. As such, it would come close to restoring the emphasis of Aristotle, with his view of man as a "political animal." (169–70)

These parallels suggest why Burke could equate "comic critique" (*ATH* 227) to "Marxist critique" (*ATH1* 2: 69), substituting one for the other in different editions of *ATH*.

In sum, Burke borrows the group emphasis in the Marxist concept of class to find a way to reaffirm *PC*'s view of the human subject as a "participant," a "cooperative" member of a "group," while at the same time shifting away from biological essentialism. One could apply one term from Burke's "Dictionary" and call this group emphasis a "bridging device" (*ATH* 224). In this borrowing from Marx, Burke exploits an ambiguity in Marx's concept of class: on the one hand, class is equivalent to division insofar as it is contrasted to classless society; on the other hand, in class solidarity one can detect a prefiguration of classlessness. It's the solidarity side of the concept that is primary for Burke, as one can see when he metaphorizes the notion of "property" to suggest, "One 'owns' his social structure insofar as one can subscribe to it by wholeheartedly feeling the reasonableness of its arrangements, and by being spared the need of segregational attitudes. Insofar as such allegiance is frustrated, both the materially and spiritually dispossessed must suffer" (*ATH* 330). In passing, it's worth noting Burke's insistence that to explain the phenomenon of class traitors, it's necessary to couple spiritual with more obvious material reasons for becoming disillusioned with a social structure (*ATH* 330–31).

Group realism allowed Burke to take a step that is small in one sense and big in another. Different groups are held together by different ideological regimes, each a collective construction. But human beings are always found in such groups, so belonging is, as *ATH* suggests, in some sense *"natural"* (330), if not quite like a heartbeat. The line between nature and culture is not bright; it's the transhistorical middle that gets excluded in an overly blunt binary opposition between essentializing and historicizing. The group is the bridge by which Burke could change his basic oppositions. Before crossing, he gave himself a choice between permanence and change, and put his real money on permanence. After crossing, permanence is split into two forms, supernaturalism and naturalism, permanency from above and below. Against both, there is "man in society": "If you would avoid the antitheses of supernaturalism and naturalism," he insists, "you must develop the coordinates of socialism — which gets us to cooperation, participation, man in society, man in drama" (TP 311). These coordinates allow Burke to resolve the essentialist–constructionist tension in *PC* in favor of the constructionist emphasis in *ATH*. "Acceptance" and "rejection" — the "attitudes" introduced on the first page of *ATH* — foreshadow the book's conceptualization of history not as a projection of biological motives but as a succession of agons of cultural constructs. The reviewer for the *New Masses* found *ATH* to be an original contribution, perhaps even more than Burke realized, "in the field of practical agitation" (Conklin 25).

In the introduction added for *ATH*'s second edition, Burke uses the term "bureaucratization of the imaginative" to single out "the process of processes" that the book investigates. The term is used in many contexts. Even the public materiality of a work of art is said to bureaucratize the imaginative (197–98). But the main use, as Burke indicates at the beginning of the section devoted to it in the "Dictionary," is to name "a basic process in history": "An imaginative possibility (usually at the start Utopian) is bureaucratized when it is embodied in the realities of a social texture, in all the complexity of language and habits, in the property relationships, the methods of government, production and distribution, and in the development of rituals that re-enforce the same emphasis" (225). Bureaucratic realities always fall short of utopian possibilities, the falling short becoming a crisis of historical proportions when the bureaucratization intensifies the "class struggle," as subjects become alienated from it while one class has "a very real 'stake in' the retention of the ailing bureaucratization" (226).[8]

The term's main purpose, then, is to identify a process that gives the dynamic of history its agonistic shape. If one wishes to conceive history as simply change over time, then everything has a history, and the history of the universe works by the same process as the history of humankind. For history to be a more useful notion, something more is needed. Burke locates it in the recognition that human social systems characteristically favor some at the expense of others and that the past is replete with struggles to correct the balance. Burke's generalization of this condition of history could, moreover, accommodate "stakes" other than the strictly economic, a possibility that one could cite to answer Schlauch, who singles out the term "bureaucratization of the imaginative" to ask why it should be preferred to the more direct economistic language of "economic exploitation, which Mr. Burke himself recognizes, though he seldom refers to" ("Reply" 252). One can defend this term, in other words, as an attempt not to predict economistically the exact basis of every agon, but to alert one to look for an agon, even if only emergent, in every historical situation.

But Burke looks to the agon of history less to theorize its formation than to analyze the problem that it poses for subjects, as has been observed.[9] Building on his Aristotelian–Marxist assumption, Burke postulates that the "individual's identity is formed by reference to his group" (TP 306). Organized around a regime of normative behavior, the group is the condition of the subject. But the regime is

8 Burke's use of the term "bureaucratization" prompted a bitter exchange, published in the *Partisan Review*, consisting of Sidney Hook's review of *ATH*, Burke's response (IMHS), and Hook's reply. (Hook quotes from one footnote on the Moscow trials found only in the first edition [*ATH*1 2: 153–54].) Trotskyites, Burke recounts in *ATH*'s third edition, routinely pinned the term "bureaucracy" on the Stalinist dictatorship (400). The term acquired in the process a rhetorical charge that Hook exploited to reduce the whole of *ATH* to a covert apology for this dictatorship, even though Burke conceives bureaucratization as a process that can occasion a revolutionary crisis. Hook relies on one passage where Burke declares that because a degree of bureaucratization is inevitable, those who cry out against it too quickly open themselves to the charge of being covert utopians (*ATH* 227). Terry A. Cooney reports that the *Partisan Review* regularly attacked Burke, Cowley, and others who "visibly supported the Popular Front"; see *The Rise of the New York Intellectuals: "Partisan Review" and Its Circle, 1934–45* (Madison: University of Wisconsin Press, 1986), p. 144. For Burke's dismissal of the Trotskyite objections to the Popular Front, see *ATH* 307. The *Partisan Review* was the center of one of the factions on the left which sometimes battled one another – see Alan Wald, *The New York Intellectuals: The Rise and Decline of the Anti-Stalinist Left from the 1930s to the 1980s* (Chapel Hill: University of North Carolina Press, 1987), p. 97. One effect of these battles was a longstanding rocky relationship between the journal and Burke (see TYL 514).

9 See Abbott, p. 224. Abbott provides an excellent summary of the Marxist ingredients in *ATH*.

a construct, so that the very formation of the subject presupposes the possibility of reconstruction. Realization of this possibility begins with the agon, as the benefiting of some at the expense of others in the bureaucratic process produces material deprivations and spiritual demoralization.

An example of the kind of difficulty that the bureaucratization of the imaginative can pose for subjects appears in Burke's paper "Revolutionary Symbolism in America," in his contrast between *"propaganda by inclusion"* and *"propaganda by exclusion"* (RSA 93). His reasoning is the same as that which we saw in the last chapter in reviewing what he says about "pure art" in "The Nature of Art under Capitalism." "Art," Burke reaffirms in the paper, "strains towards *universalization*," seeking paths beyond divisions to unity (92). Art is the most inclusive rhetoric of all. But there are limits. Artists, Burke declares to his audience of writers, should engage in the agon of history resulting from the Great Depression precisely because it militates against the artistic rhetoric of inclusion: "For a totally universalized art, if established in America to-day, would simply be the spiritual denial of an underlying economic disunity (the aesthetic of fascism)" (92). The rhetoric of inclusion is the way to go if possible, but in some situations it can defeat its own aims. The difficulty is that, according to Burke's Marxist–Aristotelian realism, the subject would normally prefer inclusion. Insofar as allegiance to the inclusive whole is impaired, the subject suffers. Even those who benefit materially from the status quo can suffer spiritually as they find that the culture's rhetoric of inclusion is no longer rhetorically sayable, but mere "casuistic stretching," like that in the examples considered earlier.

Burke devises in *ATH* the term "process-category" (68), which he conceptualizes, in his response to Schlauch, as a middle ground between permanence and change: "If an emphasis upon nouns (categories) was followed by an antithetical emphasis upon verbs (processes), why should not 'dialectic' reasoning lead us to look for a synthesis of the two, something like *categories of processes*?" (TP1 249). *ATH*'s most extensive and systematic arrangement of process-categories appears in "Poetic Categories," where Burke introduces a theory of literary genres. The chapter shows that literature is still central for Burke, but now in a different way from his earlier work. As his conceptualization of genres suggests, moreover, his search for process-categories in *ATH* points him toward the transhistorical perspective that comes into its own a few years later, as we'll see in our next chapter.

One barometer of the change is the New Critic Allen Tate's essay, "Mr. Burke and the Historical Environment." Tate is writing shortly before *ATH* appears, in response to Burke's "Symbolic War" (SW), an essay-review of proletarian literature. But Tate's arguments would, if anything, be even more applicable to *ATH*. Tate is a good barometer because he and Burke, born only two years apart, both belong to the generation that reached maturity during the 1920s. That is why Tate singles Burke out: "Mr. Burke alone of the extreme left-wing critics seems to me to possess the historical and philosophical learning necessary to the serious treatment of the literary problems of Marxism: before his 'converson' to Communism he had subjected himself to a rigorous critical discipline" (62). If even Burke's literary integrity is corrupted by his turn to the left, then there is nothing one can expect from anyone on the left – that is Tate's rhetorical logic.

What Tate especially objects to, as he stresses in his closing paragraphs, is Burke's privileging of reference to the historical environment. With this objection, one can see Burke put on the receiving end of an argument he earlier leveled at others, a reversal he experienced often at the hands of the New Criticism. In this case, one can think back to *ACR* and its typology of primary, secondary, and tertiary realities, where tertiary reality consists of the historical struggles of the day that by definition are transitory and therefore secondary to the other two realities. This typology, in short, relegates historical reference to secondary status, a position with which Tate would feel much more at home. Tate becomes uncomfortable when Burke begins elevating instead of relegating historical reference. "None of these poetic categories can be isolated in its chemical purity," Burke explains, "Our distinctions are offered only for their suggestive value, the primary purpose here being simply to indicate that, whatever 'free play' there may be in esthetic enterprise, it is held down by the gravitational pull of historical necessities" (*ATH* 57). Historical reference, in other words, is now seen not as secondary but as inescapable. Direct or indirect, it's always there.

Burke's genre distinctions, when scrutinized, reveal themselves to be an effect of this reevaluation of history. Earlier, when his primary concern was the conceptualization of aesthetic value, such distinctions were not important. Music might be elevated above other artistic genres on aesthetic grounds insofar as it is less dependent than other arts on "imparting information" (*CS* 36), but generally Burke didn't localize aesthetic value either in any artistic medium, or within literature, in any literary genre. The main concern was aesthetic value in general. The concern in *ATH* with genre distinctions is something new.

This concern is not, moreover, as it might have been, a fleshing out of an aesthetic theory. The issue is not aesthetic value but the role literature plays in the historical process. Burke's poetic categories and historical narrative are not different realms, but different perspectives on the same complex process – roughly akin to the difference between scrutinizing brush strokes and viewing a painting as a whole composition:

> In our previous chapter we discussed "frames of acceptance and rejection" as exemplified primarily in various poetic categories. Here we shall center attention upon those "collective poems" evolved by the widest group activities . . . The two emphases are not mutually exclusive, since the individual's frame is built of materials from the collective frame, but the change from one to the other shifts the emphasis from the *poetic* to the *historical*.   (111)

In the agons of history, literature divides into kinds as it sometimes reinvigorates an established historical construct, while at other times it saps its strength. "Acceptance" and "rejection" – these are Burke's encompassing categories of categories. Burke summarizes his arrangement of the categories midway through his analysis – (1) acceptance: epic, tragedy, comedy; (2) rejection: elegy, satire, burlesque; (3) transitional: grotesque, didactic (57). Burke remarks in a letter that analyzing genres in this fashion produced an "unexpected bonanza" of insight (*SCBC* 214).

The lines Burke draws between the genres, as he suggests, are not analytically clearcut. He does not draw on standard definitions of genres, such as Aristotle's of tragedy. There is no attempt to isolate genres as aesthetic forms. Rather, the genres are process-categories designed to gauge differences in literary barometric readings of the cultural weather. As he puts it at the outset of his analysis, "each of the great poetic forms stresses its own peculiar way of building the mental equipment (meanings, *attitudes*, character) by which one handles the significant factors of his time" (*ATH* 34; italics added). Each of the forms – like transcendence, as considered earlier – is a function in the historical process. Each appears in history and would disappear if history were to vanish. But each is distinctive enough to be abstracted as a transhistorical category. The abstraction does not put a form into an aesthetic heaven but serves analysis of concrete historical agons. The forms, in actual instantiations, never appear anywhere except in the historical process itself. One might use Burke's conception of these forms to rewrite Raymond Williams's term "structure of feeling"[10] as "structure of attitude," since Burke associates attitudes with the forms. His title, "attitudes toward history," is misleading insofar as it seems to put attitudes outside history looking in. They are, rather, as Hook remarks, part of "the *stuff* of history" ("Technique" 91). Burke says as much himself when he specifically cites "attitude" as an example of a process-category, explaining, "Attitudes are 'strategies.' As such, they maintain something permanent through flux, while at the same time they must adapt themselves to the specific changes of material provided by flux" (TP1 249).

The analytic strategy Burke uses to gauge differences in cultural weather is not immediately obvious. The analysis, like the historical narrative, appears Marxist in some ways and non-Marxist in others. To define the strategy, it may help to view it, at least initially, from the standpoint of the perspective by incongruity provided by Jameson's "proposition that the effectively ideological is also, at the same time, necessarily Utopian"[11] – a proposition to which we shall return in chapter 7. This equation suggests two possible starting-points: either from the side of ideology and class division, or from the side of utopian unity.

Starting from the ideological side produces the familiar features of orthodox Marxist analysis, especially as it was practiced during the 1930s. One could, for example, construe Macbeth as the tragic exemplar of bourgeois ambition, a threat to the feudal order that *Macbeth* reaffirms. One could, in other words, read the play as a class assertion of hegemony. Burke, in contrast, starts from the other side, the utopian. Using this standpoint to interpret his analysis clarifies its affinities with Marxist analysis as well as its differences. The premise of the standpoint is group realism: "man in society." The group is healthy when solidarity overrides segregation, diseased when the reverse occurs as an effect of bureaucratization. To the extent that absolute solidarity is impossible, the group is utopian – no place, but present as an aspiration. Literature may be viewed as the utopian voice in the historical process. History makes the utopian possible by creating the aspiration for it and impossible by preventing its realization. The agon of history refracts the utopian voice into the range of pitches recorded

10 See *The Long Revolution* (New York: Columbia University Press, 1961), p. 48. Williams also discusses the term retrospectively in *Politics and Letters* (London: NLB, 1979), pp. 156–65.

11 *The Political Unconscious: Narrative as a Socially Symbolic Act* (Ithaca, New York: Cornell University Press, 1981), p. 286.

by the poetic categories. Utopian unity is never heard in its purity, only indirectly, through the noise of the conflicts in the historical process. A text's genre is Burke's starting-point. In an analysis of *Macbeth*, for example, one begins with the notion of tragedy rather than with feudal ideology. What the genre says, by itself, about the health of the hegemonic ideological regime in the text's cultural context is the question to be answered. The health of this regime always falls short of utopian perfection. But it falls short in the different ways the poetic categories measure.

The regime is ultimately reaffirmed in both tragedy and comedy, but only after surviving a bout of heresy. These genres differ in that in tragedy heresy is crime, whereas in comedy it's stupidity (*ATH* 41). In depicting heresy as a crime so profound that it can shake the natural order itself, tragedy exhibits a regime that is paradoxically at once so strong that heresy is a crime of enormous proportions and so weak that heresy must be subjected to the most severe of punishments. Comedy is the reverse, exhibiting a regime so weak that deviance isn't serious enough to be criminal, and so strong that deviance need be subjected to nothing more serious than laughter. What is tragic in *Macbeth*, Burke suggests, is comic in Mandeville's *Fable of the Bees*, where private vices, by stimulating the economy, ironically become public benefits (*ATH* 24).

Contrasts of this sort interest Burke, not genres in isolated purity. Another, on the rejection side, is between burlesque and satire. Burlesque is a defense: "a writer who could imagine himself in the many humiliating roles that are in fashion today would, by this very ability, open himself to great risk. A purely *external* approach to such characters would protect him greatly" (53). In burlesque, a character exemplifying an orthodoxy's norms "driv[es] them to a 'logical conclusion' that becomes their 'reduction to absurdity'" (54). The orthodoxy is publicly humiliated from a standpoint that feels comfortable located outside it. By contrast, Burke suggests, satire's laughter is less self-confident than burlesque's. The satirist is self-divided, one side despising the orthodox regime, the other not quite able to let it go. Swift, Burke suggests, "beat himself unmercifully, eventually with drastic results" (50).

The burlesque example suggests an additional dimension of Burke's analysis, one that is not worked out as thoroughly as the discriminations among the categories but that can nonetheless be extrapolated easily enough. For Burke depicts, in the situation giving rise to burlesque, roles that are "in fashion" for some and "humiliating" for others, thus acknowledging that an orthodoxy can look different from different standpoints in a historical agon. There can be limits to the range of these differences; there could be a situation where the health of a regime is such that a particular genre is rhetorically unsayable. But normally the range is great enough to accommodate a range of genres. A simple example that engaged a whole nation for a few weeks may serve to illustrate. It occurred near the end of the Bush Administration, when Dan Quayle used the TV sitcom *Murphy Brown* to focus on "family values," the issue the Republicans hoped to use as a flag leading the march to reelection in 1992. Murphy sinned against family values when she became a mother out of wedlock. Such an event, in the Quayle faction of the culture, should be depicted, if at all, in the accents of tragedy. Motherhood out of wedlock is an enormity. But *Murphy Brown* made it a light comedy. The sitcom spoke for another faction, one that also saw motherhood out of wedlock as deviance but as a deviance that could be comic, especially for someone with a job as good as Murphy's.

In his response to Schlauch, Burke positions his approach in relation to the orthodox Marxist model of the 1930s:

the objective factors giving rise to a code of moral and aesthetic values are, of course, *economic*. They are the "substructure" that supports the ideological "superstructure." But the objective materials utilized by an individual writer are largely the *moral and aesthetic values* themselves. For instance, new methods of production gave rise to the change from feudal to bourgeois values. But Shakespeare's strategy as a dramatist was formed by relation to this conflict between feudal and bourgeois values ... Economic factors gave rise to the transition in values, but he dealt with the transition in values.

(TP 308–09)

The feudal regime, like any other, was subjected to rhetorical challenge. The state of the rhetorical conversation determines what is sayable – what is controversial, what isn't – in what genres – what is laughable, what isn't. The effects of the interaction give the writer the materials with which to start. The writer interacts, in turn, altering the materials in the process. A great writer can significantly alter the state of the conversation.

Another barometer of a text's position in its culture is "tragic ambiguity." Is the tragic hero a heretic or a prophet? Is the hero purely a negative example that serves to reaffirm a hegemonic regime? Or is the hero a prophecy of an alternative regime on the horizon of history? Burke uses the terms "reactionary" and "progressive" to mark the ends of the spectrum of possibilities (*ATH* 39). If it's easy to answer such questions, the tragedy gravitates toward either of the ends. If it's hard, it's in the ambiguous middle range.

Burke also distinguishes between "factional" and "universal" tragedy. In universal tragedy, the hero "represents everyman . . . *his* punishment is *mankind's* chastening" (188). In factional tragedy, an enemy is punished. One could imagine performing *Macbeth* either way, the universal making Macbeth sympathetic, the factional making him a monstrous tyrant. Critical commentary on the distinction usually cites it to applaud the universal against the factional, faulting the factional as a lapse into the us-against-them rhetoric of exclusion. But the universal is not immune to criticism, as Burke stresses in *PLF*, where he returns to this distinction to contrast the sacrifice of universal tragedy to the kill of factional:

> whereas on its face, the emphasis upon the sacrifice is much superior to the emphasis upon the kill, in the dialectic of concrete historical situations important matters of *insignia* figure. Both history and anthropology supply us with plenty of instances in which a priesthood has exploited the sounder method for malign purposes (in consciously or unconsciously so interweaving it with essentially unrelated structures of ownership and special privilege that in actual practice its function becomes the very reverse of a religious one). (48)

To mistake the universal rhetoric of inclusion for the reality of inclusion is to lapse into rhetorical idealism. Such a rhetoric may work against rather than for such a reality. In *ATH*, in illustrating factional tragedy, Burke cites as his example a Thomas Mann text, "Mario and the Magician," which he reads as "an admonition against Fascism" (189), an example that reminds us of Burke's own argument in "Revolutionary Symbolism in America," considered earlier (see p. 93), about the limits of the rhetoric of inclusion in the context of the Great Depression. In shifting from his early aesthetic toward his later cultural orientation, as we saw in chapter 2 in considering *CS*'s "LR," Burke recognized that neither universal tragedy, nor pure art, nor anything else can be valorized absolutely, apart from its positioning in concrete situations.[12] Positionality is inescapable.

The same holds for his comic attitude, introduced as his "propagandistic

---

12 Crusius, in "*Auscultation*," uses *ACR* as an occasion for a critique of the rhetoric of exclusion that is worth careful study. While one might ask if Crusius altogether eschews the rhetoric of exclusion himself, what most merits attention is his conclusion, where he decides what he is for. His answer is "dialogue" (378). As he says, who can be against dialogue? But if everyone is for it, it may be an empty goal, something to which everyone can subscribe without changing any of the rules of the game that benefit some at the expense of others. A rhetoric of inclusion can perpetuate exclusion. One cannot valorize any rhetoric of inclusion absolutely; one must always consider its real effects in a concrete situation.

(didactic) strategy" in *ATH* in the chapter "Comic Correctives" (166). As a poetic category, the didactic is a strategy for transition, one that divides people into "friends" and "enemies" (79). The comic softens such oppositions, but as "Comic Correctives" concludes, such softening must be evaluated contextually. The modern economy forces workers to fight one another for jobs "which, in earlier economies, would not have been performed at all except by slaves and criminals under compulsion. For alienations of this sort . . . the comic frame could not, and should not offer recompense" (174–75). This frame has value in such a context only insofar as it actually helps to produce the needed social transformation (175).

Burke introduces the notion of "symbols of authority" in carrying out the critical commitment he declares in *ATH* to "the 'revolutionary' emphasis, involved in the treatment of art with primary reference to symbols of authority, their acceptance and rejection" (200). Such a treatment, he adds, concerns itself with transition, especially "change in identity" (200). With this declaration, he completes his own transformation from a literary concern with aesthetic value to a cultural concern with historical transformation, preeminently the transformation of the subject. *PC* is transitional insofar as it turns toward culture but does so by envisioning a utopian culture with maximum aesthetic value as the telos of history. As Burke puts it in a passage noted earlier, *PC* "thinks of communication in terms of ideal cooperation, whereas *ATH* would characterize tactics and patterns of conflict typical of actual human associations." In these conflicts in history, the process of the formation and transformation of the subject centers on the contingent hierarchization and re-hierarchization of the "we's" that together, in their interaction, constitute the "I."

Theorizing such contingent hierarchization remains a major concern for Burke through a number of books. Theorizing it as effected through acceptance or rejection of symbols of authority is what is distinctive about *ATH*. Whether a symbol is accepted or rejected is a function of whether it integrates the "we's." "Acceptance," as the term suggests, reinforces the status quo. Translated into the language of the present study, art in which acceptance is dominant stays within the confines of the disciplinary agon: "If the ingredient of acceptance is uppermost, the poet tends to cancel the misfit between himself and the frame by 'tragic ambiguity,' whereby he both expresses his 'criminality' and exorcises it through symbolic punishment" (209). Deviance is thus expressed but punished, functioning in the end to reaffirm rather than to challenge the orthodoxy. If rejection is uppermost, in contrast, "there will usually be, more or less clearly limned, the outlines of a counter-authority" (209) – that is, a rival orthodoxy, the rivalry constituting an agon of history.

Rejection needs a rival orthodoxy to affirm, Burke recognizes, because the negativity of rejection by itself is too insecure to be self-sustaining. Even the poetic categories Burke puts on the side of rejection – all traditionally relegated to low rungs on the hierarchical ladder of genres – suggest as much. A step rather than a terminus, rejection by itself fragments the "we's." "Discomfitures of Rejection" – the final section (99–105) in the last chapter in part 1: "Acceptance and Rejection" – announces with its title the difficulties of transition. "Stealing back and forth of symbols" is Burke's term for the process by which a rebellious sect "maintains its integrative identification with the orthodoxy by insisting that it alone truly embodies the orthodox principle" (103; see also 328). It leans on the old to advance the new until the new is strong enough to speak for itself. Burke himself exhibits this strategy in "Revolutionary Symbolism in America" as he "steals" the "people" as the symbol for the revolutionary movement.[13] A sect might try to maintain its purity apart from the hegemonic orthodoxy – that would be an argument for the "worker" as symbol – but at the risk of making itself vulnerable to isolation and internal splintering (100–02). Rejection can sustain itself against the danger of lapsing into deviance only by outlining and fleshing out a rival orthodoxy to affirm. Burke nails the point with a maxim: "The full strategy for saying *'don't* do that' is *'do* do this'" (22).

Burke's emphasis on the discomfitures of rejection is another sign of the reorientation in his approach to the subject. When there is a foundational subject, as in *PC*, what is rejected stands in the way of the subject's return to the fullness of its transcendental being. Accepting the present is the discomfiture, whereas rejection is a return home to the sources of one's being. In contrast, when there is no foundational subject, as in *ATH*, one is constituted within an orthodoxy so that in rejecting it one in effect leaves home to go into exile. Accepting being easier than rejecting, rejection becomes the discomfiture. To sustain rejection, one needs the promise of a new home in a rival orthodoxy.

13 Lentricchia's analysis of "Revolutionary Symbolism" is a detailed and illuminating theoretical unpacking of this strategy of theft, which Lentricchia seems ready to identify as the essence of the historical process itself (24).

This new home could be a speculative fiction – Burke finds an example in Coleridge, as we'll see in the next chapter – but it becomes a historical player when it is, like the new orthodoxy Defoe exhibits in Crusoe, the cultural legitimation of a way of life that is "emergent," to borrow Raymond Williams's term.[14] Rival orthodoxies range from the utopian to the nostalgic, but only those become historical actualities that are inscribed in practices sustainable in the context of the world, both its materiality and its configurations of economic and political power.

Burke puts the notion of symbols of authority in the first of the propositions he addresses to Schlauch: *"The basic concept for uniting economics and psychology ('Marx and Freud') is that of the 'symbols of authority'"* (TP 305). *ACR*, we saw in the last chapter (p. 60), reopened the case against Marxism that Burke made in "The Status of Art," while leaving at rest the companion case against psychoanalysis. Eventually, as Burke turned his theoretical attention away from aesthetic value to the transformation of culture and the subject, he reopened that case too. The result is his version of Freudo-Marxism. As his first proposition to Schlauch suggests, the names Freud and Marx can serve to designate the two dimensions that Burke distinguishes in theorizing the process by which symbols of authority are accepted and rejected.

Such symbols, Burke suggests, include "rulers, courts, parliaments, laws, educators, constabulary, and the moral slogans linked with such" (*ATH* 329). Symbols of authority, in other words, are principles of group formation and organization. In accepting or rejecting them, one enrolls oneself within a group or exiles oneself from it. One expects this process, given the group realism that Burke finds in Marx, to be Freudo-*Marxist* rather than *Freudo*-Marxist. Reinforcement of this expectation appears in the section on "identity" in *ATH*'s "Dictionary," where Burke begins by arguing that bourgeois thought

made a blunt distinction between "individual" and "environment," hence leading automatically to the notion that an individual's "identity" is something private, peculiar to himself. And when bourgeois psychologists began to discover the falsity of this notion, they still believed in it so thoroughly that they considered all collective aspects of identity under the head of pathology and illusion. That is: they discovered accurately enough that identity is *not* individual, that a man "identifies himself" with all sorts of manifestations beyond himself, and they set about trying to "cure" him of this tendency.   (263)

14 Williams introduces this term, contrasting it with "residual," in "Base and Superstructure in Marxist Cultural Theory," *Problems in Materialism and Culture* (London: Verso, 1980), pp. 40–41.

Nonetheless, when one looks closely, *Freudo*-Marxism is what one finds.

One's relation to symbols of authority have, for Burke, two levels: forensic and pre-forensic. "Forensic" is an important enough term to find a place in the "Dictionary," where a contrast between adult and child serves to clarify its meaning. The forensic is equated with "the forum, the market place. The materials of law, parliamentary procedure, traffic regulation, scientific-causal relationships evolved by complex and sophisticated commerce (of both the material and spiritual sorts)" (254). "The child," in contrast, "necessarily develops without much awareness of this forensic material. He is concerned with his immediate relatives and playmates, his toys and animals, material objects like food, chairs, tables, trees, cellar, and attic" (254–55). *ATH*'s *Freudo*-Marxism appears in the privileging of the pre-forensic, as is evident in the following (the italics are Burke's): "Authority symbols of the mature adult involve such intellectualistic or philosophic concepts as church, state, society, political party, craft. They are largely 'forensic.' But in treating them with *engrossment* ... he is induced to integrate them with the deepest responses of his experience. These are found in the 'pre-political' period of childhood" (209).

In short, sayability in the forum is secondary to singability in the poem. "The future is really disclosed *by finding out what people can sing about*," Burke suggests, "It is in ... the active enlistment of a man's full faculties, giving *full psychological employment*, that you find the material for prophecy. You find history foretold in the areas where people cannot possibly 'sell out'" (335). As in *PC*, the poetic is production without alienation. What is new is the Freudian emphasis. "'Symbolic regression' takes place in that the poet, in the thoroughness of his sincerity, necessarily draws upon the pre-forensic, pre-political ('autistic') level of informative experience, even when symbolizing his concern with purely forensic matter" (*ATH* 209–10). Burke uses the metaphor of "rebirth" to suggest that the transformation of the subject involves a metaphoric replaying of the Freudian family romance, the attitude toward the public symbol of authority involving "symbolic parricide (when rejection is uppermost) and incest-awe, with symbolic castration (when acceptance is uppermost)" (210).[15] Even the notion of a symbol of *authority* seems to be predominantly Freudian as it deflects attention from Marx's emphasis on class toward the family romance.

Burke characterizes Freud's terminology as "individualistic libertar-

---

15 The assumptions about gender in this formulation are obvious, but Burke later recognizes that these are a function of patriarchal orthodoxy to be contrasted to matriarchal assumptions (FAP 272–74).

ianism" in the 1960s (MBU 79), after he explicitly distances himself from Freud in ways to be considered in later chapters, beginning with the next one. But even in the 1930s he sees in Freud at most some wavering between group and individual psychology, the group being the family. Freud, Burke decides, "compromises by . . . drawing individual psychology from the role of the monopolistic father, and group psychology from the roles of the sons, deprived of sexual gratification by the monopolistic father, and banded together for their mutual benefit. But note that the whole picture is that of a family" (FAP 273). Either way, in theorizing acceptance and rejection in the formation and transformation of subjects, *ATH* reverses direction, moving from group realism toward individualism. *ATH*'s "I" may be a conjunction of "we's," but it's a conjunction in which, in the final analysis, the family "we" is privileged over all others. Freud may have decentered the bourgeois individual not only by subjecting it to an unconscious, but also by making it a function of the family. Even when doubly decentered, however, the Freudian subject still possesses a unique individuality that may be privileged, as Burke illustrates, as the source of "engrossment" − singability rather than mere sayability.

ATH's reversal of direction surprises not only by undermining the premise of its group realism but also by going against the grain of the leftist culture in which Burke participated. Cowley, for example, in a retrospective look at the 1930s, cites Burke's 1933 poem "Plea of the People" (*CP* 58–60) as exemplifying the power "of the idea of comradeship, that you were no longer alone, isolated, helpless, but if you took the side of the working class you were one of a large body of people marching toward something" (TYL 504–05). Burke himself, in 1953, retrospectively contrasts his early emphasis on the individual with his later focus on "interdependent, social, or collective aspects of meaning" (*CS* 214). It's possible, in other words, to write a biographical narrative taking Burke from the isolation of individualism to the uplift of revolutionary collective action, a trajectory that no doubt helped to form his commitment to group realism. But *ATH* stops at *Freudo*-Marxism. Burke would eventually go farther, but only in later texts.

This reversal in direction may seem less surprising, however, when one considers *ATH* in the broader context of Burke's career to this point. Whatever the differences between the innate forms in his early aestheticism and the biologism in *PC*, both theorize a subject independent of history, at the generic level of the human species. Considering *ATH* from the standpoint of this earlier work, it's no surprise that it turns from a subject of history to a history of subjects gingerly, getting its feet wet but fearing to get in over its head. Further, behind Burke's aestheticism and biologism is a fundamental commitment to the view that literature, however deeply it is enmeshed in history, nonetheless cannot be contained by history. In our time, this subordination of history has been a standard rhetorical strategy for the valorization of literature. In *PC* Burke broadens his scope from the literary to the cultural text, but he does so by looking in the latter for a will to eloquence with strong ties to the former – in other words, he does so by keeping his commitment to the valorization of literature. *ATH* keeps this commitment too, in a new way, one that finds in Freud a new kind of eloquence, the eloquence of the dream.

This eloquence requires a new method for its analysis, one that receives its best-known statement in *PLF*, to be considered in the next chapter. The framework for this method appears in *ATH*'s contrast between forensic and pre-forensic, which is a contrast between the abstractions of the public forum and the concreteness of poetic expression. The latter can be sung whereas the former can only be stated. On a level of "mimetic" assertion, "the poet, feeling (let us say) agitation, gives us agitated sound and rhythm; or feeling calmness, he slips into liquid tonalities" (339). Forensic abstractions, however,

are too complex for mimetic assertion. They are "tonally opportunistic," since there is no rudimentary choreographic act related to their pronunciation...[T]he poet "reclaims" these areas, as far as possible, by using them in tonal and rhythmic contexts that give them something of a mimetic content...The "mimetic" level becomes interwoven first with the "intimate" level, in the "pre-political" or "pre-forensic" ("familiar") experiences of childhood. This "familiar" level may become so authoritative, since it necessarily is the first form in which we encounter the world at large, that its informative cues will always figure in our incorporation of later materials. (340–41)

The Freudian pre-forensic thus poeticizes the acceptance and rejection of symbols of authority. The formation and transformation of subjects is a process that is agonistic but still poetic.

The Freudian pre-forensic has one additional appeal. While it is enmeshed in the transformation of subjects in history, it seems, in *ATH*, to escape history. It is part of history but not contained by history. In "the doctrines of the psychoanalysts...to 'integrate' the rational experience of waking life with the incongruous perspectives of sleep" (180), Burke finds an exploration of levels of experience and conflicts irreducible to anything resolvable through the agon in history. He concludes,

> To sum up: For various reasons, one has many disparate moods and attitudes. These may be called sub-identities, subpersonalities, "voices." And the poet seeks to build the symbolic superstructures that put them together into a comprehensive "super-personality." Even in the "best possible of worlds," then, there will be many factors stimulating men to the construction of symbolic mergers. Even if you remove the class issue in its acuter forms, you still have a disparate world that must be ritualistically integrated.　(184)

The "class issue" refers, of course, to Marxism, and the passage registers Burke's sense of its limits. *ATH* historicizes the subject through the agon of history, but not completely. A level of conflict is resolvable through Freudian eloquence alone.

ATH's Freudian individualism is thus continuous with the earlier aestheticism and biologism, not on the level of theoretical doctrine, but on the level of commitment to the valorization of literature. Moving from innate forms in the mind, to biologism, to the Freudian pre-forensic, Burke makes a series of big leaps, but he manages in a certain sense to land on the same spot each time. The security of the spot seems to enable the broadening of theoretical scope to culture and to history. *ATH*'s turn from a subject of history to a history of subjects is thus not quite as complete as it appears at first blush. Completing the turn requires theorizing the transhistorical; one goes with the other. Considering that in *ATH* it's the privileging of the Freudian subject that inhibits completion of the turn, one might expect Burke's theorizing of the transhistorical to begin with a reevaluation of Freud. As we'll see in the next chapter, that is precisely what happens.

But first a coda for the present chapter: there is an irony in Burke's Freudo-Marxism when considered from the standpoint of his "comic attitude." For Burke draws on the century's two greatest discourses of demystification − only Nietzsche's rivals Marx's and Freud's − to devise an alternative to such demystification. Burke's comic demystification depends on the utopian aspiration in his group realism. This aspiration is the countervailing power in Burke's discourse: Freud and Marx keep Burke suspicious; the group keeps him on the lookout for the utopian aspiration that allows for the charity of comedy. Against Freud, there is more emphasis on the group; against Marx, the group is more utopian. Burke, however, goes in the wrong direction in privileging the pre-forensic of Freudian individualism insofar as that road leads more to Freudian demystification than to his comic alternative. For a more rigorous and consistent comic demystification, one must await *RM*, where Burke finds even in capitalism's celebration of raw competition among individuals a comedy of fanatical conformity to the ideal of setting oneself apart: "From the standpoint of 'identification' what we call 'competition' is better described as men's attempt to *out-imitate* one another" (131).

5

The Philosophy of Literary Form: history without origin or telos

> The critic is trying to *synopsize* the given work. He is trying to synopsize it, not in the degenerated sense which the word "synopsis" now usually has for us ... but in the sense of "conveying comprehensively," or "getting at the basis of." And one can work towards this basis ... in focussing all one's attention about the *motivation*, which is identical with *structure*. Burke, *PLF*

The centerpiece of our reading of Burke's career begins with the present chapter and continues through the next two, which examine *GM* and *RM*, the two completed parts of the trilogy Burke envisioned in conceiving dramatism. We follow Burke closely but depart from him in extrapolating a rhetoric of the subject, which is present and absent in *GM* and *RM*: present as an implication but absent as a term. Sufficient to theorize a rhetoric of the subject, *GM* and *RM* are here considered parts of a completed discourse, not parts of an incomplete trilogy. From the standpoint of our reading, as we'll see in later chapters, the projected *SM* would have been theoretically redundant.

PLF collects previously published essays and reviews from the preceding decade and adds something new in the long title essay, which is both continuous with the work of the 1930s and discontinuous with it in its anticipations of the transformations in Burke's thought that emerge with dramatism. *PLF* introduces in its subtitle, "Studies in Symbolic Action," a term that becomes a regular part of Burke's vocabulary thereafter, even appearing over two decades later in another title, *Language as Symbolic Action*. Beginning with the categories "situations" and "strategies" that serve as its theoretical armature, "PLF" conceives symbolic acts as "answers to questions posed by the situation in which they arose. They are not merely answers, they are *strategic* answers, *stylized* answers" (1; see also 8).

Jameson draws on "PLF" for a perspective on his notion of a subtext:

Kenneth Burke's play of emphases, in which a symbolic act is on the one hand affirmed as a genuine *act* ... while on the other it is registered as an act which is "merely" symbolic ... suitably dramatizes the ambiguous status of art and culture ... The symbolic act ... generat[es] and produc[es] its own context in the same moment of emergence in which it steps back from it, taking its measure with a view toward its own projects of transformation. The whole paradox of what we have here called the subtext may be summed up in this, that the literary work or cultural object, as though for the first time, brings into being that very situation to which it is also, at one and the same time, a reaction.[1]

The paradox Jameson identifies here is the paradox of rhetorical realism, which insists on the real even while subscribing to the constructionist thesis that we are always already inside constructions that bring something into being "for the first time." In their rhetorical inventiveness, constructions cannot be derived from something antecedent such as the economy, in Marxist economism; the creative subject, in romantic authenticity; or the object, in enlightenment certainty. Constructions are rhetorically sayable and sayability involves a rhetorical inventiveness that is relatively autonomous. Theorizing this paradox of rhetorical realism is the main purpose of this and the next two chapters.

Burke began revising the theoretical armature of "PLF" so soon after completing it that he added a footnote sketch of his new armature in progress. In the sketch, one can see *GM* taking form as its dramatistic pentad emerges: "And instead of the situation–strategy pair, I now use five terms: act, scene, agent, agency, purpose" (106). Further, as we'll see in chapter 6, the pentad is associated in Burke's discourse with the constitutional act, the US Constitution serving as his featured example. This historical document appears in "PLF" but simply as a specific historical *"strategy for encompassing a situation"* (109), whereas in *GM* it provides Burke, as he remarks retrospectively, a "generative model for the study of language as symbolic action" (QAP 334). More anticipations of *GM* appear in "The Study of Symbolic Action" (SSA), an important but neglected essay that appeared in 1942, one year after *PLF* and three years before *GM*. Here, the pentad is fleshed out and one sees in embryonic form some of its main uses in *GM*. The term "dramatism" appears, as do two important oppositions: action vs. knowledge, and action vs. motion (SSA 12, 7, 11–12). The concluding

---

1 *The Political Unconscious: Narrative as a Socially Symbolic Act* (Ithaca: Cornell University Press), pp. 81–82.

paragraph begins, "The work of art is an enactment. Being constitutive, it survives as a structure, or 'constitution'" (16).

It's easy enough to see anticipations of symbolic action in Burke's earlier work, but overstressing such continuities reduces Burke to saying the same thing in new ways. One must look for discontinuities to find what is new. With the emergence of symbolic action, for example, behaviorism undergoes a change of status in Burke's discourse. A part of that discourse in *PC*, it is apart from it in *GM*, where it is cast as a polemical antagonist in a line of argument that Burke often has occasion to reiterate – in chapter 8, we'll have occasion ourselves to examine a reiteration appearing in "Dramatism" (D68). In *GM*, the occasion for the polemic is its introduction of the term "representative anecdote":

Men seek vocabularies that will be faithful *reflections* of reality. To this end, they must develop vocabularies that are *selections* of reality. And any selection of reality must, in certain circumstances, function as a *deflection* of reality...

Dramatism suggests a procedure to be followed in the development of a given calculus, or terminology. It involves the search for a "representative anecdote"... For instance, the behaviorist uses his experiments with the conditioned reflex as the anecdote about which to form his vocabulary for the discussion of human motives; but this anecdote, though notably *informative*, is not *representative*, since one cannot find a representative case of human motivation in animals, if only because animals lack that property of linguistic rationalization which is so typical of human motives...

If the originating anecdote is not representative, a vocabulary developed in strict conformity with it will not be representative. This embarrassment is usually avoided in practice by a break in the conformity at some crucial point... The very man who... might tell you that people are but chemicals, will induce responses in people by talking to them, whereas he could not try to make chemicals behave by linguistic experiment.   (*GM* 59)

This polemic raises questions not only about the reason for Burke's turn against behaviorism, but also about whether this turn entails, as well, displacement of *PC*'s thesis that language is metaphoric.

Burke's distinction between motion and action, as presented in "Study of Symbolic Action," reinforces his argument against behaviorism. The conditioned reflex in Pavlov's dog was an effect of the motion of stimulus and response in a laboratory process, but this process was an effect of Pavlov's action as a scientist. Pavlov was able to conceive this process and perceive the significance of its results by virtue of the linguistic prowess that made it possible for him to enter scientific debates: "Dramatistically, *motion is deduced from action.* That is, a man acts, and uses the resources of motion as a condition or instrumentality of his action; he sets in motion the kinds of motion that serve the purposes of his act" (SSA 12). The behavioristic error is to eliminate action from its "anecdote" in order to derive action from motion: "scientifically, *action is reduced to motion.* That is, the act is dissolved into an arc of motion, an adjustment or behavior, a complex of vibrations responding to other vibrations" (SSA 12). The behaviorist is a walking contradiction, acting to persuade other scientists that "people are but chemicals" and demonstrating by this very act that people are more than chemicals. Behaviorism errs, in other words, in blinding itself to rhetoric without which there would be no behaviorism.[2]

Burke's polemic with behaviorism may be contrasted to the present text's polemic with rhetorical idealism, the differences between the polemics arising from different rhetorical situations. Today, it's easy to say that there is a constructive ingredient in our "realities," perhaps too easy. To us, it's hard, if not impossible, to see past rhetoric. Burke's situation was the opposite. His polemic with behaviorism is a strategy for establishing a beachhead for constructionism in a hostile environment, one in which it was hard even to see rhetoric in the first place. Behaviorism provided Burke a strategically effective example in the sense that the behaviorist, considered as a walking contradiction, is well suited to making a case for the reality of rhetoric. This reality is the "critical moment" that appears in *GM* as it distances itself from *PC*'s biologism in conceiving "language as the 'critical moment' at which human motives take form, since a linguistic factor at every point in human experience complicates and to some extent transcends the purely biological aspects of motivation" (318).

---

2 Burke's argument exemplifies the *argumentum ad hominem* that Henry W. Johnstone, Jr. has legitimated in his rhetoricizing of philosophy. See the essays he collects in *Validity and Rhetoric in Philosophical Argument: An Outlook in Transition* (University Park: Dialogue Press of Man and World, 1978) for various versions of this argument, conceived as necessary when *argumentum ad rem* (i.e., appeal to things antecedent to discourse) is not possible.

The line that Burke draws between action and motion, it's important to stress, is not a clean break. Physiological processes in the realm of motion are involved in the action of speaking and writing. Rhetoric is linguistic action, but language-users live and die in the biological realm of motion. Action, in short, is impossible without motion. In contrast, motion would remain if language-users were to disappear from the face of the earth. Further, while Pavlov's scientific project is an act of construction with a history, motion limits his construction. Motion is an interlocutor beyond the reach of the power of constructing and reconstructing, an interlocutor that always answers the same way, not different ways at different times and places. Motion marks the autonomy of science, that which no science can historicize away, regardless of whether its historical origins are bourgeois, proletarian, or anything else. Burke directs attention to the limits as well as the reality of rhetoric.

In using his term "representative anecdote" to dismiss behaviorism, Burke deploys a criterion of representativeness foreign to *PC*'s thesis that language is metaphor, particularly when one recalls the constructionist saturnalia that "perspective by incongruity" licenses. It's this consideration that raises the issue about whether Burke's turn against behaviorism entails displacement of this thesis in *PC*. Moreover, as we'll see in chapter 8 in examining Burke's final phase, this issue of whether there are shifts in his conceptualization of language figures prominently in current discussion of the periodization of his career, particularly its later phases. In this discussion some participants frame their periodizing narratives within the opposition between literality and metaphor: the narrative's theoretical issue is whether terminologies can be literal or are necessarily metaphoric, and the narrative revolves around Burke shifting from one side of the issue to the other.

Literality and metaphor, however, may not exhaust the possibilities. The present chapter considers an alternative, namely, that when language is conceived as action, it is strictly speaking neither one nor the other but prior to both. This alternative is also relevant to chapter 8, as it bears upon the question of periodization to be addressed in that chapter. Consideration of this alternative takes us into the area of overlap between Burke and J. L. Austin. There are important differences along with this overlap, but these can be shelved for later chapters. Burke and Austin do walk together in some ways, as illustrated by Burke himself in his own essay on Austin, which begins by identifying Austin's speech act as a dramatistic approach to language (WD 147).[3] Burke and Austin undertook in the 1940s projects that parallel one another in significant ways.[4] Coming from the different directions of literature and philosophy, they sought to reorient the discussion of language – to change the topic of conversation, as Rorty would say – in a similar manner. The irony is that the conception of language as action they share has entered literary theory mainly by way of Austin rather than Burke, even though it was Burke who stood up for literature and Austin who excluded it as parasitic upon ordinary language.[5]

One sign that Burke's turn against behaviorism necessitated a turn against *PC*'s conception of language as metaphor is that behaviorism can be construed as a metaphor, as Burke himself suggests. In *PC*, for example, he offers a list to support his claim that schools of thought have their source in fertile metaphors: "Thus we have, at different eras in history, considered man as the son of God, as an animal, as a political or economic brick, as a machine, each such metaphor . . . serving as the cue for an unending line of data and generalizations" (95). Either "animal" or "machine," depending on whether one wanted to emphasize the organic or the mechanistic, could provide a metaphor for behaviorism. An even more specific example appears in "Four Master Tropes" (FMT) – a text to which we'll return shortly – where the behavioristic "conditioned reflex" is included in a list designed to exhibit the broad range of metaphor (504). In short, while behaviorism

3 Affinities between Burke and Austin have received little attention, but they have not been ignored altogether (see Henderson, *Burke* 107–10).

4 *How to Do Things with Words,* ed. J. O. Urmson (New York: Oxford University Press, 1965) is, of course, based on lectures Austin gave in 1955. But one example in this text also appears in a 1940 essay, "The Meaning of a Word," where it is used to invoke the importance of the total speech situation in a manner that anticipates the later work; see Austin's *Philosophical Papers,* eds. J. O. Urmson and G. J. Warnock, 3rd ed. (Oxford: Clarendon Press, 1979), pp. 63–64. Austin reportedly thought his views in his 1955 lectures were formed by 1939; see J. O. Urmson, "Editor's Preface," *How to Do,* p. v.

5 Derrida's critique of Austin's exclusion of literature will be considered in the next chapter. This exclusion derives from Austin's distinction between "serious" and "nonserious" speech acts, which allows Austin to reintroduce through the back door of his text the distinction between statement and pseudo-statement that he kicks out the front. To take the brave step of dismantling literal reference from its lofty perch in philosophy, Austin evidently needed the rhetorical security of a factual world untainted by fiction, so he reconstituted positivism's narrow factual world of literal reference in the form of the broader factual world of serious speech acts. His bald assertion that facts can be cleanly separated from fictions and his deferral of the demonstration of this separation to a later day suggest he sensed both that he was vulnerable to the kind of critique Derrida mounts and that he had to sidestep this critique to get his text written – in other words, he could go as far as he did only by not going as far as the logic of his premises dictated. The rhetorical pressure under which Austin worked in his conversation with philosophers was not present in Burke's conversation with literary theorists.

doesn't qualify as a representative anecdote, it does as a metaphor.

It qualifies, moreover, even by the criteria of the modern aesthetic of metaphor. This aesthetic is often contrasted to the neoclassical aesthetic, whose *locus classicus* is Johnson's critique of the metaphysical poets in his life of Cowley. Johnson's formula is "natural and new," according to which a metaphor should be novel but not at the expense of abandoning rationalistic restraint. It's this restraint that the modern aesthetic rejects in the name of imagination. I. A. Richards exemplifies this modern preference in applauding a line in Shakespeare — "Steep'd me in poverty to the very lips" — while holding up to ridicule an eighteenth-century critic's complaint that this metaphor conceives poverty as a fluid, "which it resembles not in any manner."[6] For this critic, in other words, fluid is too unrepresentative of poverty to serve as a metaphor for it. But this rationalistic unrepresentativeness is an imaginative virtue for Richards. Analogously, the more the behaviorist anecdote fails by the logic of literal representation, the more it succeeds by the aesthetic of metaphoric imagination. Behaviorism is imaginative, as suggested by the literary tradition of animal metaphors.

Metaphor, in short, ironically fails to provide the basis for turning against behaviorism that Burke sought. But a turn away from metaphor is not necessarily a turn to literality. *GM* forges dramatism against not only behaviorism but also postivistic semantics and its privileging of literal reference:

So, one could, if he wished, maintain that all theology, metaphysics, philosophy, criticism, poetry, drama, fiction, political exhortation, historical interpretation, and personal statements about the lovable and the hateful — one could if he wanted to be as drastically thorough as some of our positivists now seem to want to be — maintain that every bit of this is nonsense. Yet these words of nonsense would themselves be real words, involving real tactics, having real demonstrable relationships, and demonstrably affecting relationships. And as such, a study of their opportunities, necessities, and embarrassments would be central to the study of human motives.   (57–58)

This positivistic charge of "nonsense," leveled at departures from literal reference, is another version of the charge of "pseudo-statement" that Richards, as noted in chapter 3 above, reversed by finding positive value in such departures. The New Criticism followed suit in its defense of the complex metaphoric language of poetry against the

---

6 "Metaphor," lecture 5 in *The Philosophy of Rhetoric* (New York: Oxford University Press, 1965), p. 104; Richards introduces here terms now commonly used in discussing metaphor: "tenor" and "vehicle."

literal language of science – an apology for poetry as a form of knowledge different from and more humanistic than science.[7] But this approach, Burke countered in *GM*, is "a lame attempt to pit art against science as a 'truer kind of truth.' The correct controversy here should not have been at all a pitting of art against science: it should have been a pitting of one view of science against another" (226). The correct controversy, in other words, is the one now commonplace in the wake of Thomas Kuhn's work.[8] Rather than continuing the conversation framed by the flat opposition between positivism's literal reference and New Criticism's metaphoric density, Burke tried to change the rules of the conversation by conceiving language as action to direct attention to the reality of rhetoric. Words, regardless of their content, are real events in the world: nonsense or not, before they are anything else they are real acts with real effects.[9]

An adumbration of this rule change appears in "Semantic and Poetic Meaning" (SPM), first published in 1938 and reprinted in *PLF*: "although the semantic ideal would eliminate the *attitudinal* ingredient from its vocabulary . . . the ideal is itself an attitude, hence never wholly attainable, since it would be complete only by abolition of itself. To the logical positivist, logical positivism is a 'good' term, otherwise he would not attempt to advocate it by filling it out in all its ramifications" (150). Burke outflanks positivistic semantics by building on a linguistic principle that informs even the language of positivism. This outflanking strategy assumes its mature form in *GM*.

This strategy marks the overlap between Burke and Austin. In the performative, Austin similarly finds language that is a real act with real (illocutionary) effects. His performative initially seems simply to fall outside the parallel distinctions between sense and nonsense on the one hand, and statement and pseudo-statement on the other, both of which Austin reviews in his first lecture in *How to Do Things with*

---

7 For a still useful summary of the New Criticism's epistemological approach, see Murray Krieger, *The New Apologists for Poetry* (Bloomington: Indiana University Press, 1963), especially section 3: "The Function of Poetry: Science, Poetry, and Cognition."

8 Regarding Kuhn's *The Structure of Scientific Revolutions*, Fish suggests that it "is arguably the most frequently cited work in the humanities and social sciences in the past twenty-five years"; see *Doing What Comes Naturally: Change, Rhetoric, and the Practice of Theory in Literary and Legal Studies* (Durham: Duke University Press, 1989), p. 486.

9 Wittgenstein effected a comparable rule change in the linguistic game. See Charles Altieri's *Act and Quality: A Theory of Literary Meaning and Humanistic Understanding* (Amherst: University of Massachusetts Press, 1981) for an authoritative account of the value to literary criticism to be derived from this rule change, characterized as a displacement of "the referential–emotive dichotomy" (9).

Words, where he introduces the "constative" as his alternative to "sense" and "statement." In other words, the performative intially seems to be neither sense nor nonsense, but something distinct from both. Later, however, the performativity of the speech act emerges as the architectonic category. Language is performative before it is anything else: "The total speech act in the total speech situation is the *only actual* phenomenon which, in the last resort, we are engaged in elucidating."[10] The performative is the whole pie, not a mere piece.

The polemical edge in Austin's text, in the context of philosophy, is its movement of constative utterance from a primary to a subordinate position. "Austin's revolution in philosophy," observes Rodolphe Gasché, "consists in restoring...the priority of real life over the abstract logical situation, and in demonstrating that the assumption by analytical philosophers that the business of language is to make statements upon facts depends on an illicit abstraction of the constative function of language from the total speech act situation."[11] One of Austin's examples of a constative is "Lord Raglan won the battle of Alma." Is it true or false? The job of epistemology is to define criteria by which to decide. Austin doesn't deny that the job needs doing, but he does insist, "The truth or falsity of a statement depends...on what act you were performing in what circumstances."[12] In one "total speech act situation," "Lord Raglan..." may count as true; in others, it may not. It is and is not literal. What Austin refuses is the positivistic abstract logical situation in which statements are true or false in an absolute sense. "Lord Raglan..." is an act of selection presupposing a strategy of historical construction in a specific rhetorical situation. Other acts, presupposing other strategies, might demote Lord Raglan to a subordinate clause or even omit him altogether, such that to say he won the battle would in effect be to speak figuratively. One may reintroduce the traditional literal–metaphor distinction, contrasting "Lord Raglan" to "the fox," "the hawk," or whatever might suit Lord Raglan. But from the standpoint of language as action, such a contrast is at most a second-tier distinction.

Burke's argument in the opening of "Study of Symbolic Action" parallels Austin's privileging of the performative in the total speech act situation against the philosophical privileging of the constative: "The proposal here is to consider poetry as a kind of *action* rather than as a

10 *How to Do*, p. 147.
11 "'Setzung' and 'Übersetzung': Notes on Paul de Man," *Diacritics* 11.4 (1981): 37.
12 *How to Do*, p. 144.

kind of *knowledge*. This is a 'dramatistic' approach to poetry, as against the customary 'epistemological' approach which has flourished along with the prestige of science" (7). The term "epistemology" here serves to identify the antagonist Burke shares with Austin. In the classical epistemological tradition descending from Descartes, epistemology is the abstract logical situation where truth and falsity in an absolute sense is possible. Contrasting dramatism to epistemology serves Burke in the 1940s as a standard strategy for introducing his dramatistic approach to language.

Burke's turn from metaphor to the representative anecdote, then, should not be equated to a simple turn to literality as it is conceived in classical epistemology. Perhaps the best vantage point from which to study Burke making this turn is "Four Master Tropes," published in 1941, the same year as *PLF*, before its reprinting as an appendix in *GM*. In its opening paragraph, Burke makes it clear that his interest in these tropes – metaphor, metonymy, synecdoche, irony – is not "with their purely figurative usage, but with their role in the discovery and description of 'the truth'" (503). Therefore, he adds, "It is an evanescent moment that we shall deal with . . . [in which] the figurative and literal usages shift" (503). His first trope is metaphor, defined as "a device for seeing something *in terms of* something else" and illustrated with the broad range of examples that includes the conditioned reflex (503–04). This range exhibits the unrestrained imaginativeness of metaphor. With metonymy Burke continues within the figurative structure of seeing something in terms of something else, but he adds an additional consideration as he indicates that the metonymic something else may take the form of an unrepresentative reductive terminology of motion, as in behaviorism.[13] With this introduction of considerations of representativeness, the shift begins from the metaphoric to the literal. These considerations come into full force with synecdoche: "Let us get at the point thus: *A terminology of conceptual analysis, if it is not to lead to misrepresentation, must be constructed in conformity with a representative anecdote – whereas anecdotes 'scientifically' selected for reductive purposes are not representative*" (510). Consistent with his analysis of these tropes, it's worth noting, Burke privileges synecdoche rather than metaphor in "PLF," "synecdochic representation . . . [being] a necessary ingredient of a truly realistic philosophy" (26).

13 Madsen is exceptional in the attention he gives to Burke's analysis of these tropes to determine the criteria of representativeness in the representative anecdote. Madsen also provides a valuable review of the literature on the representative anecdote.

There is still one more trope, irony, to which Burke turns to answer his own question, "What then, it may be asked, would be a 'representative anecdote'?" (511). His answer is an example that equates irony to dialectic and dialectic to drama, equations designed to exhibit symbolic action in action. Burke finds in synecdoche enough connection between a representation and what it represents for it to qualify as a model for the representative anecdote, but a synecdochic representation does not qualify as the "mirror of nature" that Rorty identifies as the model in classical epistemology. Synecdoches are representations that rhetorically qualify one another as they question and modify one another in a dramatistic dialectic. Irony is the structure of such qualification. It is only, Burke concludes, when one representation is abstracted from this irony – when, in effect, it is treated as a "mirror of nature" – that there occurs "the simplification of literalness" (516).[14] Burke thus distinguishes different senses of literality as he privileges the "representative anecdote" against "the simplification of literalness," just as Austin privileges literal in the sense of "Lord Raglan won the battle of Alma" against literal in the sense of classical epistemology.

Burke's dramatistic subordination of epistemology helps to explain the presence of the term "anecdote" in his conception of the representative anecdote. This term insists on the situational positionality of the model on which any terminology is based.[15] The selection of an anecdote, moreover, is itself an act in a situation. Burke's deliberations in *GM* leading to his choice of the US Constitution as his central anecdote are strategic, encompassing pragmatic as well as theoretical considerations. An act of selecting an anecdote is situated in historical processes. Terminologies always have agendas.

In "PLF," Burke offers a more concise version of the main argument in "Four Master Tropes" as he equates the situational positionality of symbolic action to the magical decree: "if you size up a situation in the name of regimentation you *decree* it a different essence than if you sized it up in the name of planned economy. The choice here is not a choice between magic and no magic, but a choice between magics that vary in their degree of approximation to the truth" (6). Only God is capable of producing a "mirror of nature": "Only a *completely accurate* chart would

14 For a similar reading of "Four Master Tropes," albeit one that doesn't consider the appearance in it of the "representative anecdote," see Leff 119–21. Hans Kellner mentions Burke along with others such as Vico in reviewing treatments of these tropes as a set of four; see "The Inflatable Trope as Narrative Theory: Structure or Allegory," *Diacritics* 11.1 (1981): 14–28.
15 Leff finds illuminating parallels between Burke and Cicero in their emphasis on the situational (Leff 118–19).

dissolve magic, by making the structure of names identical with the structure named . . . A completely adequate chart would, of course, be possible only to an infinite, omniscient mind" (7). Only God, in other words, escapes positionality to the nonpositionality of knowledge, as classically conceived. The opposition of positionality to nonpositionality stands behind the opposition of dramatism to epistemology that Burke introduces at the beginning of "Study of Symbolic Action." One can get from action to knowledge, but not to the knowledge hypothesized in enlightenment certainty. In other words, knowledge never realizes the "dream at the heart of philosophy," a phrase Rorty borrows from Derrida; Rorty equates the dream to "an ancient hope: the hope for a language which can receive no gloss, requires no interpretation, cannot be distanced, cannot be sneered at by later generations. It is the hope for a vocabulary which is intrinsically and self-evidently final, not merely the most comprehensive and fruitful vocabulary we have come up with so far."[16] Such a language is, like Burke's "completely adequate chart," available only to God.

In these varying ways, as Burke begins forging dramatism, he insists that a representation is and is not what it represents. Insisting on "is not" preserves the reality of rhetoric against the bald "is" of philosophy that would blind us to rhetoric. Burke's strongest formulation of this insistence appears in one of his best-known essays, "Terministic Screens": "Even if any given terminology is a *reflection* of reality, by its very nature as a terminology it must be a *selection* of reality; and to this extent it must function also as a *deflection* of reality" (TS 45). Burke has almost arrived at this trilogy of terms when he introduces the term "representative anecdote" in *GM*, in the passage quoted at the beginning of the present section: "Men seek vocabularies that will be faithful *reflections* of reality. To this end, they must develop vocabularies that are *selections* of reality."[17]

Throughout "PLF," Burke recurrently writes against the fear that the rhetorical reality of symbolic action will connote only unreality to his readers. He does this a final time near the end of the text, mounting an argument of particular interest because it bears on the shift from *PC* to *GM* that we've been examining. In *PC*, his strategy takes its cue from the opposition between literality and metaphor that frames his conception of language as metaphor. On one side, he invokes biological perspectivism to argue that there is perspectivism on the

16 "Deconstruction and Circumvention," *Critical Inquiry* 11 (1984), p. 5.
17 For an insightful discussion of Burke's conception of a verbal act of selection, see Schiappa 414–16.

level of sensory perception, so that even the empirical perception positivistic literality presupposes is impossible; on the other, the "as if" of metaphor is buttressed by the principle of recalcitrance. In "PLF," in contrast, his strategy takes its cue from the dramatistic conception of language as action. "Suppose," Burke suggests, "that some disaster has taken place, and that I am to break the information to a man who will suffer from the knowledge of it" (126). Verbalizing the disaster stylizes it, paradoxically responding to the disaster and bringing it into being for the first time in the sense that the verbalization is a linguistic act that selects one depiction of the disaster from multiple possibilities, each being both reflection and deflection. The verbalization of the disaster is thus a choice of disasters. Whichever one chooses, one stylizes it for the man who will suffer from knowledge of it, as well as for oneself as the bearer of bad news. Even a bare description in the seemingly neutral style of the positivist ideal would still be one stylization with its own effects. Literality is as much an act in a total speech situation as a metaphoric verbalization of the disaster designed to cushion the blow. "Stylization is inevitable" (128) — not because of metaphor, but because of the act of selection. The verbalization, in sum, is a real act with real effects. The real is determinate "in the last instance," as we saw in chapter 1, not as a verbal representation of itself, but as the necessity that forces the verbal act to hierarchize in choosing its disaster.

It may be worth noting, in concluding this section, that symbolic action is a road to constructionism that differs from the more familiar one built on the Saussurean principle that language is a system of differences with no positive terms. Perhaps, however, we have now traveled this Saussurean road long enough to take stock of just how far it allows us to advance.

This Saussurean principle underwrote structuralism but survived structuralism's demise as Derrida broadened its applicability. Structuralism used it to introduce a transindividual decentering of the individual: language speaking the individual rather than the individual speaking language. Derrida, in turn, decentered the structuralist transindividual center, opening up the centerless world of postmodern fragmentation. The homogeneous culture of structuralism gave way to the heterogeneous culture of poststructuralism. We're now used to the idea that cultures consist of fragmented systems of linguistic differences and that there is no way to privilege any system as true. But this Saussurean conception of language only deals with the formal cause of meaning. It's true that for two linguistic units to have distinct meanings, they must be formally differentiated somehow; moreover, these formal relations affect the meaning of the units, since no unit can be divorced from the relations that make it possible for it to mean. But why *this* system of differences rather than *that* one? Neither difference nor differance has proved able to answer this question.

Theoretical debates in recent decades have taught us about the limits of formalism, a discovery Aristotle made long ago. To invoke Aristotle is not to return to his metaphysics, but to suggest that the trajectory of these debates may be read as a parallel in the analysis of culture to his correction of the shortcomings of Plato's formalism, which revealed themselves in Plato's failure to explain change in the material world – maybe we are still nothing more than footnotes to Aristotle and Plato.[18] Structuralism's excessive formalism collapsed on the rocks of history. Derrida paradoxically revitalized formalism by exposing its limits, but his "there is nothing outside the text" eventually gave way to Foucault's "power is everywhere," a formula Derrida himself seems ready to embrace with a few qualifications.[19] Foucault's current ascendency may be seen as an effect of the extent to which the Foucauldian disciplining of the body corrects formalism. But as we saw in chapter 1, Foucault's correction fails to step beyond the disciplinary agon to the agon of history. For that step, we need the rhetorical realism of the act. The Saussurean formal cause is a condition of the act in the agon of history, but this act is not reducible solely to this cause because it has a directionality, one that explains why there is *this* difference rather than *that* one, even if it is itself always *in media res*, without an ultimate origin or telos.

Accompanying the emergence of Burke's conception of language as symbolic action is the equation, highlighted in the present chapter's epigraph, of motivation to structure. The main subject of the present section, this equation exhibits an early stage of the theorizing of a rhetoric of the subject that attains its mature form in *GM* and *RM*.

An act adds something new to the world. That is what gives it value

18 For a concise and authoritative summary of how Aristotle's correction of Plato led Aristotle to his theory of four causes, see Richard McKeon, "Introduction," *The Basic Works of Aristotle* (New York: Random House, 1941), pp. xix–xx.

19 *Limited Inc*, ed. Gerald Graff (Evanston: Northwestern University Press, 1988), pp. 149–50. These remarks on Foucault's "power is everywhere" are in "Afterword: Toward an Ethic of Discussion," a text first published in this volume.

for historical analysis and constructionist theory. The reality of rhetoric is paradoxically permanent and transitory: rhetoric is a permanent part of the human condition, but it is the part that is constructed and may at any time be reconstructed. A construction is an invention – an act – something that wasn't always here and that one day may live only in historical memory. The inventiveness of the act is what makes the act resistant to theoretical comprehension. Theorizing the act puts one in the paradoxical position of trying to comprehend the motivation of what by definition can change one's comprehension of motivation. The theoretical gesture, in other words, seems to put the cart before the horse of invention. In a certain sense, a theory of the act is impossible; in another, perhaps not. In the present chapter, we'll take a few steps to test this theoretical thin ice; in the next, we'll try to walk all the way across.

The easiest way to begin to comprehend Burke's equation of motivation to structure is to return to his distinction, introduced in chapter 1, between essentializing and proportionalizing. Before appearing in *GM*, where there is a proportionalizing of the act, it appears in "Freud – and the Analysis of Poetry," where Burke proportionalizes what he terms a "cluster." This term appears in *ATH*'s "Dictionary of Pivotal Terms," which cites as an example distinctive clusters of images in a text, such as those that Caroline Spurgeon uncovers in *Shakespeare's Imagery* (232). Burke's interest in such associational clusters can be traced at least as far back as his notion of qualitative form, introduced in his aesthetic period (*CS* 124–25). In *PC*, Burke characterizes as "Proustian" an example in which a man routinely hears, during a period of deep unhappiness, a peculiarly nagging ring of a nearby doorbell; and then, decades later, long after the period of unhappiness, upon hearing a similarly nagging ring, experiences a sudden, unexplained feeling of depression (76). For this man, the movement from the ring to the state of depression instantiates qualitative rather than syllogistic form, but from an aesthetic standpoint associational connections need to be communicable. What exercises Burke particularly in *PC*, as we saw in chapter 3, is the extent to which modern writers are forced to rely on personalized rather than public associations, such as the feeling of uplift that might run through a community upon hearing every Sunday morning the sound of a church bell. *PC* argues that such public versions, under conditions of cultural instability and fragmentation rooted in economic ills, are too few and too superficial to suffice for serious writers.

Clusters can thus be collective or individual, but it is the individualistic variety that receives most of Burke's attention as he evolves his method of cluster analysis, which receives its most extensive statement in "Fact, Inference, and Proof in the Analysis of Literary Symbolism" (FIP). An early version of the method appears in *ATH*, where one can see the act of selection appear as a principle: "The world contains an infinity of objects. The artist's engrossment involves a selection from among them ... The poet's selectivity is like the selectivity of a man with a tic ... You disclose the 'symbolic organization' of his tic when you have found the class of words that provokes it" (193).

In "PLF," the method assumes the shape of one of his methodological questions: what equals what? Burke finds, for example, that the Albatross in "The Rime of the Ancient Mariner" is in a cluster with Coleridge's wife, Sarah, because the Albatross and Sarah are associated with Christ, albeit in different poems (71). In passing, this mixing of passages from different texts should be underscored. In mixing them, Burke violated the New Criticism's insistence that one respect the intrinsic integrity of each individual poem, a principle with which he explicitly takes issue in "PLF" (23, 73–74). In addition, his claim that structure or form (the two are interchangeable in "PLF") is equivalent to motivation merges what the New Criticism sought to divide in its distinction between the intrinsic and the extrinsic, as illustrated by *The Well Wrought Urn*, where Cleanth Brooks selects texts from the Renaissance through the modernist period, reading them in chronological order, precisely for the purpose of uncovering a poetic structure in all of them that is indifferent to extrinsic historical differences.[20] *PLF* appeared the same year as John Crowe Ransom's *The New Criticism*, a book that gave a name to a movement, so that the two texts can be positioned as a fork in the road in the history of literary and cultural theory in twentieth-century America.

Such clusters of equations are, Burke suggests in "PLF," "unconscious or subconscious" as he categorizes this dimension of symbolic action as "dream," distinguishing it from "prayer" and "chart," prayer designating "communicative functions" and chart the "realistic sizing-up of situations" (7). In this tripartite subdividing of symbolic action, it's

---

20 See Henderson for a fine study of how Burke offers an alternative to both the intrinsic and the extrinsic; Henderson's first chapter, "The Intrinsic/Extrinsic Merger," does a very thorough job of assembling the textual material in Burke relevant to the issue. For Brooks's statement of his project, see *The Well Wrought Urn: Studies in the Structure of Poetry* (New York: Harcourt, Brace and World, 1947), p. ix.

important to add, one can see an embryonic version of the dramatistic trilogy: chart corresponds to *GM*; prayer to *RM*; and dream to *SM*. The term "dream" suggests that in his cluster analysis Burke sees the critic's relation to the writer as analogous to the psychoanalyst's to the patient (see also FAP 267). Burke seems, however, not to have derived his method of analysis from reading Freud so much as he assimilated Freud to interests that antedate this reading.[21] In any case, it is by casting himself as a proportionalizer and Freud as an essentializer that Burke opposes his method of dream analysis to Freud's, an opposition that he accentuates repeatedly in "PLF" (42, 48–49, 51–52, 56, 58, 89).

In introducing this opposition in "Freud – and the Analysis of Poetry," Burke imagines a situation in which a man is simultaneously experiencing sexual impotence, conflicts in his private life, and conflicts with fellow workers at the office – "the essentializing strategy would, in Freud's case, place the emphasis upon the sexual manifestation, as causal ancestor of the other two" (FAP 262). The proportionalizing strategy, in contrast, leaves open the possibility that any one of the three could be primary; to decide, one would have to examine the interrelations among the three, as in a narrative that includes all three and privileges one. In this proportionalizing analysis, in other words, the Freudian subject becomes a possible subject in competition with other possible subjects. Burke's treatment of Freud no doubt meets less resistance today than it once did.[22] It would be possible to apply to Burke, for example, Jameson's approbation of Deleuze and Guattari's *Anti-Oedipus* for challenging the Freudian family narrative in discrediting "interpretation in which the data of one narrative line are radically impoverished by their rewriting according to the paradigm of another narrative, which is taken as the former's master code or Ur-narrative . . ."[23] Rewriting any narrative into the terms of a master narrative of family romance, in other words, would correspond to essentializing. In refusing essentializing, Burke refuses any master narrative, embracing instead a proliferation of narratives. A narrative of sexual impotence,

---

21 These interests may be traceable all the way back to an early interest in Remy de Gourmont, whom Burke writes about in 1921 (ARG), groups with Flaubert and Pater in *CS* under the rubric "adepts of 'pure' literature" (1–28), and returns to once again in *RM*, where he reminds us of de Gourmont's role in introducing the French Symbolists (150) as he discusses de Gourmont's influence on his own thinking about the association and dissociation of ideas and images (149–54).

22 For example, in *Psychoanalysis and American Literary Criticism* (Detroit: Wayne State University Press, 1960), Louis Fraiberg finds little of value in Burke's discussion of Freud. Rueckert excerpts Fraiberg's commentary on Burke (*Critical* 335–44), but omits the portion devoted to FAP.   23 *Political Unconscious*, p. 22.

of conflict in private life, of conflict at the office – each is possible in the above example.

Applying the Jameson passage to Burke also suggests how one can add a dimension to Burke's polemic with Freud by construing it as an autocritique of *PC*'s historical narrative, which is a master narrative that rewrites the proliferation of orientations generated by trained incapacity and perspective by incongruity. In this rewriting, this proliferation becomes a cycle rooted in a master biological agon between the will to power and the will to eloquence. Proportionalizing frees proliferation from reduction to a master code. These considerations suggest that the forging of the opposition between essentializing and proportionalizing is part of Burke's turn from *PC*'s subject of history to a history of subjects. Such an autocritique is licensed by Burke's own retrospective comment: "To look over a book [*PC*] twenty years after it was first written is to discover that the author has been imaginative despite himself ... He has imagined someone who stoutly averred things that he now would state quite otherwise" (*PC* l).

Burke offers as "an explicit example of 'proportional' motivation" a summary of the commentary on Coleridge running through "PLF" (92). This summary takes the form, as in the case of Therborn's worker-qua-body, of the isolation of five problems – aesthetic, marital, political, drug, metaphysical (93–100) – each of which is a motivation that could be privileged against the others, or more generally, an area where motivations reinforce or contradict one another. The five, in other words, could be combined in different proportions in different situations. Of all the Coleridge texts that Burke cites, "The Rime of the Ancient Mariner" receives the most attention, though even that analysis is sketchy; Burke envisioned a monograph on Coleridge that he evidently left incomplete as he occupied himself writing *GM* and *RM* (*PLF* 95). There is, however, enough in place for illustrative purposes and for extrapolating from it themes important to the present study.

A key moment in the poem is the Mariner's blessing of the snakes, which he does "unaware" and which prompts the fall from his neck of the dead Albatross. The blessing instantiates Coleridge's impulsive aesthetic in which subjectivity is at one with the universe, even the seemingly lowly snakes; this aesthetic has its political analogue in Coleridge's "Pantisocracy project," a utopian plan for a community where virtue in general would be as impulsive as the Mariner's blessing in particular (96; see also *GM* 369–70). Aesthetic and political motivations, in other words, reinforce one another. Additional reinforcement, Burke suggests, can be found by linking the snakes to the benign phase of Coleridge's drug addiction, the snakes being "synecdochic representatives of the drug" such that the blessing redeems the drug (*PLF* 96–97).

This blessing, in Coleridge's symbolic act, is distinguished both from what comes before and after. Considerations of sequence arise in response to another of Burke's methodological questions: from what to what? (75). The question directs attention to the hierarchical interrelations among the multiple motivations incorporated in the act. What precedes the blessing involves mainly the marital problem, where Sarah is typically equated with Christianity and in opposition to the impulsive aesthetic and related motives (96). These marital difficulties constitute deviance from Christian orthodoxy that is dramatized when the Mariner slays the Albatross. In turn, when hung around the Mariner's neck, the Albatross becomes an image of the profound guilt attending this deviance. From the standpoint of what precedes it, therefore, the blessing, especially in its political dimension, may be seen as a shift to a rival orthodoxy. Affirming it, the Mariner moves beyond guilt, beyond the agon of deviance to a historical agon between rival orthodoxies. This historical agon is the poem's answer to Burke's one other methodological question: what vs. what? (69).

But this rival orthodoxy, the Pantisocracy project, never got much beyond the speculative stage and was, Burke suggests, probably "incapable of realization" in any case (*GM* 370). This rival orthodoxy lives only in aesthetic uplift, sometimes drug-induced or drug-reinforced. This orthodoxy is sayable, in other words, in a context that may be contrasted to the material concreteness of the new colony that Defoe could invent for Crusoe, his new subject of individualism. Imagining a colony as the personal possession of an individual entrepreneur wasn't realistic in a reportorial sense, of course, but it was sayable enough for generations of Europeans busy colonizing the rest of the world to give Crusoe mythic status.

What follows the affirmation of the rival orthodoxy in the blessing of the snakes is a movement that culminates in the Mariner's sermonizing to the Wedding-Guest, who is persuaded in the end to turn away from the marriage ceremony. Burke construes this conclusion as an explicit "preference for a religiosity-without-marriage" (*PLF* 95). How one would construe the final hierarchizing among the poem's interrelated motivational strands would depend on whether one associated this final religiosity with the initial orthodoxy or its later rival. In the process of ordering and modifying motivational discourses, however fissured the ordering, an act such as Coleridge's can become itself a new motivational discourse that, in turn, becomes part of the context of later acts. In its newness, in other words, an act can modify its conditions, by which it's constrained but not determined. Acts make history, though not "just as they please," as Marx suggests, "but under circumstances directly encountered, given, and transmitted from the past." The world is always already hierarchized for us, but it can be re-hierarchized.

Burke concludes his Coleridge interpretation by counterpointing it to Freudian essentializing:

> Thus, even if one were to begin his analysis by isolating an explicit sexual burden (such as the marital problem . . .) – the chart of interrelationships, as ultimately developed, would by no means vow one to some such simple picture of the author as writing works "caused" by this specific sexual problem.
> One would not have to consider the matter of "causation" at all. (101)

One need not consider "causation" because structure is motivation. In the essentializing that Freud exemplifies, in contrast, motivation causes a structure such as Coleridge's because the Freudian hierarchy, privileging sexuality and subordinating other motives to it, is in place prior to any structure. The motivational hierarchy causes the structure that stands as its expression. Different expressions can be invented but the hierarchy itself is fixed, not itself invented.

Proportionalizing makes invention possible at the root level of hierarchy by making hierarchy an issue rather than a *fait accompli*. In proportionalizing, there are hierarchies but none can ever stand as *the* hierarchy. The real, in rhetorical realism, imposes itself in necessitating hierarchy, but not in necessitating any particular one. Motivational discourses incorporated into the hierarchizing process may be antecedent to the structure, constituting the situation to which it responds, but only in the structural termination of the process itself is the issue of motivation settled. The motivation of the act is the structure of the act, not prior to it as a hierarchy forever fixed in place. Motivation, in other words, is constructed and the element of newness in the construction is irreducible to the antecedent situation. The act adds something to history – for example, the invention of the subject of individualism and the re-hierarchizing it entailed, as exemplified in Crusoe.

The subject, in short, is formed and transformed in the reality of rhetoric. The act is a rhetoric of the subject.

In a study of Burke's work in the 1930s that rewards careful reading, Paul Jay observes that Freud and Marx interested Burke, but "not [as] correct explanations of psychological or socioeconomic systems (although it would be wrong to suggest that he was not interested in these explanations too)" ("Motives" 537–38). Jay is right to accentuate Burke's search for an alternative to the idea of a "correct explanation," in the essentialistic sense of correctness that Burke finds in Freud. Burke writes a grammar and a rhetoric of motives, not a correct explanation. The one shortcoming in Jay's study surfaces in his parenthetical taking back of his point about Burke's interest in Freud and Marx. The need for the parenthetical hedge arises because Jay tries to force too much of the 1940s Burke into the 1930s texts. In Jay's account, Burke gets ahead of himself. Jay could make his point better with later texts.

Jay's important insight derives from developing the implication of Burke's claim in *PC* that "the assigning of motives is a matter of *appeal*" (25). This claim appears in a chapter called "Motives," a term that catches the eye because it appears in two later titles. Jay identifies this claim as "a key moment in Burke's development of a rhetorical form of cultural criticism" (541), as indeed it is, since it indicates that at an early stage Burke was ready to see motivation rhetorically, as a cultural construct. Earlier in "Motives," Burke uses a hypothetical example to elaborate:

> He was conditioned not only as regards what he should and should not do, but also as regards the reasons for his acts. When introspecting to find the explanation for his attitudes, he would naturally employ the verbalizations of his group – for what are his language and thought if not a socialized product? To discover in oneself the motives accepted by one's group is much the same thing as to use the language of one's group; indeed, is not the given terminology of motives but a subsidiary aspect of the communicative medium in general? (20–21)

A terminology of motivation is to be considered, in other words, not in terms of whether it's correct or incorrect but in terms of what it does culturally as it functions rhetorically. Even automatic writing, as suggested in chapter 1, functions rhetorically; such writing aims to free the writer from what culture put in the writer, yet it depends on a literary subculture, both to disseminate and legitimate it.

But while Burke was ready in *PC* to see motivation as a construct, he wasn't ready to theorize this view all the way down. When he got to the bottom of his text, he couldn't do without his biological essentialism. One can, as we tried to do in our analysis of *PC*, examine this essentialism in terms of its rhetorical appeal to Burke in his polemic with Marxism; in other words, one can view it as a rhetorical construction. But that is not how Burke theorizes it in *PC*. Rather, he does himself what he later faults Freud for doing. Despite its constructionist gestures, *PC* ultimately theorizes the essentialism that informs its historical narrative, with its cyclical shifts back and forth between the will to eloquence and the will to power. In contrast, a rhetoric of the subject theorizes not a subject characterized by a distinctive motivation (biological, Freudian, Marxist, whatever), but the invention of subjects. Theorizing such a rhetoric thus encounters the difficulty, noted earlier, of theorizing the new. Burke offers an example of how to meet this difficulty in the trajectory of his work during the decade from *PC* to *GM*.

In *ATH*, there is a turn from *PC*'s subject of history toward a Freudo-Marxist history of subjects. *ATH* anticipates proportionalizing in the formula that the "so-called 'I' is merely a unique combination of partially conflicting 'corporate we's'" that may get along or be at odds, since the issue of hierarchically interrelating the "we's" is not decided essentialistically in advance but left open to different proportional possibilities in the agon of history. This theoretical turn exhibits itself in the difference between the historical narratives in the two books: in *PC*, a short narrative, covering a long span of time, in which at the foundational level there is much more permanence than change in subjects; in *ATH*, a longer narrative, covering a shorter span, in which change dominates.

But in *ATH*, as we saw, Burke privileges Freudian individualism against other possible subjects in conceptualizing the processes of accepting and rejecting symbols of authority. The construction and reconstruction of subjects in history turns out to presuppose a subject that is the final arbiter of whether to reconstruct or reaffirm the existing construction. In this presupposition, *ATH* contradicts its own group realism. That Burke recognized this theoretical lapse is evidenced by his subsequent polemic with Freud in "Freud — and the Analysis of Poetry" (FAP), published two years after *ATH*. Relegating the Freudian subject of sexuality to essentialism, Burke rewrites it as one proportional possibility among multiple others. In other words, the Freudian subject becomes merely a possible subject — a view compatible with the current tendency, strengthened by Foucault, to historicize psychoanalysis. Freudian sexuality can be a proportional ingredient, sometimes even a dominant one, but it can't be an essentializing ingredient.

Motivational content such as the Freudian is thus subtracted to theorize a structure capable of generating multiple subjects. Burke's strategy is to develop ways to analyze motivation apart from the content of particular theories of motivation, not only the early biological essentialism or the later Freudo-Marxism, but any other as well. The equation of motivation with structure suggests that with each new structure, there can be a new motivation, a new subject. What is (structure) is what it does (motivation). In the act of structural hierarchizing, Burke finds a process of constituting that is irreducible to antecedent circumstances, however large a part they play in the content of the act — a molten process where existing subjects can be melted down and new ones formed.

Structure can, of course, be an escape from history, as we know from the demise of structuralism. The theoretical issue is always whether the process of structuring is dependent on the process of history. Today, for example, in the US, in the cultural struggle pitting a monocultural against a multicultural subject, these competing subjects structurally proportionalize, or hierarchize, in different ways race, ethnicity, gender, class, sexual orientation, and so on. One side seeks to preserve a traditional hierarchy with its exclusions; the other, to re-hierarchize and thereby open the culture to new combinations that privilege inclusion against these exclusions. Such structurings, in their theorization, must be seen to depend on history, since it is history that will resolve the competition between them. In the agon of history in the US today, inclusion is something for which one must struggle. To anticipate the next chapter, one could say that the multicultural subject seeks to put in place a new constitution, and like any constitution, it is an agonistic instrument that seeks, "by verbal or symbolic means, to establish a motivational fixity of some sort, in opposition to something that is thought liable to endanger this fixity" (*GM* 357). In the agon of history, inclusion is possible but only by excluding that which endangers it. Only in a utopia beyond the agon can there be inclusion without exclusion.

If one wished to argue that there is in Burke an escape from history, one could note that while there are historical narratives in *PC* and *ATH*, there is none in "PLF," *GM*, or *RM*. But there is more than one way to embed oneself in history. In *PC* and *ATH*, Burke places the position he advocates in a historical narrative, but one can also situate oneself on the transhistorical level. We question, in fact, not only whether one can historicize without a transhistorical premise, but also, as the critique of Foucault in chapter 1 argues, whether one's historicizing can be any better than one's premise. Theoretical scrutiny of the transhistorical is needed to insure that the hierarchical structuring constitutive of the subject is conceptually embedded in history rather than abstracted from it.

In "PLF," Burke formulates the goal of transhistorical analysis: "A 'logic' of history would be a set of universal statements about history. And these statements would be at such a 'high level of generalization' that they would apply to *all* historical development. In short, the 'laws' of movement cannot themselves move, if they are correctly stated" (100). Burke also relates the transhistorical to the historical with an example paralleling one, cited in chapter 1, that Marx uses for the same purpose, although Marx's focus is production, whereas Burke's is the subject. Marx contrasts the category instrument of production, considered as a transhistorical abstraction, to historical instantiations of this category, ranging from the hand used in manual labor to the capital used to finance construction of a factory. Analogously, Burke contrasts the transhistorical "people must act" to historical acts constituting subjects such as savage, priest, and mechanic (100).

The transhistoricity of dramatism makes Burke vulnerable to the charge that he kicks essentializing out the front door only to let it return through the back if one reads him from the standpoint of a flat opposition between essentializing and historicizing. This opposition, however, as argued in chapter 1, is too blunt; one needs to be more discriminating. The essentializing Burke finds in Freud is a hierarchy that is fixed: a specific motivation is always primary, always that to which others are subordinated. One may also categorize as essentialistic the transhistorical "people must act," but what the act essentializes is hierarchizing, not any particular hierarchy. The act opens up the possibility that "anybody can do anything for any reason" (SO 353), which is a far cry from what historicizers attacked in their struggle with essentializers.

The transhistoricity of Burke's act allows one to rewrite the "ideology has no history" that we saw Althusser posit in distinguishing the transhistorical from the transcendental as "the act constituting the subject has no history." The act is an abstract structure, but embedded in history at the transhistorical level so that the hierarchizing constitutive of the act is always historically contingent and therefore subject to re-hierarchizing. In "PLF," in the section "Ritual Drama as 'Hub'" (103–32), Burke situates his analysis transhistorically as he stresses that it's a matter of theoretical indifference whether his dramatistic model emerged in the historical process early, late, or somewhere along the line. In *PC* and *ATH* Burke motivated his position by making it the goal of historical narrative. But the dramatistic perspective is not, he counters in "PLF," based on such "historical or genetic material. We are proposing it as a *calculus* – a vocabulary, or set of coordinates" (105–06).

Being without history, the transhistorical is all middle, no origin or telos. Fundamentally nonnarratable itself, it swallows up the narratives in which subjects are constituted. Always *in medias res*, the transhistorical is the autonomy at the heart of the agonistic struggle of the rhetoric of the subject, the molten liquidity out of which subjects can be invented as well as melted down and transformed:

Where does the drama get its materials? From the "unending conversation" that is going on at the point in history when we are born. Imagine that you enter a parlor. You come late. When you arrive, others have long preceded you, and they are engaged in a heated discussion, a discussion too heated for them to pause and tell you exactly what it is about. In fact, the discussion had already begun long before any of them got there, so that no one present is qualified to retrace for you all the steps that had gone before. You listen for a while, until you decide that you have caught the tenor of the argument; then you put in your oar. Someone answers; you answer him; another comes to your defense; another aligns himself against you, to either the embarrassment or gratification of your opponent, depending upon the quality of your ally's assistance. However, the discussion is interminable. The hour grows late, you must depart. And you do depart, with the discussion still vigorously in progress.   (110–11)

From the "social idioms" sayable in the conversation, the dramas of subject formation are constituted (112). In their formation, "material interests" are at stake: "These interests do not 'cause' your discussion; its 'cause' is in the genius of man himself as *homo loquax*. But they greatly affect the idiom in which you speak" (111, 112).

The unending middle of this unending conversation is postmodernist insofar as it swallows the "grand narratives" *PC* and *ATH* offer with their histories, transforming them into instances of Burke putting in his "oar." The conversation does the same thing to Lukács's narrative. In other words, the grand narrative attempt to encompass history becomes an act in a historical process that cannot be encompassed narratively. In ATH, Burke anticipates this later history without origin or telos when he steps outside his historical narrative to foreground its rhetoricity.

Burke's conversation is perhaps the single most often quoted passage in all his work, though often the addendum about material interests is overlooked, an omission that courts turning his rhetorical realism into rhetorical idealism.[24] Lentricchia is not among those who overlook this addendum. Conversations frame his reading of Burke, as he, in his first chapter, dismisses Rorty's for being too idealistic, and in his last, affirms Burke's as a paradigmatic "primal scene of rhetoric" (160). Lentricchia also revises Burke to tighten the conversation theoretically (161). Burke describes the origin as beyond recovery for pragmatic reasons: no participant in the conversation now was on hand way back then. But recovery is impossible for the deeper reason that we are always already in the conversation such that any construction of the origin is an instance of putting in an oar in competition with other constructions. The conversation is the fundamental object that dramatism theorizes. Theorizing it is possible, as the next chapter argues, but paradoxically only from a position inside the conversation itself.

Jameson goes against the postmodernist grain in reaffirming the Marxist grand narrative.[25] He assumes that a progressive politics is impossible without such narrative. But the cultural conversation can become its own end in a politics of empowerment that aims, not at the perhaps impossible dream of ending the agon of history, but at leveling the playing field so that in the agon there is a more equitable balance of power. Freedom of speech is a necessary starting-point, but it needs to be supplemented with the freedom that comes with empowerment. In the US, where one Texas billionaire can with loose change buy hours of TV time to tower with his squeaky voice over millions of homeless and impoverished who appear rarely in the cultural conversation and then only as objects talked about, a politics of empowerment has perhaps enough of a progressive agenda to keep it busy for the foreseeable future.

---

24 Burke omits them himself in an earlier version of the conversation, one conceived as a process that is more syllogistic than agonistic: "And when a new thinker is born, to carry on some one historic line of thought, it is as though a man had come into a room, found people there discussing some matter, and after he had listened long enough to get the drift of their conversation, had begun putting in remarks of his own, accepting *their* remarks as the basis of *his* remarks, 'proving' his points on the strength of the points which the other speakers had taken for granted" (*ACR* 102). The explicit conception of history as a process without origin or telos is also absent from this earlier version. 25 *Political Unconscious*, pp. 19–20.

Kenneth Burke

In "PLF" Burke theorizes the rhetorical constitution of the subject in the conversation mainly with two principles, "externalizing the internal" and "internalizing the external." His example of the former is "Joyce's individualistic, absolutist, 'dictatorial' establishment of a language from within"; of the latter, Shaw's heroine in *Pygmalion*, who inscribes within herself "the linguistic and manneristic labels of the class among whom she would, by this accomplishment, symbolically enroll herself" (112). She exemplifies "prayer," the side of a symbolic act that conforms to "a public, or communicative, structure," whereas Joyce exemplifies "dream," the side that is individualistic, self-expressive (5–6). In the interplay between dream and prayer, subjects are constructed in dramas that are either disciplinary agons ending in the reaffirmation of orthodoxy or agons of history in which one orthodoxy is rivaled by another emerging to displace it. Burke's concern, he sums up in "PLF," is with "the various tactics and deployments involved in ritualistic acts of membership, purification, and opposition" (124). In these tactics, Burke argues, imagery ranging from sacrifice to the kill is prominent as either an old orthodoxy is displaced by a new one or deviance is purged in a purified return to orthodoxy.

Burke tells us in *GM* that he began dramatism with only the categories corresponding to dream and prayer, the symbolic (self-expression) and the rhetoric (communication), and that only gradually did the grammar emerge as he found himself taking notes that didn't quite fit into either of these categories, a process leading eventually to the recognition that dramatism "needed a grounding in formal considerations logically prior to both the rhetorical and the psychological" (xviii). Some of these notes appear in "PLF," most notably in the category of "chart" mentioned earlier (p. 123), but they take a back seat to dream and prayer. If one begins to think of this interplay between dream and prayer as itself a proportionalizing of proportionalizing, one can see the emergence of a need for, as Burke puts it, "a grounding in formal considerations" prior to both. The interplay can be hierarchized in either direction, as in the modernist attitude that sometimes subordinated the communicative side in a gesture of contempt for the audience, or conversely, in the postmodernist death of the author that elevates the reader to a position of supremacy. To proportionalize, in contrast, is to refuse either hierarchy as fixed. Each becomes a possibility, depending on an act of proportionalizing. The realization of either becomes a contingent act in history. In the act, in short, there is something prior to either of the categories in the interplay. In the act, as theorized in *GM*, Burke finds his formal grounding.

The act of selecting a "reality," as we saw earlier, is the side of the symbolic act that Burke categorizes as chart, as he contrasts the perfect chart available only to God to the approximative charts available to symbol-users in their positionality. In this category, *GM* is emergent. An appropriate place to conclude this chapter and to turn toward *GM*, then, is the footnote in "PLF" about this act of selection:

> it is in this "unending conversation" that the assertions of any given philosopher are grounded. *Strategically*, he may present his work as departing from some "rock-bottom fact" (he starts, for instance: "I look at this table. I perceive it to have ... " etc.). Actually, the very selection of his "rock-bottom fact" derives its true grounding from the current state of the conversation, and assumes quite a different place in the "hierarchy of facts" when the locus of discussion has shifted. (111)

In the unending conversation, the participants at any time share a situation in one sense and struggle over its definition in another. This agon of definition takes its point of departure from a pre-selected reality. The symbolic acts in the agon are simultaneously responses to a common situation and differing definitions of it, differing re-selections. Such re-selection exemplifies the paradox of rhetorical realism in bringing into being the situation to which it is simultaneously a reaction.

6

‡‡‡

A Grammar of Motives: the rhetorical constitution of the subject

‡‡‡

[W]e found our pre-pre-introduction actually taking shape. And this we found in the selection of our pentad, as a "final" set of terms that seemed to cluster about our thoughts about the Constitution as an "enactment." Burke, *GM*

[I]deology has the function (which defines it) of "constituting" concrete individuals as subjects.   Althusser, "Ideology and Ideological State Apparatuses"

A decision can only come into being in a space that exceeds the calculable program that would destroy all responsibility by transforming it into a programmable effect of determinate causes ... Even if a decision seems to take only a second and not to be preceded by any deliberation, it is structured by this *experience and experiment of the undecidable*.
                    Derrida, "Afterword: Toward an Ethic of Discussion"

Undecidability is always a *determinate* oscillation between possibilities (for example, of meaning, but also of acts).   Ibid.

GM officially inaugurates dramatism. Our chapter subtitle borrows a term from the book's longest chapter, "The Dialectic of Constitutions." In speaking of the constitution of the subject, we modify one of Burke's statements of the task he envisioned for *SM*: "The *Symbolic* should deal with unique individuals, each its own peculiarly constructed act, or form. These unique 'constitutions' being capable of treatment in isolation, the *Symbolic* should consider them primarily in their capacity as singulars" (*RM* 21–22). The "unique individual" is ambiguous insofar as it can refer to the individual either as body or as the subject constructed in the rhetoric of individualism. Our subtitle is intended to be read as the constitution of the body as a subject, one possible constitution being the subject of individualism. Insofar as a constituted individual is not the unique individual that the rhetoric of individualism sees in itself, Burke, in this formulation of *SM*'s project, may be ironically signaling its redundancy.

"The Dialectic of Constitutions," however, has been marginalized in commentary on *GM*. Viewed through this commentary, *GM* would seem to be about its dramatistic pentad – scene, agent, act, agency, purpose[1] – and not much else. Hence, before proceeding, it's necessary to reorient readers whose expectations for this chapter may be shaped by this commentary.

Critical theory in recent decades has been widely perceived and has often provocatively presented itself as anti-humanistic. *GM* was perceived similarly when it appeared in the context of the New Criticism, then still rising to the ascendency it was destined to enjoy in the 1950s. One reviewer concluded with an acerbic dismissal: "[*GM*] reduces intellectual history to matters of transformation, placement and position – in short, to the very terms of motion that the five key dramatist terms were designed to prevent" (Rosenfeld 317). This dismissal appeared in a strategically important place, the *Kenyon Review*: founded in 1939 by Ransom – whose *The New Criticism*, as noted in the last chapter, gave the movement its name – it presented itself as "a permanent manifesto of the New Criticism."[2] Ransom conceded in his own review of *GM* that in drawing on drama for his pentad, Burke displayed a commendable "humanistic bias," but Ransom wanted still more: "In general, the pentad is not so dramatic in practice as its derivation promised. More often than not, the situation examined is not felt as drama" (160, 162). Later, René Wellek, whose *Theory of Literature* (coauthored with Austin Warren) was a basic text of the New Criticism, joined the chorus, depicting Burke as writing good literary criticism in the 1920s but going steadily downhill afterwards: "Burke's charts, hierarchies, pentads, bureaucracies have nothing to do with literature."[3] In the field of literary and cultural studies, *GM* has yet to recover fully from this initial marginalization. A major text by a major figure, it has been well known in the field for fifty years, but it has never become a site of sustained critical debate. In the secondary literature that has developed, moreover, "The Dialectic

---

1 In an addendum to later editions of *GM*, Burke proposes adding the term "attitude," making the pentad a hexad (443–44).

2 John Fekete, *The Critical Twilight: Explorations in the Ideology of Anglo-American Literary Theory from Eliot to McLuhan* (London: Routledge & Kegan Paul, 1977), p. 87.

3 "Philosophy and Postwar American Criticism," *Concepts of Criticism* (New Haven: Yale University Press, 1963), p. 325; see also "The Main Trends of Twentieth-Century Criticism," p. 353. Burke responded to Wellek in the form of a letter to the editor of *The Yale Review*, where "Main Trends" appeared, but nothing came of it because Wellek wanted to confine their debate to private correspondence (*LSA* 494). Eventually, Wellek replied publicly in "Kenneth Burke and Literary Criticism" (*Sewanee Review* 79 [1971]: 171–88), to which Burke responded in AIWS.

of Constitutions" has been further marginalized. This literature is most extensive in the field of speech communication, where analysis based on *GM* is pentadic rather than constitutional (see Brock, "Dramatistic").

This inattention to "The Dialectic of Constitutions" prompted complaints from Burke himself. William H. Rueckert, for example, reports that Burke complained to him about his failure "to discuss [its] significance" (*Drama* x).[4] As if to spotlight its significance, Burke reminds us that his theorizing of the constitutional act is his "generative model for the study of language as symbolic action" (QAP 334). He also recalls his surprise when reviewers "raised objections that would have been irrelevant had this portion of the book been systematically considered" (*DD* 24; see also RPP 112).

The marginalization of this chapter is especially surprising when one considers how Burke goes out of his way in *GM* itself to call attention to its seminal role in the book's genesis. The chapter began with a different title, "The Constitutional Wish," conceived simply as an introduction to rhetoric and symbolic, at the time still his main categories – as noted in the last chapter, the grammar was posterior to these two categories, emerging only as Burke recognized that they needed a "grounding" (xviii). "The Constitutional Wish," however, turned out to need its own introduction, a pre-introduction, which in turn needed a pre-pre-introduction, and so on. He analogizes this process to being cornered by a relentless interrogator:

Q: And why did you begin with this?
A: For such-and-such reason, that logically preceded it.
Q: And why was this reason logically prior?
A: For such-and-such other reason, logically prior to that – etc.   (338)

This regressive search for a "grounding" ended with the pentad (340).

In a letter, Burke indicates that in his first draft, the pentad actually appeared not on page 1 but near the end: "The five terms with which the work now begins were settled upon toward the end of the first

4 Rueckert doesn't correct this failure in his second edition, leaving his 1963 book unchanged to indicate how Burke looked at that time and adding new material only on what Burke published subsequently. Henderson, Lentricchia, Heath, and Southwell continue the neglect in their books on Burke. Heath considers "The Dialectic of Constitutions" briefly (182–83), but he doesn't consider it in the pages he devotes to *GM* (184–92), so this chapter's significance in the book as a whole goes unrecognized. Roig's consideration of the chapter, although brief (97–98, 132–38), stands out enough for Burke to cite it as an exception to the general neglect (RPP 112). Stuart considers the Constitution, but she reads it as a text rather than as a theoretical model for symbolic action, so that she has nothing to say about its place in *GM*'s structure.

version, and the book was turned around accordingly" (*SCBC* 292; see also QAP 333). The first draft and the last are the same text written in opposite directions. Burke notes, in indicating how he came upon the pentad as a starting-point, that from the beginning the pentadic terms "seemed to cluster about our thoughts about the Constitution as an 'enactment'" (340). Constitutional enactment and the pentad, in other words, seem on some deep level to imply one another, such that one can start with either and go to the other, as Burke did in writing the book in two directions.

Reading it in two directions would seem to be equally possible. Elsewhere, we have traced the logic connecting the pentadic beginning to the constitutional ending (see "Dialectic of Constitutions"). Here, we propose to start at the end, with the Constitution, as Burke himself did, and not to turn to the pentad until much later, although there will be occasions to introduce it intermittently along the way.

Why concern oneself with constitutional enactment? Our first chapter answered this question in an introductory way by presenting the significance for a rhetoric of the subject of the constitutional game of changing the game's rules while playing the game. The present chapter addresses the problem of theorizing such a game. At its heart is the act. As noted in the last chapter, Burke and Austin are alike in their interest in the act. The act, however, also marks their difference: Burke's act is constitutive; Austin's, conformative.

Readers of Austin are familiar with his use of examples such as betting, promising, marrying, and so on – all having in their familiarity a certain solidity. For each such act to occur, Austin observes, "There must exist an accepted conventional procedure having a certain conventional effect, that procedure to include the uttering of certain words by certain persons in certain circumstances."[5] Viewed through Austin's eyes, everyday acts are performances of cultural scripts. Austin's term "performative" comes naturally to this conception of speech act. To act is to perform, and to perform is to conform to a script, though felicitous performance proves difficult: "infelicity is an ill to which *all* acts are heir which have the general character of ritual or ceremonial, all *conventional* acts."[6]

Barbara Johnson notes the irony in Austin's use of "the word that most commonly *names* theatricality: the word *perform*" when one

5 *How to Do Things with Words*, ed. J. O. Urmson (New York: Oxford University Press, 1965), p. 14.
6 Ibid., pp. 18–19.

considers his assertion that a performative is "hollow or void if said by an actor on the stage ... Language in such circumstances is ... used not seriously, but in ways *parasitic* upon its normal use."[7] A deeper irony may be that sometimes felicity is achieved even more successfully in the controlled conditions of theatrical production than in "real life." Perhaps in a moment of supreme performance an actor and actress marrying on stage may even conform to the "thoughts or feelings" — among Austin's conditions for performatives[8] — in the cultural script of marriage more closely than did newlyweds sitting in the audience. In any case, Austin's use of "act" and "performative" together reinforces his conception of the act as conformative. Contrastingly, conceiving the act as constitutive, Burke consistently uses the term "act" rather than "performance."

In reading Austin, we begin *in medias res* with conventional scripts all around us that seem, despite their conventionality, as firmly in place as the trees outside our window. These conventions seem so obviously collective that it is difficult to say much more than "the community put them there" and move on. In an authoritative study of Austin, Sandy Petrey proposes that performatives are "always representative of the collective identity they perform."[9] The collectivity of the conventions, in other words, argues for a collective cause. In one of Petrey's formulations, effect is even depicted grammatically as cause: "Because collective conventions change, societies can both do things with whatever words they choose and make words do what they've never done before."[10] Such societies are equivalent to Fish's interpretive communities.

Marriage is prominent among Austin's examples. Appearing early in Austin's text, it receives more attention than most. Austin's followers have done likewise. What conventional script is more familiar and more obviously collective in its formation? But just how collective is marriage? As I write in the US in the early 1990s, I know of no state where gays and lesbians can legally marry. Maybe there is an exception, but if so it's the exception that proves the rule. Even within the framework of heterosexuality, marriage can be a site of struggle. Consider Erica Harth's penetrating account of the British Marriage Act of 1753. This law is of interest from a speech act standpoint because it

---

7 *The Critical Difference: Essays in the Contemporary Rhetoric of Reading* (Baltimore: Johns Hopkins University Press, 1980), p. 65; *How to Do*, p. 22.   8 *How to Do*, p. 15.

9 *Speech Acts and Literary Theory* (New York: Routledge, 1990), p. 79.

10 *Speech Acts*, pp. 46–47.

invents a conventional script to define what counts as marriage. The law was passed democratically (125 for, 56 against), so it is in a sense a collective act. But the collective effect should not be allowed to conceal the agonistic cause. The law required marriages to be licensed and to occur only after publication of banns. It prohibited other forms of marriage previously accepted, which included marriage by private mutual consent (recognized under ecclesiastical law). Making marriage public enhanced patriarchal control. The opposition favored multiple forms of acceptable marriage because they weakened that control. Their existence, in effect, gave love sufficient freedom to allow wealth to circulate more freely.[11]

Marriage is a social ritual of inclusion and exclusion. It is properly viewed from the perspective of the competing regimes of orthodoxy in the expanse of history. Gays and lesbians may effectively contest current orthodoxy, making current prohibition of same-sex marriage recede into historical memory to take its place alongside the earlier prohibition against miscegenation. They are trying to change the rules of the game in the play of the game. The jury, of course, is still out. New movements are forming to reinforce the privileging of heterosexuality and they marshall considerable forces.

Behind the apparent collectivity of the conventional script of marriage there is agonistic struggle. Austin's examples discourage one from looking behind the collective façade of their conventionality because they are typically drawn from areas where normally little or nothing is at stake. Our scrutiny of marriage forces Austin's text beyond itself, shifting attention from conformity to a conventional script to the constitution of such a script. Derrida effects a similar shift in his reading of the US Declaration of Independence – a reading to receive close attention later in the present chapter. His critique of Austin notwithstanding, Derrida describes himself as "both interested in and indebted to his [Austin's] problematic."[12] The performative interests Derrida because it offers an alternative to the classical representational model of language: "It does not describe something that exists outside of language and prior to it. It produces or transforms a situation, it effects" (*Limited* 13). Austin's performative may be said to "produce or

11 Erica Harth, "The Virtue of Love: Lord Hardwicke's Marriage Act," *Cultural Critique* 9 (1988): 123–54.
12 *Limited Inc*, ed. Gerald Graff (Evanston: Northwestern University Press, 1988), p. 38. Graff's edition includes a new text, "Afterword: Toward an Ethic of Discussion," from which we draw epigraphs for this chapter. Hereafter, page references are included in the text; where necessary, the abbreviated title *Limited* is added.

transform" but in a limited way. His analysis of marriage explains only how two people, by conforming to a conventional script, produce another marriage. To realize the potentiality of the dramatistic alternative to the classical view of representation, one must focus not on the conformative but the constitutive act. Transformation, in the most complete sense, is not conforming to an established script but constituting a new one. Austin describes performatives in the theatre as "hollow or void," but it is his own performatives that sound hollow in the din of history. The act as conformative is the road to the dead-end of rhetorical idealism.

The transformative power of the constitutive act is among the first of its attributes that Burke discusses in "The Dialectic of Constitutions." He begins, not with the US Constitution itself, but with two books, one by Henry Bamford Parkes and the other by Herbert Read, confiding that while puzzling over them he began identifying "typical properties of constitutions" (344). His commentary on these books, designed "to abstract their tactics as 'Constitutions'" (360), gives us Burke's own version of the formation of his concern with constitutional enactment. In Parkes's book, *Marxism: An Autopsy*, Burke finds an illustration of transformation. Writing in 1939, Parkes proposes — by giving government more power to secure jobs for workers and more control of banking — to protect capitalism against the threat of Marxism. Burke construes this proposal as "a new constitution for *laissez-faire*," arguing that government intervention at the two most consequential sites in the capitalist free market — the labor and money markets — is a transformation of capitalism.

This analysis of Parkes leads, in addition, to Burke's conclusion, noted in chapter 1, that constitutions are "agonistic instruments" (357). Burke elaborates, "They [constitutions] involve an enemy, implicitly or explicitly ... In all such projects, the attempt is made, by verbal or symbolic means, to establish a motivational fixity of some sort, in opposition to something that is thought liable to endanger this fixity" (357). The framework for the transformation that Parkes illustrates, in other words, is not the Fishian interpretive community but the Burkean conversation. Marxism is the antagonist that Parkes selects as he puts in his "oar" to advocate a new capitalism. Orthodoxy is pitted against orthodoxy in an agon of history.

Even in a utopian world beyond this agon, a constitution would still be necessary. At the end of chapter 1, we suggested that the constitutional game of changing the rules of the game in the play of the game could be shelved only in a utopia with rules by which everyone could function materially, with no rule benefiting anyone at the expense of anyone else. According to Habermas, we have an *"emancipatory* cognitive interest" in knowledge about "ideologically frozen relations of dependence that can in principle be transformed,"[13] but in such a utopia we would no longer need such knowledge because all such relations would have been transformed. But even in this utopia, a constitution would still be needed "to establish a motivational fixity" to protect against backsliding. Such a constitution would be a final transformation, a constitutional enactment to end enactments.

Burke's commentary on Read's book, to turn to it, focuses on a tension between two levels. On one, the book is a vision containing ideals potentially at odds with one another in varying ways; on the other, the book encounters the reality that to put this vision into practice, some ideals have to be given priority over others. This tension between vision and practice leads Burke to contrast a constitution at peace to one at odds with itself: "Yet when, in the realm of the practical, a given case comes before the courts, you promptly find that this *merger* or *balance* or *equilibrium* among the Constitutional clauses becomes transformed into a *conflict* among the clauses – and to satisfy the promise contained in one clause, you must forego the promise contained in another" (349). Analogously, in the example of the multiple motivational discourses addressing Therborn's worker-qua-body, one could say that the strike call, like bringing a case before the court, ends whatever merger or equilibrium there previously was among these discourses, since responding to the call necessitates that some give way to others. In this fashion, with the example of Read, Burke introduces the constitutional principle of hierarchizing.

In theorizing the constitutive act Burke draws his terminology from his representative anecdote, the US Constitution, as is evident in his statement in constitutional terms of the tension he finds in Read. To underline the voluntaristic side of the act, Burke sometimes equates the Constitution's clauses to "wishes," adding that the Constitution doesn't textually dictate in advance which wishes should give way to which in every conflict among them. In one sense, he suggests, it's difficult to pass a law that is unconstitutional: "The law that frustrates one wish in the Constitution will, by the same token,

---

13 *Knowledge and Human Interests*, trans. Jeremy J. Shapiro (Boston: Beacon Press, 1971), pp. 308, 310.

gratify another" (378). Burke cites a 1941 *New York Times* report of a proposal to pass a law suspending the 1942 Congressional elections to facilitate rearmament by eliminating the distractions of campaign divisiveness (381). Its supporters speculated that a constitutional basis for this law could be found in either executive war powers or legislative authority to alter the times of elections, or possibly in both. Conceivably, in other words, even something as seemingly unshakeable as the wish in Article I, Section 2 that House members be "chosen every second year" could be set aside to satisfy other wishes.

Such voluntaristic wishes appear in a section on the "principles of the conflict among principles" as one kind of principle to be distinguished from another kind, the necessitarian: "Thus," Burke observes, "in the *volitional* sense, any clause ... would be a Constitutional 'principle.' But in the *necessitarian* sense, any statement would be a 'principle' if it signalized a logical or practical conflict between clauses" (374–75). This section concludes:

> In sum: There are principles in the sense of wishes, and there are principles in the sense of interrelationships among the wishes. Principles as wishes are voluntary or arbitrary, inasmuch as men can meet in conference and decide how many and what kind of wishes they shall subscribe to. But once you have agreed upon a list of wishes, the interrelationships among those wishes are necessary or inevitable. A public right, for instance, "necessarily" implies a private obligation or a private jeopardy; a private right "inevitably" implies a public obligation or a public jeopardy. Confronting such a situation, you could, "of your own free will," draw up a Constitution that merely proclaimed a set of public rights and a set of private rights (or a set of public and private obligations); but in doing so, you would have made it "mandatory" that, in all specific cases, a conflict must arise out of these implications.   (375–76)

This necessitarian principle forces the act: "where the attempt to carry out the wishes of a Constitution in specific legal cases involves a conflict between Constitutional wishes, what is really mandatory upon the Court is a *new act*" (376).

The cultural debate over abortion can illustrate. On the voluntaristic side, there are principles asserting the fetus's right to life and the woman's right to choose whether to give birth. These are both constructs introduced into the cultural conversation. Whatever conflicts arise between them is in part an effect of discursive construction. There would be no such conflict in a culture subscribing to neither or to one alone. But conflict between them is not only a function of their construction. By virtue of constructing them, we encounter material conditions, beyond our constructive power to alter, that necessitate one wish having to give way to the other on occasion. We cannot construct a world in which the two principles can always be honored. The act hierarchizing the principles is necessarily partial, its constructive power falling short of God's. "A Constitution," *GM* stresses, "is but a partial act; the only truly total act would be the act of a Supreme Founding Father who founded the Universal Substance, the Constitution-beneath-the-Constitution, the scene in which the Constitution of 1789 was an enactment" (374).

We can conclude this section with one additional example, involving the tension between private and public that Burke cites in the quotation above. This tension is present in a current area of constitutional controversy centering on the "takings" clause in the 5th amendment prohibiting governmental seizure of property for public use without just compensation. Conservatives are forcing the issue by seeking to broaden the definition of a taking to include any legislation affecting property values. In Lucas v. South Carolina Coastal Council, a case the court decided in its 1991–92 term, Lucas had paid $975,000 for oceanfront lots, only to see their value plummet to virtually zero when the Coastal Council, because of the hurricane threat, prohibited new development in the area. The court sided with the conservatives in ruling 6–3 that a taking had indeed occurred even though the government didn't take Lucas's property, but added that a number of additional factors had to be considered at the state court level before determining whether Lucas was entitled to compensation.[14] Conservatives, in other words, are seeking to effect a constitutional act that restructures the hierarchical balancing of private property rights and the public interest such that legislative action in the public interest could come with a prohibitively high price-tag.

Such a constitutive act exemplifies the Althusserian *"lived* relation" to the world – "conservative, conformist, reformist or revolutionary" – that is the domain, as we saw in chapter 1, of ideology as rhetoric.

The constitutive act of changing the rules of the game in the play of the game theorizes the invention and reinvention of orthodoxies and their subjects. With the constitutive act, Burke completes his theoretical journey from a subject of history to a history of subjects.

Subjects are invented in constitutive acts. The act adds something

14 *New York Times*, 30 June 1992.

irreducible to its antecedents. However much an act may be a function of its circumstances, there is some modicum in the act that makes it magical, a "new thing" (65): "There must, in brief, be some respect in which the act is a *causa sui*, a motive of itself" (66). In proportionalizing, the act incorporates discourses antecedent to it as its conjunctural context, but the form of the incorporation is open, not determined essentialistically in advance. The act can contingently hierarchize antecedent subject positions this way or that, or it can invent a new position that rearranges interrelations among the old. The contingent response to the conjunctural is equivalent to the new; they are two ways of saying the same thing. Speaking pentadically, the constitution is an "agent" when considered as a batch of voluntaristic "wishes" potentially at odds with one another in varying ways, but it is an "act" in the contingent hierarchization of these voluntaristic principles that adds something new to the world. The new is not in the imagination in an agent but in an act in the world. Paradoxically, it is the necessitarian principle, rooted in the real, that motivates the invention of the new act.

Cultures, of course, construct acts for us prior to our arrival in history *in medias res,* and they labor mightily to suit us to perform them, but no act is fixed forever. Constituted in history, acts can always be agonistically melted down and reconstituted — "constitutions are agonistic instruments." Gayatri Chakravorty Spivak's powerful essay, "Can the Subaltern Speak?"[15] poses a question that would, to return to an earlier example, be pertinent in a patriarchal culture in which there was no discourse for a woman's right to choose whether to give birth. A subaltern who cannot speak today, however, may be able to speak tomorrow. A new act can re-hierarchize old cultural priorities to establish new ones. An act, in its novelty, is irreducible to its antecedent circumstances however deeply it is shaped by them. In this irreducibility resides the act's constitutional capacity to go beyond its antecedent situation in transforming it.

To accentuate his location of the new in the act rather than the agent, Burke takes care to stress the act's independence of the agent, exhibiting in doing so his recognition of a tendency in his audience to assume that any reference to action presupposes an autonomous agent as its authentic origin. Despite Burke's care, however, one can see this assumption control even a sympathetic reading such as Lentricchia's: "Burke has argued forcefully that behind all theories of the act, no

15 In *Marxism and the Interpretation of Culture,* eds. Cary Nelson and Lawrence Grossberg (Urbana: University of Illinois Press, 1988), pp. 271–313.

matter how secularized, there lies the model of God's creative act: God is ur-model of action, pure origination, pure consciousness, and pure reason — the lucid subject of all subjects" (114).[16] Burke, however, explicitly cautions against such a reading:

> The modicum of novelty in the act would seem to be the element that justified Coleridge's view of poetry as a "dim analogue of Creation." However, that formula was obscured by the idealist stress upon *agent*, as locus of the "shaping spirit of Imagination" . . . [T]o glimpse more clearly the independent claims of the term, act, we might better go back to Spinoza who . . . defined the universal Substance as the "cause of itself." (68).

Contrary to Lentricchia, in modeling the act on God's creative act, Burke accentuates its independence of the agent:

> If we think of "the Creator" as an "agent," we might contend that the motives of the act are here situated outside the locus of the term *act* and within the locus of the term *agent*. Yet the statement [William James's] that God's creative act "has its motive within the creative circumference" comes quite close to satisfying our motive assignable under the heading of *act* itself. And the requirement is still more fully met if we recall the scholastic definition of God as "pure act." (66)

For Burke, in sum, it's the something out of nothing — the something in the act irreducible to its antecedents — that is decisive, not any attributes in an agent.

Lentricchia's reading exhibits how the rhetoric of individualism, having penetrated our culture so deeply, coaches us to look past the act to the agent for a privileged point of origination. We value *Robinson Crusoe* because while in it the "individual" proves dominant, its dominance doesn't "go without saying" from the beginning but has to establish itself through rhetorical struggle with a rhetoric that would subordinate the entrepreneur to the obedient son. The text allows one to see individualism taking form as a re-hierarchizing, a constitutive act that proved itself in the agon of history. To remind oneself that individualism need not be the dominant subject position, it's useful to consider Clifford Geertz's "Person, Time, and Conduct in Bali." Geertz's study is especially valuable because Balinese culture recognizes the unique individual in a personal-naming system that distinguishes individuals even more rigorously than our own. Duplication of personal names within a community is avoided, and the names are not even associated with families or any other group. They are purely

---

16 For a more detailed assessment of Lentricchia's reading, see Wess, "Lentricchia's."

individual. But the personal name is not one's only name, and of all the names it is at the bottom of the hierarchy. The personal name carries little rhetorical weight. Personal names are "arbitrarily coined nonsense syllables" that disappear at one's death. Viewed condescendingly as "child" or "little" names, they are allowed to "play very little public role." The personal dimension of one's cultural definition "is highly muted," Geertz sums up, "And with it are muted the more idiosyncratic, merely biographical, and, consequently, transient aspects of his existence as a human being (what, in our more egoistic framework, we call his 'personality') in favor of some rather more typical, highly conventionalized, and, consequently, enduring ones."[17]

The personal name in Balinese culture is, in effect, an inversion of the example of automatic writing subjected to Foucauldian analysis in chapter 1. In automatic writing, the individual carries so much rhetorical weight that it is sought even though it is buried far below the discourse by which one normally lives and is accessible only through the extraordinary labor of automatic writing. Further, the enigmatic images that this labor produces are preserved as carefully in the dignified form of poetry as the nonsense syllables of the Balinese personal name are forgotten forever. At the top of one hierarchization, the unique individual is at the bottom of the other. The unique body, in its life and death, exists in all cultures, and one may expect it always to be signified somehow, but the signification's rhetorical weighting can vary from culture to culture. Placing the individual prior to culture, as in romantic authenticity, is a strategy of rhetorical weighting devised within an agon of history.

After equating the act to the new, Burke moves on, in the same chapter, to his notion of circumference, indicating as he turns to it that he begins "almost anew" (77). Almost but not quite – the act can't be left behind. Burke borrows the term "circumference" from the James statement that God's act "has its motive within the creative circumference." Burke underlines the importance of circumference in responding to critical commentary on *GM*, emphasizing that it needs to be used along with any application of the pentad (QAP 333, 334).

In a section entitled "Strategic Choice of Circumference for 'Freedom,'" Burke argues that Parkes posits the free market as a circumference for freedom so that to be free is to be able to buy and sell (354). Parkes,

---

17 *The Interpretation of Cultures* (New York: Basic Books, 1973), pp. 369–70.

in his essay-review of *ATH*, faults Burke for failing to recognize that
one needs an objective standard for rational choice (114–15, 118–19).
Burke counters that Parkes's objective standard – his circumference – is
a strategic selection: an act in his agon with Marxism (354, 359). This
critique amounts to a rhetorical demystification. Such demystification
works by situating a text in the agon of the Burkean conversation, a
context that exposes, as Paolo Valesio puts it, "the inevitable
stylization ... that is the ontological basis of rhetoric."[18] Valesio
illustrates this stylization with an example he finds in "PLF," where
Burke proposes: "suppose that you wanted to weaken a stateman's
reputation in the most 'scientific' manner. A very good method
would be ... to send forth investigators armed with questions that
constantly harped upon the matter of the man's integrity ... The man's
integrity, which might otherwise have been taken for granted,
becomes a 'problem'" (67). Simply making integrity an issue rhetorically
"stylizes" the conversation, and ironically the more objective the
discussion of the issue, the more rhetorically effective the stylization.
Parkes's choice of circumference is similarly a "stylization" in privileging
free-market terminology. Any hegemonic terminology functions as a
constitution insofar as it authorizes evaluating acts in its terms but not
others (*GM* 368).

One always has, Burke insists, "*a great variety of circumferences* to
select [from] as characterization of a given agent's scene" (84): "one
must see things 'in terms of ...' [Burke's ellipsis]. And implicit in the
terms chosen, there are 'circumferences' of varying scope" (77). In
Joyce's *A Portrait of the Artist as a Young Man*, Stephen Dedalus places
himself in scenes of increasingly wide circumference when he writes
under his name: "Class of Elements," "Clongowes Wood College,"
"Sallins," "County Kildare," "Ireland," "Europe," "The World," "The
Universe." Stephen is constituted differently within these different
circumferences. One can move from one of these to another, but no
two can be circumferences at the same time: to see Stephen as Irish is
one thing; to see him as an Irish boy in Europe another. Choice of
circumference is necessary. Further, whichever one is chosen, it is – like
Austin's "Lord Raglan won the battle of Alma" – neither literal nor
metaphoric, but an act of selection.

Circumference thus makes the constructionist point that representa-

---

18 *Novantiqua: Rhetorics as a Contemporary Theory* (Bloomington: Indiana University Press,
1980), p. 31.

tions of reality are never simply reproductions of reality without any intervention on our part. Burke makes this point most directly against his behaviorist opponent:

[W]hen the behaviorist experiments with animals to discover, under "controlled laboratory conditions," the springs of conduct that operate also in human beings, we consider his experiment fully as important as he does, though for a totally different reason. For we take it to indicate, with the utmost clarity possible, the terministic relationship between the circumscription and the circumscribed. For no matter how much a matter of purely empirical observation it may seem to be, it actually is a very distinct choice of circumference for the placement of human motives. By the very nature of the case it chooses to consider human motives in terms of an animal circumference, an acutely terministic matter, not a matter of "empirical observation." (78)

Within a circumference, one can make true and false statements within the terms that the circumference sets, but the selection of the circumference itself is an act. Act first, knowledge second.

Burke thus arrives through rhetoric at a point analogous to Althusser's that "it is impossible to prove the ultimate principles of materialism just as it is impossible to prove...the principles of idealism."[19] Philosophy for Althusser is the site of the struggle between materialism and idealism: it is class struggle on the level of theory. Analogously, for Burke, the issue of circumference is resolved through the rhetorical struggle of the cultural conversation, not through an epistemological judgment of truth and falsity. Terminologies do not "correspond" but "reduce": "A cosmology, for instance, is a reduction of the world to the dimensions of words; it is the world *in terms of* words...[A]ny terminology of motives reduces the vast complexity of life by reduction to principles, laws, sequences, classifications, correlations, in brief, abstractions or generalizations of one sort or another" (96). One must choose one's reduction, and in doing so, one constructs one's reality. There is no truth of motives.

But there is "a grammar of motives." A selection of a circumference "is in itself an act, an 'act of faith,' with the definition or interpretation of the act taking shape accordingly" (84). Ungrammaticality arises when a circumference dissolves the act in interpreting it. Behaviorism's terminology of stimulus and response, for example, reduces action to motion (78–79). Behaviorism stands for Burke as the paradigmatic instance of ungrammaticality because its reliance on animal experiments

---

19 *Lenin and Philosophy and Other Essays*, trans. Ben Brewster (New York: Monthly Review Press, 1971), p. 56.

methodologically excludes language. For this reason, as we saw in the last chapter, Burke rules that behaviorism is unrepresentative by the standard of his representative anecdote. It is unrepresentative not in the correspondence sense of representation, but in Burke's grammatical sense: because it is itself an act, a terminology must, to be grammatical, "represent" its own possibility.

Circumference appears regularly in Burke's pentadic rewritings of terminologies. While it is perhaps easiest to think of circumference from the standpoint of scene, as in the range of scenes in which Stephen Dedalus places himself, circumference is not limited to scene. In the chapter on idealist terminologies, for example, Burke marks the shift from Berkeley's agent to Hume's as a "narrowing of circumference" (181). Excessive narrowing risks ungrammaticality, materialisms typically running the greatest risk. In the case of Hobbes, for example, the appearance of action in his terminology marks an ungrammatical break in its overall "symmetry" (135). In the Epicurean universe, atoms fall but some "swerve," a detail that Burke highlights as a move that opens up space for action and that thereby keeps this discourse grammatical, albeit just barely (159). Instruments are mechanistic but they are also products of human design so that agency retains room for action within its "circumference of motives" (283). As Booth observes in his study of pluralism, Burke's pentad is pluralistic only to a point because it rules out some terminologies on the grounds of ungrammaticality ("Burke's Comedy" 121–22).

For Burke, behaviorism stands for science in general insofar as science tries to override the contingency in the act:

> If I conceive of my act as enacted in a scene that includes a whole pantheon of gods, it's one kind of act ... If I conceive of it in a scene reduced to terms of nature, it's another kind. And so on. Now, there is nothing in science that can justify the use of one particular circumference ... At that point [choice of circumference], science is out. (D67 357)

Science acts as it limits its circumference to motion. As a result of this limitation, however, it can't account for its own existence, but must turn this job over to the philosophy, or some equivalent, that Althusser conceives as class struggle on the level of theory. In science, Burke suggests, "Men can so arrange it that nature gives clear, though impartial and impersonal, answers to their questions ... Stated broadly the dialectical (agonistic) approach to knowledge is through the *act* of assertion, whereby one 'suffers' the kind of knowledge that is the reciprocal of his act" (*GM* 38). Science contrives experiments that demonstrate scientific laws by identifying circumstances in which the realm of motion can be counted on always to say the same thing. But such laws do not explain the enterprise of science itself, which is an act in history that occurs within a circumference larger than that of motion. To explain this act, science would have to posit in the material world a telos driving it to explain itself to itself, at which point it would no longer be science.

In sum, Burke rhetoricizes grammar by anchoring it in the act. Such an anchor is at once fixed and mobile, since acts are all the same and all different. Terminologies of motives can be alike in being grammatical and unlike in their circumferential scope, so that what is sayable in one historical context may be unutterable in another.

As we saw at the end of the last chapter, in theorizing the conversation that it introduces, "PLF" relies mainly on the traditional rhetorical paradigm of speaker and audience, conceiving these as the complementary processes of "externalizing the internal" and "internalizing the external." Tensions between the two are resolved through the agon of the conversation, the ultimate arbiter of what is rhetorically sayable. "Chart," the other category in "PLF," remains comparatively underdeveloped, not coming into its own until *GM*, where Burke focuses mainly on philosophical "charts," using in his analyses, in addition to circumference, the pentadic categories, which yield five species of substance:

> scene: materialism
> agent: idealism
> act: realism
> agency: pragmatism
> purpose: mysticism　　　　　　　　　　　(128)

This rhetoric of substance supplements the rhetoric of circumference: the latter rhetoricizes the grammar of motivational discourse; the former rhetoricizes the semantics of such discourse. Like Austin's "Lord Raglan won the battle of Alma," substance is selected rather than given.

Dramatism both deploys the notion of substance and dramatistically demystifies it by rhetoricizing it, both from within and without. From without, substance is a constitution:

Men's conception of motive, we have said, is integrally related to their conception of substance. Hence, to deal with problems of motive is to deal with problems of substance. And a thing's substance is that whereof it is constituted. Hence, a concern with substance is a concern with the problems of constitutionality... A constitution is a *substance* – and as such it is a set of *motives*. (337–38, 342)

In hierarchizing competing wishes or motivational discourses, an act constitutes a conception of substance, implicitly or explicitly, from which its hierarchizing derives. "Substance" and "circumference" are Burke's terms for "retotalization," the term we borrowed from Laclau and Mouffe in chapter 1, where Lukács's proletarian subject of history exemplified the totalization of the transcendental; Therborn's subject, the retotalization of the transhistorical. As a constitution, substance is constructed in the historical process. It is constructed against history in the sense that, as a fixed structure of motivation, it attempts to end Burke's conversation. It is, to quote again from Rorty's commentary on the "dream of philosophy," a terminology that sees itself as "intrinsically and self-evidently final." But the conversation swallows such attempts to establish motivational fixity, transforming them into assertions, instances of putting in an "oar" – the same fate of historical "grand narratives" such as Burke's in *PC* and *ATH*. Dramatistic demystification of philosophy is designed to uncover "the nature of philosophy as an assertion" (130): "Every philosophy is in some respect or other a *step away from* drama. But to understand its structure, we must remember always that it is, by the same token, a step away from *drama*" (230). Burke, as one commentator concisely puts it, is "less interested in 'substance' than in 'substantiating'" (Durham 358). If the Supreme Court were to be thoroughly explicit about its motivation, Burke suggests, "it would have to formulate a theology, or a metaphysics, or a physics, or at least a philosophy of history as the ground of its decisions" (377).[20]

From within, the competing wishes a conception of substance retotalizes are related rhetorically, as suggested by the constitutional anecdote itself, since the wishes the court hierarchizes appear before it in the rhetorical combat of lawyer against lawyer. A 6–3 ruling is a proportionalizing, a rhetorical weighting, of the arguments in behalf of the competing wishes in the case. Consider, for example, the wish for

20 Given Burke's consistent opposition of action to motion, the presence of "physics" in this sentence seems incongruous. He may be thinking of something like an Aristotelian physics with its unmoved mover, which is considered in *GM*'s chapter "Act."

fetal right to life. Its advocates often make exceptions in cases of rape or incest, even though from the standpoint of the fetus, rape or incest is a matter of indifference. For these advocates, in other words, subordinating the woman's right to choose is rhetorically sayable, but only up to a point. Even for them, there are situations in which the woman's right has too much rhetorical weight to be brushed aside.

Substance evolves from and is absorbed by the agonistic struggle among discourses in the conversation, a struggle that Burke equates not only to drama but also to dialectic. "Dialectic in General," *GM*'s last chapter, begins by defining dialectics in the most general sense as "the employment of the possibilities of linguistic transformation" (402). For Burke, in other words, dialectic is not a master historical narrative in the manner of Hegel and some versions of Marx. *GM* exhibits the postmodern loss of confidence in "grand narrative." Burke's dialectic in general examines the operations involved in dialectical construction, opposition, and transformation in the agon of the conversation. Of these operations merger and division are the most fundamental (418–19), particularly because they structure transformations (e.g., 405–06, 420–21). These operations offer the most comprehensive view available to us.

The horizon of Burke's dialectic, in other words, is the horizon of the conversation. There is no origin or telos, only a middle. In hierarchizing, the act requires a totalizing substance, but there is no totalization of totalizations. There are only new acts. Verbalizing the necessitarian principle, substance transforms the necessity of hierarchy into motivation for hierarchizing this way rather than that — different substances, different acts. Such transformations can be examined with Foucault's power/knowledge nexus, as in the example in chapter 1 of the invention of the subject of sexuality, when it is shifted from his disciplinary agon to an agon of history. The necessitarian is a function of the real; its verbalization as substance, a function of rhetoric. In this verbalization of the real resides the paradox of rhetorical realism, considered in the last chapter, by which discourse is a reaction to the very situation that it brings into being for the first time. Participants in the Burkean conversation simultaneously share a situation and struggle over its definition. Definitions of substance compete and the agon of history arbitrates. The bourgeoisie (power), through a re-hierarchizing that displaced the privileging of the body as family blood in favor of privileging it as sex (knowledge), succeeded in constituting "personal virtue" as a cultural standard of standards. The subject of sexuality (power/knowledge) is a reaction to the situation it brings into being as it transforms the cultural game. Substance, in sum, is a rhetorical strategy in which a historically contingent constitution appears in the form of the knowledge of necessity.

To conceive Burke's step from "PLF" to *GM*, one can start with the speaker–audience paradigm if one adds that the interaction of speaker and audience, or writer and reader, presupposes assumptions about who we are and whom we're addressing. Without such assumptions, we could not proceed. Such assumptions inform rhetorical interaction even when they presume levels of motivation beyond our conscious reach. In "Freud, Morality, and Hermeneutics," Rorty works from a Burkean premise — "For finding good reasons to act requires, as a preliminary, finding a good description of oneself and one's situation. One cannot isolate one's psychophysiology from one's ethics, any more than one's cosmology" — as he proceeds to ask if in a Freudian culture literature could do anything "except to provide training in how to live as an ironist."[21] No less than any other, the assumption of an "unconscious" leaves an imprint on "conscious" rhetorical interaction. Such considerations lead to the conclusion that prior to the question of speaker and audience, there is the question posed in *GM*'s opening words: "What is involved, when we say what people are doing and why they are doing doing it? An answer to that question is the subject of this book" (xv). In answering it, one can either philosophize rhetoric or rhetoricize philosophy. Philosophizing rhetoric answers with an essentialized version of human nature. Rhetoricizing philosophy answers with a rhetoric of the subject.

 GM recognizes that no rhetoric is more powerful than the rhetoric of substance, so much so that the traditional philosophical project has been to claim jurisdiction over substance and to place it beyond the reach of rhetoric. *GM* reverses this jurisdictional claim in summing up the rhetorical strategy of strategies: "men induce themselves and others to act by devices that deduce 'let us' from 'we must' or 'we should.' And 'we must' and 'we should' they deduce in turn from 'it *is*' — for only by assertions as to how things *are* can we finally substantiate a judgment" (336–37). What a constitution does, *GM* postulates, is "to *substantiate an ought* (to base a statement as to *what should be* upon a statement as to *what is*)" (358). Burke's concern with substance

21 *New Literary History* 12 (1980): 178, 179.

contrasts with his earlier socialized version of "the nature of 'reason'": "the only way in which one *can* rationalize a private act is by reference to a public effect (showing that it is 'good' for someone beyond the self, that it is to be tested by reference to a field varying in scope, such as family, class, or nation" (*ATH* 164). But the ultimate test is not a group, however large, but substance. To call something "merely utopian" depicts it as unrealizable in the world that "is." Identifying an act as conforming to substance claims that it is feasible and sustainable. Substance is the ultimate trump card in the constitutional game of changing the rules in the play of the game.

GM's substance displaces *ATH*'s symbol of authority. In *ATH*, there is a history of subject positions, but insofar as Burke relies on psychoanalytical coordinates to theorize acceptance and rejection of symbols of authority at the deepest level, he inscribes his history within a privileged subject position. In *ATH*'s historical context, this position comes with credentials making it rhetorically easy to use, something that more or less "goes without saying." But the credentials making it easy to use also make its historicity easy to forget. A higher level of theoretical abstraction is required to get to the concrete of history.

Burke's proportionalizing-essentializing distinction recognizes this requirement. Forged in his polemic with Freud, this distinction opened the road to Burke's discovery of his grammatical alternative to "correct explanation," to recall Jay's phrase from the last chapter. By the logic of this distinction, the Freudian subject can be rewritten as but one possible subject. Freud's conceptualization of sexual motivation may be a proportional ingredient and, in some cases, the dominant one, but only in some cases, not all. Extending this logic, one can entertain the theoretical possibility that all essentializations of the subject can be rewritten as proportionalizations — that is, as possible or constructed subjects. This rewriting strategy takes its final form in "a grammar of motives."

A rhetoric of the subject resists the temptation to privilege any subject position, no matter how impressive its credentials. A rhetorical subject is apart from subjects in its transhistoricity and a part of them in its concreteness, appearing only in historical forms. A theoretical abstraction that only historical subject positions can illustrate, it makes historicity impossible to forget.

As a constitution, a subject can be reconstituted. But the possibility of reconstitution does not preclude a constitution of substance from going very deep, as deep as Foucault's analytic of power/knowledge can trace it, as in his analysis of the constitution of the subject of sexuality. We see ourselves making choices daily, but these are typically made from within subject positions constituted so deeply that they seem "natural," not contingencies that can be reconstituted. At this depth, we are the decentered effect of choices made elsewhere, choices that hierarchized for us the world into which we entered. Such decentering appears in one of Burke's examples, where he uses ironic contrasts to register the historicity of the subject constituted within a circumference, like Parkes's, where to be free is to be free to sell one's labor:

if you have an unpleasant piece of work to be done, and don't want to do it yourself, in a slave culture you may get this done by force, compulsion, threat. Or in a pious culture you might get it done "religiously," if those who are asked to do the work are moved by such motives as devotion, admiration, sense of duty. But in a capitalist labor market, all that is necessary is for you to say, "Who'll do this for five dollars?" – and men press forward "independently," of their "own free will," under orders from no one, to "voluntarily" enlist for the work. (*GM* 93)

Despite the depths to which the constitution of the subject can penetrate, reconstitution is nonetheless always possible because the constitution is rhetorical, not genetic (if there is contingency in genetics, it's not rhetorical). A subject position that seems "natural" is one that carries so heavy a rhetorical weight that challenging it seems inconceivable. Yet challenges do arise. Rhetorical weight can be shifted.

This process of reconstitution, however, cannot be theorized from the standpoint of the unique individual, either the rational individual of the enlightenment or the authentic individual of romanticism. The Lockean individual starts in the state of nature and reconstitutes itself through the rational act of entering the social contract, but it remains independent of this contract in reserving to itself the right to revise it. The authentic individual, suspecting that this rationality is internalized from the outside, seeks to uncover beneath it a spontaneous, authentic self, believing that from that vantage point reconstitution is possible. But we postmoderns realize that searching for such authenticity is like peeling an onion: there is nothing at the core; beneath every construct there is still another. Even the body's immunity to constructive power – e.g., we can't construct away death – is not total as constructing can penetrate such levels as sensory and sexual experience.

Constituted to this depth, there is no place within from which to reconstitute oneself. Rather, reconstitution is possible only from the standpoint of the agon of history in the Burkean conversation, where "constitutions are agonistic instruments." It is only in the context of the historical agon of orthodoxy against orthodoxy that there are rhetorical challenges with enough power to challenge the "naturalness" of established constitutions, as in Crusoe, where the rhetorical force of the old orthodoxy burdens him with his "original sin," a rhetorical weight so heavy that only God can lift it to legitimate his individualism, but lift it He does.

Autonomy, as we saw in chapter 1, is in the agon of history, not prior to it. The rhetorical analogue to the enlightenment individual is the autonomy in the agon. One is never as free as this individual, but one approximates it most closely in the historical struggle of orthodoxy against orthodoxy, where old subject positions are melted down and new ones formed. In such transformations, there is autonomy, albeit always relative to what history puts on one's plate.

Evidence that reconstitution occurs in the agon of history rather than the individual appears in "Declarations," where Derrida narrates his reading of the US Declaration of Independence.[22] As noted earlier, Derrida's reading of the Declaration redirects speech-act theory from the conformative to the constitutive act.[23] The constitutive act initially deployed in "Declarations" is the signature, an individualistic model, introduced in the neon of italics as a map for reading the Declaration: *"who signs, and with what so-called proper name, the declarative act which founds an institution?"* (8). The inadequacy of this model becomes evident later, when Derrida adds a countersignature, which is and is not a signature. Perhaps against his will, Derrida ends up reading the Declaration as a constitutional act in an agon of history.

The signature, in Derrida's analysis, is simultaneously invention and imitation. We invent the signature that we leave at a bank, but we are subsequently constrained in our banking to imitate it slavishly. Furthermore, insofar as a truly inimitable signature could not be a signature, even the first signature is always already an imitation, fissured in its "origin" between an instance of signing and a signature

22 "Declarations" is short for "Declarations of Independence," *New Political Science* 15 (1986): 7–15; page references are included parenthetically.
23 See also "Psyche: Inventions of the Other," in *Reading De Man Reading*, eds. Lindsay Waters and Wlad Godzich, Theory and History of Literature 59 (Minneapolis: University of Minnesota Press, 1989), pp. 25–65, where Derrida's interest in the constitutive act takes the form of an examination of invention, a traditional concern of rhetoric, as Derrida notes (25–27, 50–51). In a section subtitled "Beyond the Speech Act," Derrida doubts that speech-act theory, "in its present state and dominant form," is capable of accounting for invention (34–35).

signable anytime, anywhere – "signature is imitable in its essence" (*Limited* 34). This signable signature is prior not only to signings subsequent to the first but even to the first insofar as any form is prior to its instantiations. Although a signature's form doesn't exist until the completion of the first signing, it is nonetheless prior to this signing in a "fabulous retroactivity" ("Declarations" 10). The signature, then, is a constitutive rather than a conformative act. In Austin's performatives, a speech act conforms to a preexistent script, but in Derrida's signature, instantiation and authorizing script appear together, the instantiation constituting what it conforms to.

Its "fabulous retroactivity" enables the signature to serve as Derrida's initial map for reading the Declaration's undecidability, "One cannot decide – and that's the interesting thing, the force and the coup of force of such a declarative act – whether independence is stated [constative] or produced [performative] by this utterance" (9). Like a signing that retroactively constitutes its authorizing script, the Declaration is "producer and guarantor of its own signature," retroactively constituting a "people" with the authority to declare independence: "They [the people] do *not* exist as an entity... *before* this declaration, not *as such*... This signer can only authorize him- or herself to sign once he or she has come to the end... of his or her own signature, in a sort of fabulous retroactivity" (10).

Derrida's signature later proves inadequate as a reading map because it isn't abstract enough to get to the historical concreteness of the Declaration – a failure that confirms Marx's analysis of historical method, reviewed in chapter 1. A signature is a function of culture, and as such it is part of an orthodoxy that constrains it in all sorts of ways. Extrinsic constraints, for example, limit who can leave an authorized signature at a bank. Once there were gender constraints; today, there are still age constraints. Intrinsic constraints largely determine in advance the form of a signature. A surname is a "last name" in our culture; in others, a first. In US culture, furthermore, where an individualistic ethos unites individuals in the desire to be different – a coming together that ironically drives apart – it's likely that there is greater latitude than in other cultures in the use of initials, nicknames, and diminutive forms of names. Derrida adds an additional intrinsic constraint, showing that even in signing itself, where the relative uniqueness of handwriting produces an imitation fingerprint, there is a structural constraint that ironically makes a signature an effect of an orthodoxy retroactively of its own making. By confining himself to this constraint, however, Derrida sees only the tip of the iceberg above water, whereas to see the signature in its historical concreteness, one needs an abstraction that comprehends the part below water as well.

In focusing on this tip, Derrida privileges it against other dimensions of signature, reflecting it and deflecting attention from them. This privileging occurs within the rhetoric of individualism that shadows his analysis because his signature is not abstract enough to displace it. It's true, of course, that in "Signature Event Context" he deploys the signature to decenter Austin's "I." Instead of an "I" present to itself before discourse, Derrida gives us an "I" that can sign itself only through a form absent from itself, a form signable even by machines at different places at the same time. But Derrida's decentering needs itself to be decentered. Derrida sometimes dramatizes his decentering by speaking of signing as a death, a metaphor Peggy Kamuf unpacks concisely: "When I sign, I am already dead because . . . [the signature's] singular referent — me — will have already submitted to the requirement of its generalization in order to signify itself . . . 'I' spells the death of me; it is already the effacement of a singular nature in a common sig-nature."[24] This analysis is misleading, however, insofar as it implies that an antecedent "me" is "there" to die. This death of the "I" thus ironically resurrects the "I." Derrida's decentering is a pathos of individualism.

In selecting the handwritten signing as his focus, Derrida privileges against other dimensions of an orthodoxy of signature the one dimension that originates in the "I." However fissured the signing, the "origin" of its fingerprint uniqueness is the "I," the same "I" that can alter it in a new signing. Derrida's signature thus locates the autonomy of constituting in the "I" rather than in the agon of history. In the case of the Declaration, Derrida is not talking about handwritten signing, as he is in "Signature Event Context," but by starting with the model of such signing, he initially depicts the Declaration as a voluntaristic self-constitution, however fissured the moment of creation and however undecidable the question of whether the Declaration performatively invents a people or constatively reports their existence.[25]

24 *Signature Pieces: On the Institution of Authorship* (Ithaca: Cornell University Press, 1988), p. 5.
25 Derrida remarks in "Declarations" that the signature always reminds him of the Francis Ponge lines: "By the word *by* begins thus this text / Of which the first line says the truth" (10). In "Psyche: Inventions," cited above, Derrida analyzes this Ponge text at length, suggesting that its first line, by performatively bringing into existence what it constates, is "a sort of poetic performative that simultaneously describes and carries out, on the same line, its own generation" (33).

The signature is, of course, among the last places that would come to mind as a site for a historical agon. Like Austin's examples, the signature is a site where nothing is apparently at stake. Considered as a subject position, it is normally constituted so deeply that it seems "natural," immune to rhetorical challenge and reconstitution. But there are exceptions, the Declaration being one. That the paradox of the signature, Derrida observes, "should also be an everyday occurrence should not make us forget the singular context of this act [the Declaration]. In this case, another state signature had to be effaced in 'dissolving' the links of colonial paternity or maternity" (11). This case, in other words, was an instance of the constitutional game of changing the rules in the play of the game. The stakes were huge: nothing less than the right to sign with the authority of sovereignty. The signature was a site of a historical agon of orthodoxy against orthodoxy in which a British subject constituted rhetorically in the colonies was melted down and reconstituted rhetorically as a US subject. The Declaration is a new signature, constituted as a revolutionary assertion of the right to sign against the authority that heretofore reserved that right to itself. As a new constitution, this signature is an "agonistic instrument," not an individualistic self-constitution. We can recall here our discussion of Foucault in chapter 1. One can use his "power is everywhere" formula to theorize the inculcation of the orthodoxy of a signature. But this formula is inadequate when one turns to the constitution of a new signature. To theorize the newness of the Declaration, one needs to recognize that power is also "somewhere," as evidenced by the power Britain amassed to beat back this revolutionary assertion.

The revolutionary agon in which the colonists found themselves, like the strike call facing Therborn's subject, is the kind of crisis situation in which the necessitarian principle appears most dramatically. A function of the real, the necessitarian dictates that the hierarchical setting of priorities is a necessity, not a choice; hierarchizing happens no matter what happens. Derrida recognizes this necessity when, in the paragraph immediately following recognition of the agon of signature, he introduces a hierarchizing principle, casting it as a countersignature: "And yet another instance still holds itself back behind the scenes. Another 'subjectivity' is still coming to sign, in order to guarantee it, this production of signature" (11). Derrida immediately adds, "In short, there are only countersignatures in this process" (11), thus mastering this reversal in his narrative through a retrospective rereading. Just as the "people" was the countersigner who guaranteed the signing by Jefferson and the other drafters of the Declaration, "God" is the ultimate countersigner: "They [the people] sign in the name of the laws of nature and in the name of God" (11). But Derrida leaves unexplained just how radically this rereading displaces the signature model with which he started. Signing can never legitimate itself, self-constituting its own authority, because signing can be forged, as Derrida would be the first to acknowledge. Signing requires witnessing, countersigning. Signing is constitutional in the sense that it's agonistic, an assertion against counterassertions that might contest it. Such considerations take us below the tip to the historical concreteness of the iceberg of signing. Concreteness enters Derrida's reading as an effect of its recognition of the agon of history – the abstraction that is the road to the concrete.

God, Derrida adds, "founds natural laws and thus the whole game which tends to present performative utterances as constative utterances" (11). This is the game of the realist rhetoric of substance. Derrida contributes to this rhetoric in his analysis of the undecidability of the Declaration's God. Commenting on the Declaration's assertion that the colonies "are" and "ought to be" independent, he finds the textual function of God: "'Are and ought to be'; the 'and' articulates and conjoins here the two discursive modalities, the to be and the ought to be, the constation and the prescription, the fact and the right. *And* is God" (11).

Derrida thus keeps "are" and "ought" distinct in their undecidable conjunction, whereas Petrey, rejecting Derrida's interpretation, flatly equates the "are" to the "ought," lapsing into rhetorical idealism: "The ahistorical permanence of Nature and Nature's God isn't a given fact but a collectively validated convention enacted in language... The Declaration of Independence *performed* both God and the United States of America, and the fact that the performance was explicit in one case and implicit in the other is trivial."[26] The issue here is not, of course, whether "God" exists but whether anything "is"; "God" is simply the Declaration's word for "is." Petrey equates "is" to "holding constative truth to be self-evident and hence independent of performance," a possibility that he idealistically denies, insisting on "the identity of referents produced and referents affirmed, of history

26 *Speech Acts*, p. 161.

and eternity, of a congress newly assembled and Nature's timeless God. All are the effect of collective action and collective speech."[27] That there is no self-evident "presence" in the classical metaphysical sense, however, does not mean that there is nothing "there," nothing "independent of performance." It only means, as rhetorical realism concedes, that there is no access to what is "there" independent of our constructions or constitutions. Anything performatively brought into existence can be erased: what performance put here, performance can take away. To decide whether there is anything "independent of performance," one must ask whether there is anything that cannot be performed away. That is the question rhetorical idealism shies away from asking.

As Burke underlines in his reading of Austin (WD 147), Austin indicates in the opening sentence of *How to Do Things with Words* that the only merit he claims for the book "is that of being true, at least in parts." What Austin discovered is not that there is performance of collective action and speech but that it occurs in heretofore unsuspected places, so many in fact that he concluded that performativity is inescapable. That conclusion is what gives his book its theoretical interest and power, a power that Petrey seeks to enhance in applying Austin to issues in literary theory. Any performance that occurs could by the same token not have occurred – that is what makes it a performance – but in its inescapability performativity is something different. Performativity means that we are always already performing: not to perform this is to perform that; if not "Nature's timeless God," maybe "God is dead." In its inescapability, performativity cannot be performed away. In this sense, it is "independent of performance." Performativity is Petrey's God, the motive of his theoretical act.

The motivation of the Declaration, Derrida proposes, may be construed

as a vibrant act of faith, as a hypocrisy indispensable to a politico-military-economic, etc. coup of force, or, more simply, more economically, as the analytic and consequential deployment of a tautology: for this Declaration to have a meaning *and* an effect, there must be a last instance. God is the name, the best one, for this last instance. (12)

The Declaration's effect depends on a last instance to interpret the necessitarian in the constitution of a subject of revolution. God is tautological, in one sense, as a logical law that excludes no possibilities,

27 Ibid.

which in this case are the motivations ranging from hypocrisy to faith. Part of the interest of this range is that the possibility of faith is a necessary part of any contemporary theory of ideology, or of a rhetoric of the subject, that follows Althusser's reconception of ideology as the formation of the subject rather than as an instrumental "false consciousness." As Althusser observes, "[T]he ruling class does not maintain with the ruling ideology . . . [a] relation of pure utility and cunning . . . In reality, the bourgeoisie has to believe its own myth before it can convince others."[28]

Derrida's range of motivation also qualifies an often cited passage from de Man's reading of Rousseau: "A text is defined by the necessity of considering a statement, at the same time, as performative and constative . . . It seems that as soon as a text knows what it states, it can only act deceptively, like the thieving lawmaker in the *Social Contract*, and if a text does not act, it cannot state what it knows."[29] For de Man there is only the hypocrisy of the "thieving lawmaker"; for Derrida, the range of motivation doesn't stop there. What interests de Man is a tension between performative and constative that he derives from a rupture between positionality and nonpositionality. A constative aspires to be nonpositional: "With the constative," Austin observes, "we abstract from the illocutionary . . . aspects of the speech act, and we concentrate on the locutionary . . . We aim at the ideal of what would be right to say in all circumstances, for any purpose, to any audience, &c. Perhaps this is sometimes realized."[30] The "perhaps" registers skepticism, though whether it is absolute may be open to question. But there is no question about the absoluteness of de Man's skepticism. For him the rupture is permanent: a text "knows what it states," constating nonpositionally, only by deceptively concealing its positionality as an act, yet without the act there wouldn't be the constative in the first place.[31] In the legal text, de Man sees an exemplary instance of this tension: the law is nonpositional in the purported generality of its application, yet this generality is called into

---

28 *For Marx*, trans. Ben Brewster (New York: Pantheon Books, 1969), p. 234.

29 *Allegories of Reading* (New Haven: Yale University Press, 1979), pp. 270. De Man reads the full range of Rousseau's texts, but he singles out the *Social Contract* as making explicit features of textuality obscured elsewhere (p. 269), so to Burke's privileging of the US Constitution there is in de Man a parallel.

30 *How to Do*, pp. 144–45.

31 Michael Sprinker has shrewdly read de Man's formulation as a textual model of "the ideological relation to the real conditions of human existence which Althusser has claimed is a permanent feature of human society"; see *Imaginary Relations: Aesthetics and Ideology in the Theory of Historical Materialism* (London: Verso, 1987), p. 264.

question by the positionality of the act of its formulation. In the example of the "thieving lawmaker," de Man identifies a self-serving relation of the act to the law that corresponds to hypocrisy in Derrida's range of motivation. The limitation in de Man is that this one relation is put forward as the only possible relation, even though the positional, in its relation to the nonpositional, may be self-sacrificing as well as self-serving. One may defend the freedom of the speech one hates as well as the speech one wants to give; both possibilities are equally effects of the relation of the positional to the nonpositional. Derrida's tautological inclusion of both is a more rigorous formulation than de Man's.

The distinctness and inseparability of the positional and the nonpositional are together an effect of language, conceived dramatistically as action. "Lord Raglan won the battle of Alma" is a selection of one version of "is" from a range of possible descriptions of the battle – all of which could be "true" – and as a selection it conforms to an "ought." Petrey selects performativity and his ought, like any other, is implicit in his project's strategy of intervening in the contingencies of the conversation in which this project is his "oar." As an act, Petrey's text is positional. His oar is in his text in the sense that his theoretical claim is to be found in it, but in a deeper sense, the oar is apart from his act, nonpositional rather than positional, since its whole point is to theorize what happens at many times and places, maybe even all. One needs to look at the text to find the oar, but one need not be at the time and place the text appeared to comprehend or to apply it to one's own or other situations. The oar's nonpositionality is its empowerment, which can no more be separated from Petrey's positionality than it can be reduced to it.

Considered as an oar, the Declaration is similarly positional and nonpositional. From the standpoint of its enlightenment positionality, it selects a God as a substance that verbalizes the necessitarian imperative as a "circumference" from which revolutionary action can be derived. "When in the Course of human Events," the Declaration begins,

> it becomes necessary for one People to dissolve the Political Bands which have connected them with another, and to assume among the Powers of the Earth, the separate and equal Station to which the Laws of Nature and of Nature's God entitle them, a decent Respect to the Opinions of Mankind requires that they should declare the causes which impel them to the Separation.

The colonists thus present themselves as instantiating nonpositional "Laws of Nature" that "impel" their action. God is selected, yet He logically compels.

Dramatism demystifies the nonpositionality of philosophical logic by exposing its grounding in the positionality of selection: its rhetoricity. *GM* insists that "a document, arising at a given period in history, should not be treated (if we are to understand its nature as an *act*) simply as though its 'principles' were something eternal, for eternal things do not have a beginning, and these did" (365). As we saw earlier (p. 155), Burke reverses philosophy's traditional jurisdictional claim over substance in seeing the deduction of "we must" from "it is" as the rhetorical strategy of strategies. That passage appears at the end of his deliberations leading to his choice of the Constitution as his representative anecdote, where he adds that the constitutional translation of selection into logic is "the purification of war" (337). In this translation, the rhetorical subject is constituted in verbal action. The "purification of war" is best read as equivalent to what Burke terms the "critical moment" in distinguishing dramatism from *PC*'s biologism in a passage we quoted early in the last chapter: "language ... [is] the 'critical moment' at which human motives take form, since a linguistic factor at every point in human experience complicates and to some extent transcends the purely biological aspects of motivation" (*GM* 318). The constitutional act is this "critical moment." However a terminology of motivation sees itself as it is deployed in the attribution of motives, Burke's constitutional analysis exposes it as a rhetoricizing of philosophy in an agonistic struggle. We purify war as we fight about what "is."

The "and" that Derrida identifies with God conjoins the positional "ought" and the nonpositional "is" tautologically and undecidably: inseparable yet distinct. With "ought" alone, one lapses into rhetorical idealism; with "is" alone, one returns to the traditional philosophical logic based on the intuition of self-evidence. When both are undecidably distinct — inseparable yet neither reducible to the other — one has rhetorical realism: "Lord Raglan won the battle of Alma" can be read as reflecting something that is, and as such it can serve as a premise from which other things logically follow; yet it is also an act of selection that conforms to an "ought" prescribed in a mode of historical analysis, and as such it is a reflection that is also a deflection from what other modes might select, some of which might ignore Lord Raglan altogether.

We are almost ready to turn to Burke's pentad, but first we need to consider an additional Derrida text in which there appears a distinctive rhetorical structure where logics and selections intersect in undecidable inseparability and distinctness.

This text is section "v" of "Limited Inc," where Derrida is commenting on John Searle as well as Austin. We'll also consider a Fish text on Searle that facilitates extrapolating a conversational interaction between Searle and Fish. In effect we'll reconfigure "v" to read Derrida as commenting not only on Searle but also on this hypothetical interaction, a reconfiguration that Derrida invites in exhibiting an interest in theorizing the unending conversation (*Limited* 120, 127).

This interest may be significant in ways that elude Derrida insofar as it forces a reevaluation of his refusal of metadiscourse. In contrast to Austin's modest claim to truth, quoted earlier, Derrida insists that although the texts in his debate with Austin and Searle, theirs as well as his own, all analyze speech acts, they are not "discourses dominating the *ensemble* of this field and stating the truth about it. Rather, they will have constituted elements of that *ensemble . . . examples* of events, to which all the questions and categories accredited by the theory of speech acts will still be applicable and reapplicable" (*Limited* 39). Because analysis of speech acts is itself a speech act, part of the ensemble of speech acts, such analysis is, Derrida concludes, "essentially *interminable*" (39). This disclaimer refuses metadiscourse, but consider that the implication of this refusal is that Derrida's text, because it's a speech act, is on the same level as any other speech act, such as a bet on a football game at the local tavern. One can concede that both are speech acts, but to stop there is to attend too much to identities, not enough to differences. More importantly, to claim that analysis is "interminable" because no analysis can be final is to make a metadiscursive claim that has its own kind of finality – the "essentially" interminable is as terminal in its way as the terminable is in its. The refusal of metadiscourse involves a metadiscursive, transhistorical claim that cannot be refused. The "essentially interminable" needs to be not simply invoked but theorized.

Midway through section "v," Derrida emphasizes, "The matter we are discussing here concerns the value, possibility, and system of what is called *logic*" (92; italics added). He introduces this theme at the section's beginning by quoting a long passage from Searle, a small portion of which we quote here:

there could not ... be promises made by actors in a play if there were not the possibility of promises made in real life. The existence of the pretended form of the speech act is *logically dependent* on the possibility of the nonpretended speech act in the same way that any pretended form of behavior is dependent on nonpretended forms of behavior.   (89; italics added)

Derrida places this assertion of logical dependency – Searle's "metaphysical decision" (93) – in a long tradition: "Metaphysics in its most traditional form reigns over the Austinian heritage: over his legacy and over those who have taken charge of it as his heirs apparent" (93).

Searle's "metaphysical decision" restates Austin's argument that fictional speech acts such as those by actors in the theater are "parasitic" upon speech acts in "real life." This argument is the target of Derrida's well-known critique of Austin. Promises on the stage and in the street cannot be separated cleanly, Derrida counters, because both conform equally, on some level, to the same cultural script. The promise in the street cannot be separated from the fictionality of the script to which it conforms. So, Derrida concludes, the logic Searle asserts – fact first, fiction second – can be turned upside down. One could just as well start with the fictionality of the script and demonstrate that promises in life are "logically dependent" on it. This alternative logic – fiction first, fact second – is asserted by Fish against Searle in "Fact and Fiction."[32] Fish argues that all we have are fictions. At any point in time, one is singled out as "fact" and the others are distinguished from it as "fictions." But this arrangement is never fixed. What is fact today may not be fact tomorrow.

The interaction between Fish and Searle, then, is an opposition between two logics – fiction:fact vs. fact:fiction. Disseminators of Derrida's critique of Austin, like Fish, typically go no further than to invert Searle's logic, even though this inversion is only the first step in Derrida's method of "double writing," which Derrida explicitly mentions at the end of "Signature Event Context," where he characterizes it as "a *reversal* of the classical opposition *and* a general *displacement* of the system" (*Limited* 21). Section "v" interests us because in it Derrida's main concern is with the second of his two steps. After repeating, from his critique of Austin, his argument for inverting Searle's logic, Derrida goes on, "And *vice-versa*, for I do not mean simply to *invert* the order of logical dependency" (91). At this point, the issue becomes the unde-

---

32 This is a section in "How to Do Things with Austin and Searle: Speech Act Theory and Literary Criticism," reprinted in *Is There a Text in This Class? The Authority of Interpretive Communities* (Cambridge: Harvard University Press, 1980), pp. 231–44.

cidability of logic itself, and Derrida becomes the theorist of the conversational interaction between Searle's logic and Fish's.

Among the commentators on Derrida's critique of Austin, Spivak is exceptional in the emphasis she gives the second step of Derrida's double writing. Correcting readers like Fish, she stresses that Derrida takes care not to "privilege fictional and theatrical uses of speech acts ... The 'theater' does not win out over 'real life.' The two are seen as indistinguishably and structurally implicated. 'As though literature, theater, deceit, infidelity, hypocrisy, infelicity, parasitism, and the simulation of real life were not part of real life!' [*Limited* 90]."[33] The play is not between the words "fact" and "fiction" but between the existences "theater" and "real life."

From the vantage point of this second step, one can deconstruct not only Searle but also Fish. Searle's "The Logical Status of Fictional Discourse" begins with factual discourse before going on to show that fictional discourse is logically dependent on it. Searle starts with two passages that both appear to be factual reports. But one is a news report from the *New York Times* and the other a passage from a novel, so the two pose the question of how we recognize that one is factual discourse and the other fictional. Searle answers that factual "assertion is a type of illocutionary act," going on to detail a four-part script of conventions to which any statement must conform to be recognized as factual.[34] In short, factual discourse is a speech act, and like any speech act, it must conform to a conventional script: a fiction. Searle argues that fiction is dependent on fact, yet by his own account, an assertion of fact, to be recognized as such, is dependent on fiction. He must systematically ignore this dependency of fact on fiction to write his discourse about the dependency of fiction on fact.

Fish exhibits a comparable blindness. He gives particular attention to one passage, quoting it at length, in which Searle uses the phrase "shared pretense" to describe the process by which characters in a novel exist. Fish takes the phrase and reinterprets it from the standpoint of his logic: "'Shared pretense' is what enables us to talk about anything at all. When we communicate, it is because we are parties to a set of discourse agreements which are in effect decisions as to what can be stipulated as fact."[35] First fiction — "shared pretense" — then fact. But this process of shared pretense is something that actually

---

33 "Revolutions That As Yet Have No Model: Derrida's 'Limited Inc,'" *Diacritics* 10.4 (1980): 38. For a persuasive case that typical distortions of Derrida can be traced to the failure to take this second step, see Jeffrey T. Nealon, "The Discipline of Deconstruction," *PMLA* 107 (1992): 1266–79.　　34 *New Literary History* 6 (1974–75): 322.　　35 *Is There a Text?*, p. 242.

happens at a place and time because, as Fish argues, shared pretense can change from one historical situation to another. Shared pretense is thus a historical event – a fact – by Fish's own account. Fictions are part of life, and, as such, they are as factual as any other part, as Derrida accentuates in the passage that Spivak quotes. Just as Searle's text has to blind itself to its dependency on fiction, Fish's has to blind itself to its dependency on fact. Each is an act of selection, and as a selection it is necessarily also a deflection.

Deconstruction, then, positions us outside both logics, where we can theorize their conversational interaction, though it is difficult, Derrida suggests, to determine exactly where this place is. Advancing beyond the specific logics that Searle and Fish articulate, Derrida poses the problem in general terms: "The analysis must now go further (higher or lower, whichever one prefers). Logic, the logical, the *logos* of logic cannot be the decisive instance here: rather it constitutes the object of debate . . . No constituted logic nor any rule of logical order can, therefore, provide a decision or impose its norms upon these prelogical possibilities of logic" (92–93). We need to move from the "prelogical possibilities of logic" to a logic. The difficulty is that while this move seems logical, it can't be logical, since the whole point is to get to logic from a place prior to it. We need a logic that isn't a logic, something alien to the jurisdiction of philosophy. The prelogical possibilities of logic, Derrida goes on,

are not "logically" primary or secondary with regard to other possibilities, nor logically primary or secondary with regard to logic itself. They are (topologically?) alien to it, but not as its principle, condition of possibility, or "radical" foundation; for the structure of iterability divides and guts such radicality. It opens up the *topos* of this singular topology to the un-founded, removing language, and the rest, from its jurisdiction. (93)

The pun by which the term "topos" seems to enter this text – perhaps speaking Derrida as much as he it – seems to confirm his earlier remark that the sophists "haunt" his debate with Austin and Searle (*Limited* 42). Rodolphe Gasché quotes from this passage in section "v," using it in deriving major deconstructive themes compatible with the rhetorical conversation – e.g. (1) "a unity of combat" that refuses sublation of contradiction to a higher unity (the conversation offers no teleological promise of unity); (2) positionality is "a form of constitution by means of which something becomes what it is through its relation to something other" (constitutions are agonistic instruments) – but he leaves out the last sentence, where the rhetorical term "topos" appears, thus not availing himself of rhetoric in theorizing these themes.[36] A thorough examination of the rhetoricity of Derrida's thought remains part of the unfinished business of contemporary rhetorical theory.

Using the term "topos" to return to Searle and Fish from the general level at which Derrida fomulates the undecidability of logic and the consequent necessity of a "decision" prior to logic, one can derive Searle's fact:fiction and Fish's fiction:fact from the fact/fiction topos – two logics deriving from the same discursive "place." This move from topos to logics contradicting one another is "alien" to logic. The space for the topos is opened by Derrida's structure of iterability – identity and difference such that any element is divided a priori (*Limited* 53) – as this structure "divides and guts" the presupposition of logical dependency that one thing is the "foundation" or "condition of possibility" of another. Searle sees the fact as the condition of fiction, but the fact is already fiction in being inseparable from the fiction by which it is recognized. Fish's inversion privileges fiction as the condition of fact, but fiction is already fact by being a thing in the world, like any other fact. Philosophical logic anchors itself, Derrida observes, in "presence": "presence of the thing to sight as *eidos* . . . temporal presence as point . . . the self-presence of the cogito . . . and so forth."[37] From such self-evident starting-points, philosophy derives the coherence of system. What corresponds to presence in rhetoric is the seeming self-evidence of a discursive site such as the fact/fiction topos, but what derives from this rhetorical starting-point is not coherence but the contradiction of rhetorical point-counter-point.[38] The deconstructive

---

36 *The Tain of the Mirror: Derrida and the Philosophy of Reflection* (Cambridge: Harvard University Press, 1986), pp. 149, 152, 158.

37 *Of Grammatology*, trans. Gayatri Chakravorty Spivak (Baltimore: Johns Hopkins University Press, 1976), p. 12.

38 This paragraph reaches the outer edge of the present study. The proposal advanced here that the topos is rhetoric's substitute for philosophy's presence is a project in itself, one that extends beyond the present study and even beyond the contemporary revival of rhetoric, which has yet to return topoi to the prominence they've previously enjoyed. Carrying out this project would no doubt do well to begin by returning to the historical record, partly to select from all the things called topoi in their long tradition those that can substitute for presence, but mainly to explore this substitution more deeply. This exploration might well begin not in antiquity but in the seventeenth century, when modern philosophy seems to have got itself started by trashing the topoi. "Trashing" is not too strong a word to describe the treatment they receive in 1662 at the hands of Antoine Arnauld in part 3, chapter 17 of *La Logique, ou l'art de penser* (the Port-Royal Logic), a text Derrida recalls – in the previously cited "Psyche: Inventions" – in the course of revisiting the rhetorical tradition of invention. Perhaps the best place to begin is Vico's defense of topoi against the new philosophy in general and Descartes in particular. For a review of the issues, see Ernesto Grassi, "Critical Philosophy or Topical Philosophy? Meditations on the *De nostri temporis studiorum ratione*," trans. Hayden V. White, in *Giambattista Vico: An International Symposium*, eds. Giorgio Tagliacozzo and Hayden V. White (Baltimore: Johns Hopkins University Press, 1969), pp. 39–50.

bet is that any discourse that thinks itself to be other than rhetorical can be reinscribed in an undecidable topos out of which it emerged and which it has subsequently erased from its memory.

The topos from which Searle and Fish begin is a textualization of existence in which fact and fiction, as existences in the world, are undecidably inseparable yet irreducible to one another. We recognize Searle's and Fish's different logics as in competition with one another rather than as incommensurate ships simply passing one another in the night. This competition is a rhetorical commensurability of discourses, one quite different from the conversation-ending epistemological commensurability that Rorty refuses.[39] Rhetorical realism joins Rorty in this refusal, but not in his assumption that epistemological commensurability is the only kind there is. Refusing commensurability altogether, Rorty becomes a rhetorical idealist. Rorty's exhortation to keep the conversation going is an unnecessary gesture; the conversation has kept itself going for centuries in the face of one conversation-ending epistemological claim after another. The conversation is indomitable, showing as it swallows one philosophy after another that philosophies do not provide final answers. Rhetorical commensurability suggests why. What a topos such as fact/fiction demonstrates is that something is "there" but that (1) our only access to it is through discourse and (2) no statement of it is definitive.[40] Our access to what is there is thus not through classic representation – a "mirror of nature" – but through the conversation, where the vulnerability of every statement to critique keeps the conversation going interminably. Rhetorically considered, knowing isn't a process in which raw experience is processed by mental faculties such that knowledge, as Kant thought, may be said to begin with experience but not to derive solely from experience; rather, knowing is a process in which sayability is mastered through the development of the capacity to critique and to produce discourse.[41]

A topos is a site of constructions, but the site itself cannot be

---

39 *Philosophy and the Mirror of Nature* (Princeton University Press, 1979), pp. 315–22.

40 In recounting the origins of his rhetoricizing of philosophy, Richard McKeon includes insights, which he states aphoristically, occasioned by passages in Plato and Cicero: "the true is sometimes false and sometimes true"; "there is a sense in which truth, though one, has no single expression" – "A Philosopher Meditates on Discovery," *Rhetoric: Essays in Invention and Discovery*, ed. Mark Backman (Woodbridge, Connecticut: Ox Bow Press, 1987), pp. 203–04. Rhetorical realism assumes that at the site of any topos capable of substituting for philosophical presence there is an analogue to the relations, suggested by McKeon's aphorisms, of truth to expression and to history.

41 Compare Karl R. Popper, "Epistemology without a Knowing Subject," in *Objective Knowledge: An Evolutionary Approach* (Oxford: Clarendon Press, 1981), pp. 140–41.

constructed away. It can, however, be marginalized. One can shift from site to site. A simple example from the recent history of literary theory can illustrate. The New Criticism succeeded in making the intrinsic/extrinsic tension the dominant topos of the day, using it to frame issues in a manner suited to formalism's interests. The fallacies the New Criticism legislated against – intentional and affective – closed off movement to the extrinsic author, on the one hand, and the extrinsic audience, on the other. Both ironically proved to be sites where later theorists dislodged the New Criticism. On the side of the author, E. D. Hirsch intervened to argue that the autotelic text itself yielded an indeterminate range of meaning. One had to turn to the author for a determinate meaning. On the side of the audience, Fish, along with others, championed the multipicity of reader-response generated meanings, making indeterminacy a virtue. In the process, the intrinsic/extrinsic topos receded to the periphery as the determinacy/indeterminacy topos took over.[42] We can recall here Burke's point, reviewed at the end of the last chapter, that the philosopher who purports to start from a "rock-bottom fact" really starts with the current state of the conversation. This state can be defined in terms of topoi structuring the issues of the day.

Rhetoric's struggle among discourses replaces philosophy's self-evident presence. In the absence of such presence, there is no horizon beyond the conversation to resolve rhetorical struggle once and for all. Topoi are places or sites in discourse that serve as the beginnings of new discourses, none of which can close off the production of still more discourses. Burke charts such places with his pentadic terms.

Early in *GM*, Burke notes that these terms yield ten "ratios": "scene-act, scene-agent, scene-agency, scene-purpose, act-purpose, act-agent, act-agency, agent-purpose, agent-agency, and agency-purpose" (15). Later, he revises this list: "the ratios could be reversed, as either a certain kind of scene may call for its corresponding kind of agent, or a certain agent may call for its corresponding kind of scene, etc. The list of possible combinations would thereby be expanded to twenty" (262). The pentad thus yields twenty discursive sites, or topoi, at which there is a play of existences like that between fact and fiction. "At every point where the field covered by any one of these terms overlaps upon the field covered by any other," Burke proposes in *GM*'s introduction,

---

42 See Williams for an expert reading of Derrida and Burke from the standpoint of the determinacy/indeterminacy topos.

"there is an alchemic opportunity, whereby we can put one philosophy or doctrine of motivation into the alembic, make the appropriate passes, and take out another" (xix). A fixed and unchanging integration of all pentadic relations is specifically identified as an impossibility (19, 82) – the impossible other of rhetoric.

Pentadically considered, what is at stake at each ratio, or topos, is which of the competing pentadic terms is primary. The generic term "substance" is used in place of the pentadic multiplicity at the level of constitutional analysis, where the concern is with the agonistic constitution of substance in general rather than the pentadic definition of different species of substance in particular. Burke characterizes the pentadic terms as a revision of Kant – "Instead of calling them the necessary 'forms experience'... we should call them the necessary 'forms of *talk about* experience'" (317) – thereby effecting a radical dramatistic shift from mental faculties processing experience to the rhetorical sayability of discourse mastery, conceived as a comprehensive spectrum ranging from metaphysics to gossip (xv). *GM* considers mainly philosophical texts because in their complexity and thoroughness they are especially exemplary of the terminological operations Burke investigates. At the same time, the insult, "you're a bastard," posits a substance in presupposing a whole philosophy of how to define what human beings are. The category "agent" appears in Kant as well as in the street.

In narrating how he wrote *GM*, Burke recounts that he decided that the pentadic terms could simply be stated, and "their justification could *follow*, as one noted their place in the 'collective revelation' of common usage, and showed the range of their applicability" (340). He thus begins with rhetorical topoi rather than philosophical presence. The self-evidence of the pentadic terms – their "collective revelation" – shouldn't be confused with the consensus informing Fish's interpretive communities or Austin's conventional scripts. Topoi result in the discord of Burke's conversation rather than the concord of Fish's interpretive community. The operative collective revelation in the example of Fish and Searle is the distinction between fact and fiction, the underpinning of the rhetorical commensurability in their competition with one another. We know the distinction only through the statements of it, yet no single statement can end the conversation about it once and for all.

A topos is relatively autonomous, as the fact/fiction topos can illustrate. In the contemporary context, the constructionist accentuation of fiction is progressive in challenging essentialist undergirdings of patriarchy, racism, and so on. But in the cultural struggle between Richardson and Fielding in the 1740s, it was the defender of the old order, Fielding, who accentuated fictionality, repeatedly calling attention to the fictionality of his texts, most notably in *Tom Jones*, as he sought cultural legitimation through the art that he put on parade and sanctioned with the aura of his classical learning, which was still culturally potent. In opposition, Richardson eschewed fiction, even posing as an editor of real correspondence that happened to come to him. He used an epistolary technique to privilege a "writing to the moment" that purports to reproduce reality, often in extraordinarily factual detail. The rhetorical strategy is clear: the more real Pamela appeared, the more convincing *Pamela*'s assertion of equality against aristocratic hierarchy. In both these contexts, the line between fact and fiction appears, registering something that is "there," autonomous in its independence of different historical situations. But this autonomy is relative because this line appears not as a presence but in competing discursive formulations, with the stakes in the competition differing in the two historical situations. The relative autonomy of the topos is the dramatistic analogue to the relative autonomy of science. Insofar as it's possible to put to motion a question that motion always answers the same way regardless of the historical position from which the question is put, science is autonomous; insofar as the formation of such a question is itself a historical act, science is relatively autonomous. A topos is autonomous insofar as it registers something "there," something beyond the power of discourse to construct out of existence. But this something never appears independent of historically varying constructions. There is never a construction to end constructions.

With a subject of history, history has the capacity to intuit "presence" – in Lukács, for example, proletarian true consciousness is to return history to the light of presence after the darkness of false consciousness – but with a history of subjects, history can select different logics at the site of the same topos at different times. What is "there" at the topos is the basis of a logic but it never appears independently of competing acts of selection that articulate it in different ways. The conversation involves something independent of the agon of history, yet this something never appears independently of this agon. With a subject of history, history is a philosopher, whereas with a history of subjects, it's a rhetorical realist.

In a retrospective comment, Burke says that the pentad's ratios are its most important feature (QAP 332), but his practice in *GM* says something else. He begins with ratios — the first two sections being "The Scene-Act Ratio" and "The Scene-Agent Ratio" — but he doesn't systematically examine them in opposite directions, as in our example of Searle and Fish.[43] Further, ratios become secondary in "The Philosophic Schools," the second of *GM*'s three parts and its most extensive application of the pentad, where texts are classified and analyzed as unified around single pentadic terms. By relying on single terms rather than ratios, "The Philosophic Schools" is overly formalistic, deflecting attention away from the conversation and history. In the process, the pentad is transformed into a formal typology that makes it vulnerable to Lentricchia's charge that it's a "full-blown structuralism" (67). The core problem, which Lentricchia leaves unaddressed, is the relation of the pentad to the constitution.

The more the pentad is its centerpiece and the constitution its forgotten piece, the more *GM* is vulnerable to Perry Anderson's critique of structuralism and poststructuralism:

The supremacy of *langue* as a system is the cornerstone of the Saussurian legacy: *parole* is the subsequent activation of certain of its resources by the speaking subject. But the priority of one over the other is of a peculiar sort: it is both unconditional and indeterminant. That is to say, an individual speech-act can only execute certain general linguistic laws, if it is to be communication at all. But at the same time, the *laws* can never explain the *act* ... A total initial determinism paradoxically ends in the reinstatement of an absolute final contingency, in mimicry of the duality of *langue* and *parole* itself. The most striking example of this irony is Derrida's work ... Writing is ... inescapably the same in its general structure and inexplicably differing and deferring in its particular textualizations.[44]

Derrida eludes Anderson's net insofar as he theorizes the agon of history and is caught by it insofar as he does not. Derrida's seeming ambivalence in "Declarations" is explicit in "Differance":

I will say, first of all, that differance, which is neither a word nor a concept, seemed to me to be strategically the theme most proper to think out, if not master (. . .), in what is most characteristic of our "epoch." I start off, then, strategically, from the place and time in which "we" are, even though my

43 Or as in Brummett's deriving different positions in gay rights controversies from act:agent on one side and agent:act on the other.
44 *In the Tracks of Historical Materialism*, The Wellek Library Lectures (London: Verso, 1983), pp. 48, 50.

opening is not justifiable in the final account, and though it is always on the basis of differance and its "history" that we can claim to know who and where "we" are and what the limits of an "epoch" can be.[45]

Rhetorical realism would say that we simultaneously share an "epoch" and struggle over the definition of its substance.

Anderson's critique may be analogized, along the lines suggested in the last chapter, to Aristotle's of Plato. Excesses of formalism keep apart what the pentad and the constitution are designed to put together — although perhaps not altogether successfully, judging from the marginalization of the constitution in the reception of *GM*. On the one hand, *GM* is structuralist insofar as the pentad decenters the subject in the structuralist and poststructuralist sense. In the first paragraph of "The Philosophic Schools," Burke accentuates that the pentad is conceived as "anticipat[ing]" individual discourses: "In treating the various schools as languages, we may define their substantial relationship to one another by deriving them from a common terminological ancestor . . . an Edenic 'pre-language,' in which the seeds of all philosophic languages would be implicit" (127). In short, the pentad speaks us. Consider also how — in the context of his retrospective comment, noted earlier, that the ratios are the pentad's most important feature, and in response to William F. Irmscher's equation of the pentad to topoi like Aristotle's — Burke contrasts himself to Aristotle: "My job was not to help a writer decide what he might say to produce a text. It was to help a critic perceive what was going on in a text that was already written" (QAP 332).[46] In other words, instead of centering the writer in a position of control over topoi, Burke deconstructively conceives the writer as posterior to and apt to forget them. Burke reads against the grain of a text to uncover the dialect of "pentadese" that it speaks whether it knows it or not.

On the other hand, *GM* protects itself from Anderson's critique by supplementing the pentad with the constitution. The pentadic linguistic laws are executed in the constitutional act. Connecting the pentad to the constitution more visibly would have required Burke to add to his pentadic readings of texts constitutional readings situating them as acts in the conversation of their day. Occasionally, there is a short step in that direction, as when Burke turns to Kant (186–87), but never more

45 *Speech and Phenomena: And Other Essays on Husserl's Theory of Signs*, trans. David B. Allison (Evanston: Northwestern University Press, 1973), pp. 135–36.
46 For Irmscher's equation, see *The Holt Guide to English: A Contemporary Handbook of Rhetoric, Language, and Literature* (New York: Holt, Rinehart, and Winston, 1972), p. 28.

than that. Reading texts both pentadically and constitutionally would have made a long book much longer, perhaps even putting it in competition with Richardson's *Clarissa*. The only alternative would have been to read far fewer texts, a choice that would have weakened *GM*'s rhetoric in the conversation of its day. As comprehensive a survey as possible was essential. At the end of *GM*'s introduction Burke contrasts "synoptic" and "historical" strategies for achieving comprehensiveness, and it's clear that the most economical strategy is the synoptic method of classification and exemplification that *GM* deploys (xxii–xxiii). Lentricchia castigates structuralism and the pentad for their "voracious synchronic totalization" (67). However valid this judgment when viewed from our standpoint in the 1990s, at the initial stage of a constructionist reorientation like Burke's in the 1940s and structuralism's later, the rhetorical situation requires a totalizing strategy. If one can't find a constructionist ingredient in everything, one is vulnerable to the charge that one has left some things out simply because they are without any such ingredient. Burke needed a comprehensive demonstration that texts speak "pentadese" whether they know it or not. Only later, when the constructionist premise is established, can one dispense with such totalizing and its admitted liabilities.

Constitutional analysis uncovers the rhetorical situation within which the pentad functions, as is relatively easy to see when considering a text such as President Reagan's 27 October 1983 speech to the nation, which was prompted by the bombing in Beirut that killed more than 200 Marines and the invasion of Grenada the same week.[47] The voluntaristic principles assumed in Reagan's speech are principally three: (1) the wish for national security, (2) the wish to be proud of US acts in the world, and (3) the wish not to see US soldiers die on foreign soil. The necessitarian problem, made dramatic by the Beirut disaster, is that satisfying (1) and (2) can preclude satisfying (3). Reagan's rhetorical problem is to sell the sacrifice of US life, as is evident from the question posed early in the speech, "Why should our young men be dying in Lebanon?" This loss of life must be given enough rhetorical weight to give these men great respect – respect needed to motivate other young men to put their lives on the line – yet not so much weight as to interfere with Reagan's foreign policy. The unifying pentadic term needed to solve this rhetorical problem is the one that

47 *The New York Times* printed the speech on 28 October 1983.

offers the best strategy available, in Reagan's historical situation, to make this case. References to the Soviet threat appear here, as is usual in Cold War rhetoric, but 1983 was post-Vietnam, a time when this threat was still necessary but not always sufficient in such rhetoric. The pentadic category that solves Reagan's rhetorical problem is "agent." Reagan's closing paragraphs spotlight not the Soviet threat – the "scene" – but bravery: a Marine in a hospital, with an extraordinary number of tubes entering and exiting his body, writes on a pad "semper fi," which Reagan elaborately explains is shorthand for the Marine motto, "Semper Fidelis, Always Faithful." US machismo is Reagan's idealist substance, the hierarchizing principle in his symbolic act that interprets the necessitarian imperative in his rhetorical situation.[48]

A text that suggests how Burke conceived the need to deploy pentadic and constitutional analysis in tandem is "Symbolic Action in a Poem by Keats" (SAK), published in 1943 and reprinted as an appendix to *GM*. *GM* is correcting this essay when, as we saw, Burke stresses that the novelty in the act should not be confused with Coleridge's view of poetry as a "dim analogue of Creation," because romantic idealism is based on the agent rather than the act. For this essay confuses precisely this point as it equates this "dim analogue" to action (SAK 455). This confusion can be traced to an attempt to map the idealism of "Ode on a Grecian Urn" directly onto the structure of the act, an attempt that in the end Burke abandons: "Unfortunately, I must break the symmetry a little. For poetry as conceived in idealism (romanticism) could not quite be equated with *act* ... [W]e might use the italicizing resources of dialectic by saying that for Keats, beauty (poetry) was not so much 'the *act* of an agent' as it was 'the act of an *agent*'" (460). This concession signals a problem that *GM* solves by making the constitution the model for the act. Within this model, there is a role for substance, which may be played by any of the "isms" that the pentad distinguishes, including of course Keats's idealism. Rewriting the Keats essay from the standpoint of *GM*, one could feature agent from the beginning and simply say that it is primary in Keats's act, which hierarchizes competing discourses in its historical context, specifically the discourses of science and poetry, in "'estheticizing' the

---

48 See Birdsell for a purely pentadic analysis of this speech, one selected, moreover, to illustrate Burkean analysis in an anthology designed to exhibit the major critical methods used in speech communication. In such analysis, the rhetorical functioning of pentadic terms is often observed, but without the benefit of a constitutional analysis of the rhetorical situation, precisely the analysis most essential in a Burkean analysis of a text as a symbolic act.

true" (459). The act selects the pentadic term that organizes the dialect of "pentadese" articulated in the act. Acts come in the form of many different isms.

The constitution and the pentad ultimately seem to entail one another as they put together what Anderson faults structuralism and poststructuralism for keeping apart. Because the pentadic terms always, as quoted earlier (p. 139), "seemed to 'cluster about [Burke's] thoughts about the Constitution as an 'enactment,'" Burke is actually coming full circle when, in turning to the constitution, in *GM*'s third and last part, he immediately indicates that, like any typical systematic terminology of motivation, it incorporates all the pentadic terms (341). *GM*'s theorizing of the act begins and ends with the constitution. The pentad is the loop from one to the other. It became a big loop as Burke found himself writing *GM* instead of the chapter he originally envisioned, "The Constitutional Wish," in a process that he analogizes, as noted earlier (p. 138), to being cornered by a relentless interrogator. For he found in the pentad the answer that finally quieted this interrogator.

Burke saw in the constitution a terminology with which to theorize symbolic action. The problem, as the interrogation suggests, was to legitimate this terminology. Previously, he buttressed his case with the prestige of Marxist and Freudian discourses, as in *ATH*'s Freudo-Marxism. But as we'll see in the next chapter, *RM* decisively makes both these discourses posterior to dramatism. In effect, Freud and Marx helped Burke get to symbolic action, but once he got to it, he ironically used it to leave them behind. He left them behind, however, for a constructionism difficult to legitimate in the absence of the widespread rhetorical support for it today.

His constructionism is evident when he introduces "act" not by empirically observing that people act but by considering implications of the pentad, noting that one tends to look for motives of action under "the heading of *scene, agent, agency,* or *purpose,* but hardly under the heading of *act,*" a tendency that robs the act of its distinguishing feature: "[T]here could be *novelty* only if there were likewise a locus of motivation within the act itself, a newness not already present in elements classifiable under any of the other four headings" (65). For Burke, one must begin with terms because they shape observations: "Not only does the nature of our terms affect the nature of our observations, in the sense that the terms direct the *at*tention to one field rather than to another. Also *many of the 'observations' are but* *implications of the particular terminology in terms of which the observations are made"* (TS 46). Because it's an act, a terminology is a selection. It's active, simultaneously a reflection and a deflection, not a passive mirror. Burke's problem, in sum, was to convince his interrogator, in a context dominated by positivist semantics, that one must start with terms rather than observations. To make his case, he looked for terms behind all observations: the pentad. Behind the pentadic terms, there is nothing; they can only be applied: "If you ask why, with a whole world of terms to choose from, we select these rather than some others as basic, our book itself is offered as the answer. For, to explain our position, we shall show how it can be applied" (xv).

But as the big loop from the constitution back to the constitution, the pentad never stops making the case for the act, which is the claim of claims in the dramatistic view of language as action. In a later text, Burke even indicates that if he were to rewrite *GM*, he would reconceive the pentad so that scene, agent, agency, and purpose would be viewed as all implicit in the term "act" (*DD* 21). In *GM* itself, circumference is deployed as a grammatical principle to insure that discourses are legitimated as grammatical only if they, in their varying ways, legitimate action. In the pentad, all roads lead to the act – that is, to the constitution.

The pentad and the constitution coalesce in "The Dialectic of Constitutions," where Burke uses the pentad to lay out a terminology of motivation featuring "act" as its key term. One can read the pentad as the container of the constitution, since Burke's constitutional terminology of action can be placed alongside the other terminologies of action surveyed in the chapter "Act." But this reading becomes structuralist if it isn't qualified by the reverse reading in which the constitution is the container of the pentad. For it is the constitutional act that instantiates uses of the pentadic grammar in the agon of history.

Lentricchia's reproof that the pentad is a structuralist totalization registers the current widespread suspicion of totalizing discourse. The pentadic topoi are most useful if positioned alongside others in a field of places with no commanding place of places that totalizes them typologically. There is no place of places, only different places. Any discourse privileges something in organizing itself, making itself readable as putting forward a place of places, but in reality all it is doing is trying to shape the conversation's agenda, saying in effect "rather than talk at that place, let's talk at this one and let's do so in this way." The present discourse is no exception. The Burkean conversation –

with its rhetorical commensurability, which distinguishes it from the Rortyian conversation – swallows us all.

By now, some readers may have wondered why, even though the term "substance" appeared in this chapter many pages ago, nothing has yet been said about *GM*'s paradox of substance, which Lentricchia highlights by identifying with Derrida's undecidability (74), and which is the theme of a whole chapter, "Antinomies of Definition." Perhaps foregrounding "Antinomies" by considering it in the final section of the present chapter can compensate for the neglect of it thus far, especially since its neglect is more apparent than real insofar as this paradox's deconstructive theme has been a major concern, so much so that relatively little needs to be said about "Antinomies."

The notion of "economic man," suggests Burke in one example, reveals "the paradox of substance in that the given subject both is and is not the same as the character with which and by which it is identified" (32). This example reminds one of Defoe's Crusoe, who is often identified as an embodiment of economic man. As a substance defining human nature, economic man is a hierarchizing principle. Crusoe as son is subordinated to Crusoe as entrepreneur, and this subordination of family is further accentuated when his life as husband and father is reduced to a few words: "I marry'd, and that not either to my Disadvantage or Dissatisfaction, and had three Children, two Sons and one Daughter: But my Wife dying . . ." – that is the last we hear about wife or children as Crusoe goes on, in the novel's closing paragraphs, to record how his nephew, a voyager himself, prompted his own return to his island. Further, considering that Crusoe comes from a culture not shy about sex, his lack of sexual desire is another striking hierarchical subordination, one that Michel Tournier revises in *Vendredi*, his 1967 rewriting of Defoe's novel. Being marooned alone does nothing to diminish the hierarchical prominence of sexual desire in Tournier's Crusoe. The possibility of such re-hierarchizing confirms Burke's point that a definition of substance is and is not at one with what it defines. If there were simply the "is" without the "is not," a definition could get it right, identifying the one true hierarchization fixed once and for all time in "human nature." The "is not" marks the gap that insures that "economic man" is simply *a* rather than *the* substance.

The paradox of substance is as much a paradox of definition as of substance. Substances of various sorts provide Burke his main examples throughout "Antinomies," but these serve to illustrate a paradox of definition that Burke claims could be found in the definition of anything at all (24). The paradox of substance arises from, Burke makes explicit, "the systematic contemplation of the antinomies attendant upon the fact that we necessarily define a thing in terms of something else" (33). Between the "thing" and the "something else" – *definiendum* and *definiens* – there is always a difference that when scrutinized reveals that this "something else" is an act of selection, a construction as much as a representation. Burke's act of creation, as a definition of the act, is and is not the act: it defines the "modicum" of novelty in the act that is and is not the act. In taking us to the heart of the matter, definition falsifies the matter, thereby exemplifying "the paradox of purity" (35–38). Because of this antinomy of definition there is always a difference between discourse and its subject-matter such that discourse can never efface itself – no philosophical presence, only rhetorical topoi. The paradox of definition generalizes the pun that Burke finds in the term "substance." The term names a thing's essence but refers to something beneath the thing: substance is "sub-stance" (22):

But returning to the pun...the word "substance," used to designate what a thing *is*, derives from a word designating something that a thing *is not* ... [T]he word in its etymological origins would refer to an attribute of the thing's *context*, since that which supports or underlies a thing would be a part of the thing's context. And a thing's context, being outside or beyond the thing, would be something that the thing is *not*. (23)

As this example suggests, Burke takes puns seriously.

An ambiguity arises in Burke as he sometimes speaks of symbolic or verbal action, which implies that there is action without language, while at other times he speaks simply of action, as in the first sentence of "Act," a chapter in "The Philosophic Schools," "Since our entire book illustrates the featuring of act, there is less call for a special section on it" (227). An example may help to clarify the sense in which language is not only itself action but also the condition of action in general, for the linguisticity of action is the basis of dramatism's opposition to behaviorism. Language works, Burke suggests in "Terministic Screens," by means of "terms that put things together, and terms that take things apart" (TS 49). In teaching, I've illustrated Burke's point with a puzzler, now getting old but still capable of stumping some students: a father and son are driving, the car crashes and the father dies at the scene of the accident, the son is rushed to a hospital and into its operating room, the surgeon on duty is called, the surgeon arrives, takes one look at the boy, and says, "I can't operate on my son." This narrative puzzles if and only if the term "surgeon" is constituted as entailing the term "male": the father is dead — how can he turn up in the operating room? But once there is a reconstitution that allows "surgeon" to go with "female" as well as "male," the puzzle disappears. A student in one class challenged this interpretation, arguing that male and surgeon go together simply because in our experience everytime we see a surgeon it's a male; language has nothing to do with it. A confirmed empiricist, this student took the world as it appears "before our eyes." But this empirical world is a culture hierarchized for us by a constitution that put "male" and "surgeon" together and regulated action accordingly, such that while surgery occurs in a material world — the patient bleeds — the act of surgery is nonetheless cultural, one sign of this being the use of biological difference to suit agents to this act. Language no less than action involves the materiality of the world — speaking and writing involve the materiality of the body in their production — but it is language that constitutes in this materiality the culturality of action.

"Dialectically considered (that is, 'dramatistically' considered) men are not only *in nature*," Burke postulates. "The cultural accretions made possible by the language motive become a 'second nature' with them. Here again we confront the ambiguities of substance, since symbolic communication is not a merely external instrument, but also intrinsic to men as agents" (*GM* 33). Language is not apart from the world, epistemologically commenting on it literally or meta-phorically, but a part of it, constituting our Althusserian "lived relation" to the real. The analysis of motives must begin with verbal action but more than language is involved by virtue of acts being in the world (33). In his reading of Burke, Southwell argues that "language creates the alternatives that require the choice that is the act" (32).[49] But this formulation is only partially right: language creates voluntaristic principles, but the necessity of choice among them arises from the necessitarian principle that imposes itself because language is in the world. Neglect of the necessitarian risks abstracting the act from the world. The constitution is a rhetorical substance: on the one hand, the necessitarian forces the act; on the

---

49 Southwell goes on to insist that there must be something "beyond language" that makes the choice (33), a beyond that in his view is metaphysical. For a strong critique of his metaphysical reading of Burke, see McWhorter and Williams.

other, the act of language is a rhetorical invention. The act is determined in being necessary and undetermined in being free to be this hierarchization or that. The new is possible.

Burke calls his constitution an ontology (336–37). As such, dramatism seems to be an oxymoron: a rhetorical ontology. What entitles rhetoric to ontological status resides in the paradox that language is beyond the reach of its own constructive power. It can construct and reconstruct but it is itself a reality that cannot be constructed out of existence. Burke opposes his ontology to historical narrative unified, like Lukács's, by a futuristic promise (332–36). The verbal act is not a predestined moment in a narrative with a direction but a transformation *in medias res* in a postmodern narrative with neither beginning nor end. Burke's ontology is the act at the transhistorical level, where it is simultaneously apart from and a part of history. In claiming ontological status for rhetoric, however, one should not claim too much. As a transhistorical structure, the constitution could disappear from the universe – history disappearing with it – and the universe would still be here. The constitution is and is not an ontology.

7

A *Rhetoric of Motives*: ideological and utopian rhetoric

... pure persuasion in the absolute sense exists nowhere ...   Burke, *RM*

... the effectively ideological is also, at the same time, necessarily Utopian ...
Jameson, *Political Unconscious*

Under Burke's criterion of circumference, many terminologies qualify as grammatical. Equally grammatical terminologies, however, may not work equally well in a specific situation. By what criterion, in the absence of an epistemological criterion of truth, can one choose among the available grammatical alternatives?

In confronting this wide range in the choice of circumference for the location of an act, men confront what is distinctively the human freedom and the human necessity. This necessity is a freedom insofar as the choice of circumference leads to an *adequate* interpretation of motives; and it is an enslavement insofar as the interpretation is *inadequate* ... (*GM* 84; my italics)

Burke borrows this notion of adequacy – equally applicable to the choice of substance, circumference's companion – from Spinoza, who thought that "through the cultivation of 'adequate ideas,' one could transform the passives (of human bondage) into the actives (of human freedom)" (*GM* 139).[1]

Dramatism, Burke indicates, prefers Spinoza to Descartes: Descartes put in place the epistemological subject–object opposition that dramatism is designed to displace, whereas Spinoza's adequate idea puts a dramatistic emphasis on activity and passivity, "freedom" and "enslavement" (*GM* 146–47). But Burke revises Spinoza by considering activity and passivity not in Spinoza's metaphysical context but in the dramatistic context of act and historical situation. For instance, in Burke's example of Parkes, considered in the last chapter (p. 148), the

---

1 For a discussion of this notion, see Feehan, "Co Haggling" and Wess, "Question."

adequacy of the market that Parkes posits as his circumference depends on the extent to which the market is a constitution to end the constitutional game of changing the rules of the game in the play of the game. In other words, does it constitute a world in which everyone can function materially and in which no one benefits at the expense of anyone else? The classical argument for the market's adequacy is Adam Smith's "invisible hand," which putatively transforms individual self-aggrandizement into social gain through capitalist accumulation, such that there is the adequacy of activity without passivity, as the activity of license to pursue individual gain produces an accumulation from which everyone benefits. Has Smith's prophecy proved true?[2] Is continuous accumulation, the prophecy's linchpin, compatible with the ecological health of the planet?

This revision of Spinoza appears in Burke's "Dramatist Grammar for Marxism," which "'class-angl[es]' Spinoza's solution of the problem as to when ideas are 'active'" (*GM* 212–13). Burke presents his combination of Marx and Spinoza in a series of twenty-three propositional paragraphs, six of which are quoted below. In these Burke also broadens the term "property" beyond its normal meaning:

(1) Each social class, insofar as it has a way of life distinct from that of other classes, is distinct in *actus*, hence in *status*.

(2) Its distinctness in status involves a corresponding distinctness in *properties*. ("Properties" here comprising any kind of characteristics: A house is a property, a way of speaking or thinking is a property, even a condition of total impoverishment is, in this usage, a property.)

(5) From the standpoint of society as a whole, an idea is "active" insofar as it is "adequate" (that is, insofar as it does accurately name the benign and malign properties of that society).

(14) Insofar as the changes of property relations would produce the desired betterment of society as a whole, the revolutionary effort is rational, hence active.

(17) Insofar as the [revolutionary] act succeeds, a new status is established.

(21) Insofar as all members of a society profit by the new status, the passion of class antagonism is transformed into the action of general cooperation.

(211–12; numbers added)

In a retrospective comment, Burke identifies the 1930s as the time that he began thinking of property less as a thing than a function, such that "manifestations as varied as jobs, honors, and familial

2 See Wess, "Question," for an argument that from the standpoint of rhetoric the judgment of truth, in the sense of adequacy, is a prophecy. To equate truth in this sense to prophecy is equivalent to saying that it's under the jurisdiction of deliberative rhetoric, as distinct from forensic and epideictic, as Aristotle defines these in the first book of his *Rhetoric*.

affection could all be rated as kinds of private property, with corresponding kinds of personal gratification, that in turn had their corresponding kinds of personal unrest insofar as the gratifications were, or seemed to be, threatened or withheld" (*CS* 216). One can see Burke broadening the notion of property from an economic to a cultural context in *ATH*'s inclusion in its "Dictionary of Pivotal Terms" of notions such as "'Earning' One's World," "Repossess the World," and "Stealing Back and Forth of Symbols."

"The Identifying Nature of Property," an early chapter in *RM*, stresses that all such properties can become sites of struggles. The subject is

surround[ed] ... with properties that name his number or establish his identity ... [But] its relation to other entities that are likewise forming their identity in terms of property can lead to turmoil and discord. Here is *par excellence* a topic to be considered in a rhetoric having "identification" as its key term. And we see why one should expect to get much insight from Marxism, as a study of capitalistic rhetoric.   (24)

Burke indicates, in responding to Jameson's critique, that it was through reading Marx that he shifted from *CS*'s conception of ideology as belief to *RM*'s rhetoricized conception of it as identification (MP 402–03). Drawing on Marx on the one hand, however, Burke distances himself from him on the other, as he proposes in *RM* that linguistic classification is "'prior' to classification in the exclusively social sense. The 'invidious' aspects of class arise from the nature of man not as a 'class animal,' but as a 'classifying animal'" (282–83). Starting with language in this fashion allows one to broaden the terrain of ideological analysis in ways that have become familiar in contemporary theory. Conceived in Burke's cultural sense, properties function in identifications of varying sorts, not only class, but also ethnicity, gender, race, sexual orientation – all current sites of struggle in the agon between monoculture and multiculture. Such properties have long qualified some at the expense of others in ideas of property relations – sexist, racist, homophobic, and so on – whose "adequacy" is now contested.

As theorized in *RM*, rhetoric derives its incentive from the oppositions and alignments in the Burkean conversation:

In pure identification there would be no strife. Likewise, there would be no strife in absolute separateness ... But put identification and division ambiguously together, so that you cannot know for certain just where one ends and the other begins, and you have the characteristic invitation to rhetoric. Here is a major reason why rhetoric, according to Aristotle, "proves opposites." (25)

As we saw in chapter 1, Therborn's theory of ideology as the interpellation of subjects overlaps with Aristotle's *Rhetoric*. It also overlaps with Burke's *RM*, as Therborn charts an "ideological universe" containing multiple bases for identification and division. Therborn stresses that in even the most class-polarized societies, other ideologies will unite those divided by class and divide those united by it.[3] For example, Joseph Urgo shows how some proletarian fiction depicts workers united in opposition to their bosses but divided in various ways as men and women.[4]

In the interplay between division and identification, rhetoric is both ideological and utopian. This tension can be found even in the subject, Burke suggests, when one broadens rhetoric beyond its traditional bounds to encompass

an intermediate area of expression that is not wholly deliberate, yet not wholly unconscious...For instance, a man who identifies his private ambitions with the good of the community may be partly justified, partly unjustified. He may be using a mere pretext to gain individual advantage at the public expense; yet he may be quite sincere, or even may willingly make sacrifices in behalf of such identification. (*RM* xiv)

In "Rhetoric – Old and New" (RON), Burke proposes, "The key term for the old rhetoric was 'persuasion' and its stress was upon deliberate design. The key term for the 'new' rhetoric would be 'identification,' which can include a partially 'unconscious' factor in appeal" (203).

In the old rhetoric, Burke thus suggests, the rhetor was centered, whereas his new rhetoric decenters the rhetor in introducing a level of motivation beyond its deliberate control. A similar decentering occurs in Bender and Wellbery's account of the contemporary revival of rhetoric, considered at the beginning of chapter 1. Their terms for old and new are "rhetoric" and "rhetoricality": "Certain old rhetorical terms have come to designate general processes...across the entire field of discourse, that are anterior to any instrumental choices a writer might make...Exactly this shift in the theoretical function and significance of concepts is what we are calling the move from rhetoric to rhetoricality." This contrast appeals to contemporary theory, which

3 *The Ideology of Power and the Power of Ideology* (London: Verso, 1980), pp. 22–26.
4 "Proletarian Literature and Feminism: The Gastonia Novels and Feminist Protest," *the minnesota review* ns 24 (1985): 64–84.

views itself as breaking radically with the past, but classical rhetoric may not be as centered as is thought. Bender and Wellbery's own narrative of the blow romanticism dealt rhetoric ironically calls into question their claim about "rhetoricality": "the evacuation from cultural memory of the topoi — those dense and finely branched semantic clusters that had since antiquity governed discursive invention — coincided exactly with the emergence of Romanticism." In other words, it appears that classical topoi stood so much in the way of the romantic centering of the subject that they had to be forgotten.[5]

RM makes the *SM* Burke projected a redundancy. In his critique of Burke, Jameson claims that Burke never theorizes his way out of the rhetoric of individualism, even though he "anticipated many of the fundamental objections to such a rhetoric of self and identity" (521). Jameson's claim applies to *ATH*, but not to Burke across the board. Even in *ATH* there is a step beyond individualism as well as a lapse into it. In responding to Jameson, Burke insists that he distinguishes individuation by the body from the very different individuation by culture: "I locate the *individual* (as distinct from the kind of 'ideological' identity that is intended in a social term, such as 'individualism') in the human body, the 'original economic plant,' distinct from all others owing to the divisive centrality of each body's particular nervous system" (MP 404; see also M/A 813–14). The ideological individual, Burke agrees, "dissolves into quite a complexity of *identifications* in the sociopolitical realm" (MP 413). Since this ideological individual seems to be the "unique individual" envisioned as *SM*'s focus (*RM* 21), Burke's recognition of it as an ideological construct may explain his tabling of *SM*. If the subject of individualism is simply one subject alongside others, there is no reason to privilege it as a separate theoretical category, meriting the independent treatment that *SM* promised. One may claim that individualism is central in modern culture, but that is a historical rather than a theoretical claim.

RM rhetorically demystifies individualism in demonstrating that specific modes of it are effects of orthodoxy. *RM*'s technical term for orthodoxy is "consubstantiality": "A doctrine of *consubstantiality*, either explicit or implicit, may be necessary to any way of life ... [A]

<hr />

5 "Rhetoricality: On the Modernist Return of Rhetoric," *The Ends of Rhetoric: History, Theory, Practice,* eds. John Bender and David E. Wellbery (Stanford University Press, 1990), pp. 30, 15–16. Notably, the chapter that Burke devotes to his decentering term "identification" draws heavily on topoi (55–59).

way of life is an *acting-together*; and in acting together, men have common sensations, concepts, images, ideas, attitudes that make them *consubstantial*" (21). A parallel to these demystifications appears in a later text, Burke's essay on Austin.

Austin's "I," Burke claims, is a "methodologically grammatical excursion around such prior approaches, as with German metaphysicans who build from an Absolute Ego..." (WD 156). Austin would no doubt be upset to see himself put on the same platform with Hegel, but a claim similar to Burke's appears in Gasché's critique of speech-act theory, which suggests that Austin looks different when considered from the standpoint of continental rather than analytical philosophy. To illustrate, Gasché shrewdly spotlights a passage in Austin that speech-act theorists generally ignore, one where a quasi-Hegelian subject of history makes an appearance: "[H]istorically, from the point of view of the evolution of language, the explicit performative must be a later development than certain more primary utterances... 'Bull' or 'Thunder' in a primitive language of one-word utterances could be a warning, information, a prediction, &c... [D]istinguishing the different *forces* that this utterance might have is a later achievement of language."[6] About this narrative, Gasché comments, "The becoming explicit of the 'I' as the utterer of a speech act is indeed the telos of Austin's history of language."[7] However different their contents, Austin's history parallels the form of Lukács's, examined in chapter 1. Austin's history is a sign that his "I" is transcendental.

Burke's rhetorical demystification of Austin's "I" builds on the premise that every speech act is "in the *collective* realm of 'culture'... [and] in each user's *individual* physiological 'nature'" (WD 168). The cultural "I" corresponds to action; the biological, to motion. This action–motion distinction forces itself on Austin's text as Austin contrasts (1) the uttering of noise, an effect of the motion of the vocal organs, to (2) the uttering of an illocution, an effect of "the conventions of illocutionary force as bearing on the special circumstances of the occasion of the issuing of the utterance."[8] The blindness in Austin's text is that it never crosses the line that makes it possible to see the "we" in the cultural script as the condition of the "I" performing the speech act. Instead, the speech-act "I" is mistakenly identified with the biological "I." The "I"

---

6 *How to Do Things with Words*, ed. J. O. Urmson (New York: Oxford University Press, 1965), pp. 71–72.
7 "'Setzung' and 'Übersetzung': Notes on Paul de Man," *Diacritics* 11 (1981): 38.
8 *How to Do*, p. 114.

that makes a promise is a scripted character that can inhabit an indefinite number of bodies and is not to be confused with the body that it happens to inhabit in any instance of promising.

Burke's distinction between biological individuation and cultural individualism appears in *RM*'s chapter devoted to Veblen, which demystifies the competitive individualism of capitalism, whose prototype is Crusoe, his epic enterprise on his island mythically rooted in the "state of nature." "[W]hen you discuss competition as it has actually operated in our society," Burke counters, "you discover that the so-called ways of competition have been almost fanatically zealous ways of *conformity* . . . From the standpoint of 'identification' what we call 'competition' is better described as men's attempt to *out-imitate* one another" (131). Burke spells out his theoretical premise, "Imitation is an essentially dramatistic concept. It makes for consubstantiality by community of ways ('identification')" (131). Competitive individuals "out-imitate" one another in conforming to the cultural script of the competitive individual. This conformity, which ironically sets them at odds, is "constitutional," an orthodoxy, one mode of consubstantiality among others. The same is true of the various modes of romantic authenticity, such as the example of automatic writing that we saw in chapter 1. Automatic writing is freedom from orthodoxy authorized by orthodoxy.

This distinction between biological individuation and cultural individualism doesn't lessen Burke's interest in the body. If anything, it increases it. What changes is that the body is emptied of the humanistic motives that *PC* attributes to it as Burke goes to the opposite extreme to separate the body from complications that language adds. In "The Thinking of the Body," he even feels compelled to X-rate his scrutiny of texts for imagistic "connotations of physical excretion" to forewarn readers who wish not to cross the boundary of what is "suitable for discussion in the drawing room" (TB 308). In the case of the competitive individual, Burke concedes that to a point one can find an antecedent biological level in the acquisitiveness that animal behavior evinces but counters, "once a high development of public property has accumulated, private property is rather a function of that accumulation than an expression of the original biologic goading that is located in the divisive centrality of the nervous system. The cult of property comes to reflect public norms, norms identified with social classes which are differentiated by property" (130). There is, of course, no bright line between these two levels, bodily motion and cultural action. For Burke, action never occurs independently of motion, and there is interplay between the two levels, in both directions. Angelism, the thesis that the intellect is independent of the body, is explicitly rejected (SAU 345). All these qualifications notwithstanding, there is a difference, one that explains why Crusoe's behavior on his island cannot be reduced to "biologic goading."

In his response to Jameson, Burke cites the demystification of individualism appearing in *RM*'s chapter on La Rochefoucauld's *Maxims*: "I note how the individualist aspect of the *Maxims* can be analyzed as an 'ideology,' insofar as the strategic concept of 'self-love' involves identification with a 'courtly morality'" (MP 404). Burke sees this "individualist aspect" as bourgeois individualism filtered through an aristocratic terministic screen, since he suggests that "self-love" is an aristocratically dyslogistic term that counters such eulogistic bourgeois terms "as 'ambition,' 'private enterprise,' perhaps even 'dignity of the individual' and 'respect for the person'" (149). In La Rochefoucauld's analysis self-love appears not once but twice: the courtier's "devotion to princes is a second self-love" (147). Second self-love, Burke suggests, exhibits "such reversal as Marx sees in 'ideology'" (147). That is, self-love is a class orthodoxy, deriving from the courtly rhetoric of advantage, but La Rochefoucauld projects it backwards onto the individual as something inborn, so that when he turns to this rhetoric he calls it a "second" self-love, deriving it from the inborn first. Burke concludes, "following a Marxist kind of analysis, we would contend that La Rochefoucauld has the two motives [class orthodoxy and individual] 'ideologically' reversed" (147). Had La Rochefoucauld read Hegel, Burke quips, self-love might have become a subject of history: "he would probably have given the second self-love some such title as *Ur-Höflichkeit*, to designate an innate, 'pre-historic' tendency towards courtship, an 'idea' which, in its evolution towards self-consciousness, at one stage of its historical unfolding manifested itself both as a devotion to princes and as *amour-propre*" (148). The individualism of self-love, which La Rochefoucauld posits as prior to courtier orthodoxy, is actually posterior to it. The dog wags the tail, in short, not the tail the dog.

Burke's critique of La Rochefoucauld, *mutatis mutandis*, applies to any individualism, including any *SM* might have theorized. For any individualism must someday find a "second" version of itself upon encountering the orthodoxy – the consubstantiality – that produced it. From the standpoint of *RM* one can reconsider *ATH*'s Freudian individualism, which serves, as we saw, to theorize that accepting and rejecting symbols of authority occurs in the final analysis at the Freudian level of pre-forensic singability rather than the public level of forensic sayability. This Freudian eloquence is uncovered by Burke with his cluster or "dream" analysis, designed to uncover those equations or associational linkages unique to the individual. Applying *RM*'s critique of La Rochefoucauld to *ATH*, this unique individual would correspond to La Rochefoucauld's first self-love, since *ATH* posits Freudian eloquence as the site of acceptance and rejection across history. What would correspond to second self-love — that is, what historically situated orthodoxy is responsible for Freudian eloquence, as the courtier orthodoxy is for self-love?

CS and *PC* suggest ways to situate Freudian eloquence historically. *CS* classifies historical periods as objective or subjective. In an objective age there is "a general agreement as to what is heroic, what cowardly, what irreligious, what boorish, what clever, etc." (192). When this agreement breaks down, the writer is forced to retreat from the objective to the subjective: "he will, that is, tend to found his art upon an irreducible minimum of belief. This irreducible minimum is, obviously, his personal range of experiences, his own exaltations and depressions, his specific kinds of triumph and difficulty" (194). Singability depends on a bedrock of associational linkages, but history decides whether this bedrock is communal or individualistic. As we saw earlier, in chapters 3 and 5, *PC* applies this contrast in analyzing its contemporary context, where the bedrock is more individualistic than communal (58). This individualistic orthodoxy valorizes Freudian eloquence. In this situation, a "second" Freudian individual appears, encountering the orthodoxy from which it derives. *PC* envisions a return to eloquence in the traditional, "objective" sense, but in the interim, Freudian eloquence is the best available.

RM explicitly faults psychoanalysis for concealing social conflicts behind "terms of the universally sexual and the universally famil-ial . . . speciously universal terms" (280). This "error is not rectified," Burke adds, "by a stress upon individualistic aggression, compensation, inferiority, and the like. For individualism acts as strongly as universalism to conceal the 'mysteries' of class" (280). Burke may seem to contradict himself when he goes on to propose that psychoanalysis errs in making "the 'unconscious-irrational,' a psychological source . . . [prior to] the *dialectical*, a formal source" (283).[9] But this proposal appears on

---

9 This statement makes explicit what is already implicit in "Freud — And the Analysis of Poetry," where Burke proposes that Freud's "critique of the family . . . [suggests] ways in which the informative experience with familiar [sic] roles may be carried over, or 'metaphored,' into the experience with extra familiar [sic] roles, giving these latter . . . a structure of interpretations and attitudes borrowed from the former" (FAP 284–85).

the same page as the one, quoted earlier, that we are a "classifying animal" first, and a "class animal" second; Burke's universalism, instead of concealing classificatory oppositions, directs attention to them. These two proposals together mark the distance between *ATH*'s Freudo-Marxism and *RM*'s rhetoric of the subject.

In a series of chapters early in *RM* (27–35), Burke analyzes the situation of the scientist in the US during the Cold War. An analogue to Therborn's worker-qua-body, Burke's scientist is a body constituted as a subject in the context of a conjunction of four subject positions: scientist, parent, citizen of a nation, and citizen of the world. Ideally, the four would reinforce one another in reproducing day in and day out a subject whose research as a scientist enhances its credibility as parent and citizen on the one hand, and contributes to building the society it desires as parent and citizen on the other. But the Cold War made such reproduction a problem rather than a foregone conclusion, for as scientific research fell under the direction of the military, scientific activity ran counter to concerns of parents and citizens. As the occasion for this crisis among subject positions, the Cold War is an analogue to Therborn's strike call.

This crisis exhibits the fashion in which the reproduction of the subject in particular intersects with the reproduction of the social formation in general, as a solution for a social formation pursuing militaristic aims becomes a problem for a scientist who, as parent and citizen, questions these aims. Reproduction of the formation works with the efficiency of a machine if and only if the hierarchization in each subject suits it to the needs of the formation. Althusser depicts such efficiency in sketching a formation in which each subject "is practically provided with the ideology which suits the role it has to fulfill in class society."[10] Such passages lend credence to a charge like Eagleton's that Althusser's theory of ideology is "functionalist" in making subjects cogs in a structuralist machine.[11] This charge weakens, however, when sufficient attention is paid to the significance of the theory's methodological starting-point: "reproduction." Althusser even says, "The ultimate condition of production is ... the reproduction of the conditions of production."[12]

---

10 "Ideology and Ideological State Apparatuses (Notes towards an Investigation)," *Lenin and Philosophy and Other Essays*, trans. Ben Brewster (New York: Monthly Review Press,1971), pp. 155–56.   11 "Ideology, Fiction, Narrative," *Social Text* 2 (1979): 62–63.
12 "Ideology," p. 127.

Althusser starts with reproduction; Lukács, with production. Lukács's theoretical bet is that alienation in the process of production will, by historical necessity, awaken proletarian consciousness to its predestined role. The loss of this bet teaches the lesson that Therborn exhibits in his example, where Lukács's discourse functions, in effect, as one discourse among others, all having varying rhetorical weights. Which discourse prevails is contingent, not predetermined. Reproduction is a machine only in the sense that it is a contingency that may break down, be repaired, or be adjusted — a point Althusser accentuates in his postscript to "Ideology and Ideological State Apparatuses." Reproduction thus provides a methodological standpoint from which to examine why Lukács lost his bet, as the breakdown he theorized didn't materialize. What repairs or adjustments staved off the breakdown?

Staving off breakdown in the reproduction of the scientist, Burke suggests, is the rhetorical weight of the discourse of the disciplinary autonomy of science, which legitimates scientific research regardless of its effect:

If the technical expert, as such, is assigned the task of perfecting new powers of chemical, bacteriological, or atomic destruction, his morality *as technical expert* requires only that he apply himself to his task as effectively as possible. The question of what the new force might mean, as ... surrendered to men whose *specialty* is *professional killing* — well, that is simply "none of his business," as specialist, however great may be his misgivings as father of a family, or as citizen of his nation and of the world. (30)

Autonomy, in such a case, is a strategy for living with fragmentation. This autonomy is essentializing as opposed to proportionalizing, not in the sense that Burke distinguishes these in his polemic with Freud, but in the sense that appears in constitutional analysis — the sense applied to Lukács in chapter 1 — where proportionalizing considers a measure from the standpoint of all the clauses in the Constitution and essentializing, from the standpoint of one clause alone. Essentializing in this sense is hierarchizing by marginalizing, a form that contemporary theory has made familiar — "false consciousness" is Lukács's marginalizing strategy. The rhetoric of the autonomy of science sustains the hierarchization needed for the reproduction of the social formation, but in a form that relates scientist to parent and citizen not by integration but by fragmentation — that's "none of his business."

Burke suggests that this fragmentation is a dramatic instance of a commonplace pattern, so common that it is taken for granted: "The extreme division of labor under late capitalist liberalism having made dispersion the norm and having transformed the state of Babel into an ideal, the true liberal must view almost as an affront the Rhetorical concern with identifications whereby the principles of a speciality cannot be taken...simply as the motives proper to that speciality" (30–31). Reproduction by Babelistic fragmentation thus effects a blindness that Foucault, a generation later, also sees as normative: "People know what they do; they frequently know why they do what they do; but what they don't know is what what they do does."[13] Reproduction became a crisis in the case of the scientist when the atomic bomb made it impossible for scientists not to know what they do does.

Lentricchia generalizes from Burke's critique of autonomy to define the proper function of the intellectual at the present time: the "writer, teacher...is always enrolled in (identified with), all democratic myths of the Adamic self to the contrary notwithstanding, a class or at least an 'interested' socioeconomic 'group.' To exist socially is to be rhetorically aligned. It is the function of the intellectual as critical rhetor to uncover...all such alignments" (148–49). The intellectual should function, in other words, as a countervailing power against fragmentation, aiming to transform rather than reproduce the social formation, trying to do for culture in general what the atomic bomb did for some scientists in particular.

RM's extensive consideration of the rhetoric of autonomy is the first extended illustration of the "invitation to rhetoric," defined as the interplay of identification and division making it possible, as noted earlier, to "prove opposites":

The fact that an activity is capable of reduction to intrinsic, autonomous principles does not argue that it is free from identification with other orders of motivation extrinsic to it...The human agent, *qua* human agent, is not

13 Quoted as a "personal communication" in Hubert L. Dreyfus and Paul Rabinow, *Michel Foucault: Beyond Structuralism and Hermeneutics*, afterword by Michel Foucault (University of Chicago Press, 1982), p. 187. Compare Roy Bhaskar, *Reclaiming Reality: A Critical Introduction to Contemporary Philosophy* (London: Verso, 1989), p. 80: "The conception I am proposing [of the relationship between society and people] is that people, in their conscious human activity, for the most part unconsciously reproduce (or occasionally, transform) the structures that govern their substantive activities of production. Thus people do not marry to reproduce the nuclear family, or work to reproduce the capitalist economy. But it is nevertheless the unintended consequence (and inexorable result) of, as it is also the necessary condition for, their activity." The parenthetical "or occasionally, transform" is more Burkean than Foucauldian.

motivated solely by the principles of a specialized activity ... Any specialized activity participates in a larger unit of action. "Identification" is a word for the autonomous activity's place in this wider context ... The shepherd, *qua* shepherd, acts for the good of the sheep ... But he may be "identified" with a project that is raising the sheep for market. (27)

Proving opposites here derives from the intrinsic–extrinsic topos.[14] The New Criticism, as the last chapter noted, put this topos at the center of the conversation at mid-century, the time of the writing of *RM*, and in fact Burke does digress briefly to consider the autonomy of art, concluding, "In accordance with the rhetorical principle of identification, whenever you find a doctrine of 'nonpolitical' esthetics affirmed with fervor, look for its politics" (28).

Fragmentation, for Burke, is not a postmodern absolutizing of fragmentation in which immobilization becomes the mobilization of choice. Rather, fragmentation is a state of rhetorical silence among subject positions. But this silence can be broken. Not even the silence of fragmentation is immune forever to the din of history. In the scientist's crisis, the rhetoric of silence is broken when its culture begins proving opposites, valorizing scientific activity from the intrinsic standpoint and questioning it from the extrinsic standpoint of parent and citizen. The potential for this crisis, by virtue of the intrinsic–extrinsic topos, was at hand at any time, but the atomic bomb in the agon of history brought the crisis to a head at a particular time. In this din, the scientist's crisis became a constitutional crisis. As the competition between the intrinsic rhetoric of autonomy and the extrinsic rhetoric of parent and citizen became a real one, a necessitarian imperative took form.

"Dual Possibilities of Science," the last chapter in the series devoted to the scientist, is in effect a consideration of different ways this

14 According to Aristotle (*Rhetoric* 1358a13–24), a topos, in the strictest sense, is universal. His example is "more or less," easily applicable to "essentially disconnected subjects – right conduct, natural science, or anything else whatever." The narrower the scope of the topos, "the nearer one comes, unconsciously, to setting up a science" (Ingram Bywater trans.). Derrida suggests how the intrinsic–extrinsic topos can be universalized when, as noted in chapter 3, he remarks that calling into question the classical philosophic opposition between essential and accidental attributes has always been the point of deconstruction. For the essential attributes of anything are "intrinsic," which makes everything else "extrinsic." Like fact–fiction, intrinsic–extrinsic is a distinction that we know, since we can recognize competing versions of it, yet we know it only through these competing versions. There is no metaphysical "presence," only the rhetorical presence of the conversation. Derrida teaches us how to see the intrinsic–extrinsic competition everywhere, thus qualifying it to stand alongside Aristotle's "more or less."

constitutional case might turn out. One possibility – the constitutional act or road not taken – was advocated by the Federation of American Scientists, who observed the second anniversary of Japan's surrender with a proclamation from which Burke quotes: "We assert that national security cannot result from military preparedness or the support of science for its war potential" (33). Whether this act would have been preferable to the road that was in fact taken is perhaps best left to the first post-Cold War generation to judge, for its independence of Cold War partisanship suits it to assess the long-term effects of Cold War expenditure of national treasure and to inquire into the full extent to which US citizens became unwitting guinea pigs in government-sponsored research.

"Dual Possibilities" concludes with Burke's fears, as he suggests that subordinating scientific development to military preparedness will replace the scientific "norms of *universal clarity* with the divisive demands for *conspiracy.*" This subordination the scientist must "reject and resist in ways that mean the end of 'autonomy,' or if he accepts, he risks becoming the friend of fiends."

Scientific discoveries have always, of course, been used for the purposes of war. But the demand that scientific advance *per se* be guided by military considerations *changes the proportions* of such motivation tremendously. Scientists of good will must then become uneasy, in that the morality of their specialty is no longer enough. The liberal ideal of autonomy is denied them, except insofar as they can contrive to conceal from themselves the true implications of their role. (35)

Through concealment, the extrinsic rhetoric of parent and citizen would be relegated to a state of rhetorical silence. The most dangerous form of such concealment would be through "the function of the scapegoat," whereby the guilt from the silencing of this extrinsic rhetoric would be assuaged through victimage (34).

The scapegoat function is a recurring theme in Burke, one that in his final phase, to which we turn in the next and last chapter, is more prominent than ever before, becoming virtually as inevitable as death and taxes. In *PC*, in contrast, as "an error in interpretation" (14), scapegoating is correctible. A "trained incapacity," scapegoating shares features common to all trained incapacities, but as "faulty means-selecting," arising from a faulty view of cause and effect (15–16), it is correctible, most definitively by reality's "recalcitrance" (255). In

RM's example of the scientist, the scapegoat temptation is traced to an act that subordinates science to military preparedness. For science to avoid this scapegoating temptation, Burke suggests, it should undertake a different constitutional act, one like that advocated by the Federation of American Scientists in the agon of history in which, we now know, it was on the losing side. Insofar as scapegoating may be considered a form of mental disease, the ultimate implication of Burke's analysis of the scientist's crisis is that mental health can be dependent on a healthy society, one governed by "adequate ideas."

The significance of Burke's rhetoric of identification in the tradition of rhetoric is astutely pinpointed by Maurice Charland as he draws on Burke, as well as Althusser, in analyzing the rhetorical constitution of a subject, the *peuple Québécois*, to whom we'll return later. Traditional rhetoric, Charland observes, presupposes "transcendental subjects, whom discourse would mediate. In other words, rhetorical theory usually refuses to consider the possibility that the very existence of social subjects ... is already a rhetorical effect" (133). Burke's theory is different: "identifications are rhetorical, for they are discursive effects that induce human cooperation. They are also, however, logically prior to persuasion. Indeed, humans are constituted in these characteristics; they are essential to the 'nature' of a subject and form the basis for persuasive appeals" (133–34). In *RM*, identification is the condition of persuasion: "You persuade a man only insofar as you can talk his language by speech, gesture, tonality, order, image, attitude, idea, *identifying* your ways with his" (55). By constituting subjects as participants in a distinctive culture, identifications on a sub- or unconscious level make possible the activity of persuasion on a conscious level.

This activity is passivity insofar as it is a decentered effect of identifications always already in place. The rhetoric of identification, however, is written in a concrete that is always harden*ing*, never harden*ed*. The condition of persuasion, identifications can themselves change through the agency of the agon of history, so that what persuades today may not persuade tomorrow. In Burke's example of the scientist, a new identification of scientist and militarist is taking form that prompts a crisis of hierarchizing penetrating to the depths of the subject. Priorities must be sorted out among the subject as scientist, as parent, and as citizen of a nation and the world; and the sorting must occur in a social context such that however they are sorted the scientist will be identified with one side or the other in an agon of history. This agon's flashpoint is the reconstitution of the subject as scientist through a new hierarchical subordination of scientific research to military preparedness. To resist or not to resist this reconstitution is the crisis. Burke accentuates the depth of the crisis when he suggests that scientists may even, as quoted earlier, "conceal from themselves the true implications of their role," a possibility that prompts him to add that "there is a wide range of ways whereby the rhetorical motive, through the resources of identification, can operate without conscious direction by any particular agent" (35).

As identifications are constituted and reconstituted in the agon of history, Burke's rhetorical unconscious is approached best from the standpoint of the Marxist rather than the Freudian unconscious. Of the modes of unconsciousness Burke surveys in "Mind, Body, and the Unconscious," one derives more clearly than any other from his dramatistic view of language: "there is the sheerly terministic situation whereby *any* 'conscious' nomenclature gives rise to a corresponding realm of the 'unconscious,'" a situation Burke illustrates with a Marxist example: "By Marx's scheme, if the bourgeois conceives of all mankind in terms of the bourgeois, said bourgeois has *unconsciously* represented (or revealed) his bourgeois *consciousness*" (MBU 70). *RM*'s chapter "Marx on 'Mystification'" analyzes traditional Marxist demystification as a contribution to rhetoric, rewriting it with a terminological triad: individual, specific, generic. In the case of the bourgeoisie, its conception of itself as universal is generic, this generic consciousness functioning as a mystification in its unconsciousness of itself as a specific class. "Then," Burke concludes, "according to Marx, only by the abolition of property relationships that make for such specific, or class motives, might we hope to get truly universal motivation. And such universal or generic motivation would, by the same token, mean the freeing of the individual" (110). Acting generically, in the interest of humankind, the individual acts in its own deepest interest as well.

By itself, such demystification is too narrow an interpretive strategy, concludes Jameson in his study of the "political unconscious": "an enlarged perspective for any Marxist analysis of culture ... can no longer be content with its demystifying vocation ... [It] must also seek, through and beyond this demonstration of the instrumental function of a given cultural object, to project its simultaneously Utopian power as the symbolic affirmation of a specific historical and class form of collective unity."[15] Jameson thus iterates Althusser's postulation that the ruling class must believe its own ideology and Derrida's proposal that the motivation of the Declaration of Independence ranges from opportunistic hypocrisy to faith, far beyond de Man's single category of motivation, the "thieving lawmaker."

Anticipating Jameson's formulation in its concern with "symbolic affirmation," *RM* writes against the economistic grain of an earlier Marxism, without, however, abandoning its materialist commitment altogether. "Marx on 'Mystificaton,'" for example, is coupled with "Carlyle on 'Mystery,'" where Burke considers Carlyle's symbolism of clothes as "visible emblems" of the invisible spiritual bonds uniting humankind (121). Burke paraphrases Carlyle: "But because the world's 'Clothes' symbolize this profounder, divine order, we must reverence them too, insofar as they are representative of it. In ultimate reality, all men are united — and it is by reason of this ultimate union that the different classes of men can communicate with one another" (122). Burke's reading of Carlyle is a Marxist demystification to the extent that he demystifies Carlyle's divinization of the human. But this demystification does not extend to communication. In communication, however impure, Burke finds the possibility of the mystery of utopian identification.

Burke anticipates Jameson most concisely in his thesis, "Ideology cannot be deduced from economic considerations alone. It also derives from man's nature as a 'symbol-using animal'" (146) — a thesis quoted in chapter 1 to suggest that so far have the theoretical scales tipped since its postulation that one would today have to reverse Burke's formulation to repeat his point. Burke elaborates,

And since the "original economic plant" is the human body, with the divisive centrality of its particular nervous system, the theologian's concerns with Eden and the "fall" come close to the heart of the rhetorical problem. For, behind the theology, there is the perception of generic divisiveness which, being common to all men, is a universal fact about them, prior to any divisiveness caused by social classes. Here is the basis of rhetoric. Out of this emerge the motives for linguistic persuasion. Then, *secondarily*, we get the motives peculiar to particular economic situations.

In parturition begins the centrality of the nervous system. The different nervous systems, through language and the ways of production, erect various communities of interests and insights, social communities varying in nature and scope. And out of the division and the community arises the "universal" rhetorical situation. (146)

15 *The Political Unconscious: Narrative as a Socially Symbolic Act* (Ithaca: Cornell University Press, 1981), p. 291.

Through identification, divided bodies can commune with one another. This identification, however, is simultaneously a new division, one among groups rather than bodies, but it sees itself as identification atop all division. Ideology (a "specific" class motivation) thinks itself universal ("generic" motivation), its unconsciousness of itself as division being a condition of its possibility. That this unconsciousness is necessary, however, is an oblique sign of a utopian unconscious. Following Jameson, the effectively ideological may be considered proto-utopian insofar as the ideological identification of divided bodies effects a prefiguration of utopian cooperation.[16] An effect of history, the utopian unconscious presupposes not something prior to history but a possibility beyond history.

A few pages before this theoretical formulation of the "rhetorical situation," Burke concludes a chapter in which he takes the reader "to the heart of the rhetorical problem" with a mythic narrative (137–42). The concern of Burke's myth is the same as that articulated in a late Foucault text, which merits consideration here:

The analyses I have been trying to make have to do essentially with the relationships of power. I understand by that something other than the states of domination... This analysis of relations of power... sometimes meets what we can call facts or states of domination, in which the relations of power, instead of being variable... find themselves firmly set and congealed. When an individual or a social group manages to block a field of relations of power, to render them impassive and invariable and to prevent all reversibility of movement – by means of instruments which can be economic as well as political or military – we are facing what can be called a state of domination.[17]

This text would seem to concede that power is sometimes somewhere rather than everywhere, even if at that point power is renamed domination, but we quote it here because it opposes "reversibility" of hierarchy to the rigidity of domination. This opposition has classical precedent in Aristotle's thesis that the only true citizens are those capable and willing not only to rule but also to be ruled (*Politics*, Book 3, Chapter 13, especially 1284a1–3). This principle of taking turns subordinates hierarchy to the ends of utopian cooperation, a hierarchizing of hierarchy itself.

It's relevant here to recollect Wood's argument, considered in chapter 1 in the context of our argument in behalf of the transhistorical. To repeat chapter 1's quotation of Wood, "It is difficult to avoid the

---

16 *Political Unconscious*, pp. 286, 291.
17 "The Ethic of Care for the Self as a Practice of Freedom," Interview, *The Final Foucault*, eds. James Bernauer and David Rasmussen (Cambridge: MIT Press, 1988), p. 3.

conviction that even classless society will require some form of *representation*, and hence *authority* and even *subordination* of some people to others." Reasoning from this premise, the problem becomes one of instituting reversibilities to foster cooperation strong enough to keep "states of domination" at bay. Instituting these, however, is easier said than done. In principle, hierarchy is reversible; in history, it's reversible too, although it usually takes the hard work of the agon of history. Mystification stands in the way, Burke observes, as it translates the reality of the necessity of hierarchy in general into the illusion of the necessity of *a* specific hierarchy (141).[18]

The Christian version of reversibility – the first shall be last and the last first – is taken up by Burke in the context of his myth. He reads it first on the level of principle: "The state of first and last things, the heavenly state, is the realm of *principle*. In this state . . . the reversal of social status makes as much sense as its actual mundane order" (138). Then he rereads it on the level of history: "The reduction of such reversibility to the world of property can add up to political or social revolution, as the 'Edenic' world of universal principle is ironically broken down into divisions of property, confronting one with a choice between the frozen order of the *status quo* and the reversal of that order, through its 'liquidation.' We are then in the state of the 'fall'" (138–39). Both the nightmare of domination in this fallen state and the Edenic wish for reversibility in utopian cooperation are encompassed in Burke's myth.

Creatures from the sea live on the land in this fallen state, their attempts to overcome the divisiveness of nightmarish states of domination having run the gamut: "first, ideally, love, charity, the attempt of the divided beings to overcome division; then, when the tension increased, the various departures from love . . . and finally, the organization of hate and war, the farthest stage of division . . . where 'spies' go by the name of 'intelligence'"(139). This division makes these creatures nostalgic for the sea. When they first arrived on land, how could they have anticipated, Burke asks, "the speed-up of a Detroit factory, and . . . atomic and bacteriological war?" (139). But would the sea remove this division? "Is not the sea itself a jungle of divisiveness?" (139). Prior to the identifications and divisions of rhetoric, there is the biological division of one central nervous system

---

18 States of domination benefiting some at the expense of others often try to perpetuate themselves forever by privileging biological significations that are seemingly immutable, such as aristocracy's family blood, patriarchy's sexual difference, and racism's skin pigmentation.

from another. So, Burke concludes, the myth of return to the sea points toward "a myth still farther back, the myth of a power prior to all parturition. Then divided things were not yet proud in the private property of their divisiveness" (140). The myth's lesson: "Are we proposing that men cannot resolve their local fights over property until they have undergone the most radical revolution of all, a return to their source? . . . We are not – but we do take our myth seriously to this extent: It . . . suggests how thorough our shrewdness about property and hierarchy must be, before we could build a whole human society about the critique of ambition" (140).

RM's third and last part considers the utopian from the standpoint of the subject, introducing the term "ultimate" in its first chapter and adding an illustration in its second, "Ultimate Elements in the Marxist Persuasion," which in effect theorizes the rhetorical appeal of Lukács's historical narrative, with its subject of history:

much of the *rhetorical* strength in the Marxist dialectic comes from the fact that it is "ultimate" in its order. The various classes do not confront one another merely as parliamentary voices that represent conflicting interests. They are arranged hierarchically, each with the disposition, or "consciousness," that matches its peculiar set of circumstances, while the steps from feudal to bourgeois to proletarian are grounded in the very nature of the universe.
  Precisely by reason of this ultimate order, a spokesman for the proletariat can think of himself as representing not only the interests of that class alone ["specific" motivation], but the grand design of the entire historical sequence, its final outcome for all mankind ["generic" motivation].   (190–91)

The rhetorical appeal resides in the narrative's promise that one is acting generically as one acts specifically. As this passage suggests, Burke contrasts this identification of specific and generic to a parliamentary wrangle among subject positions, where positions hear one another – rather than ignore one another, as in absolute fragmentation – but to mixed effect: "the voices . . . confront one another as somewhat disrelated competitors that can work together only by the 'mild demoralization' of sheer compromise" (187). "Ultimate" corresponds to "circumference" and "substance," designating the rhetorical side of these grammatical principles, for the proletariat, as it plays its role in a narrative "grounded in the very nature of the universe," acts in accord with a substance that translates the necessitarian imperative into a hierarchy to which to conform.
  This identification of specific and generic is analyzed in epistemological

terms by Lukács, such that the proletariat is the first and only class in history to pierce the veil of "false consciousness" and arrive at knowledge of the historical process. In Burke's rhetorical analysis, this identification becomes a general formula for rhetorical appeal. The appeal of this identification is also apparent, indirectly, in its negation, as in Burke's example of the "Negro," who demonstrates that in a racist culture, a black, acting specifically as a black, cannot ascend to the generic (193) – a black must sell out (Malcolm Little's conk) or fight back (Malcolm X).[19] In the US today, multiculturalism struggles to reconstitute an existing culture of mono ascent to the generic as a culture of multiple ascents. Whether a relation of specific to generic is rhetorically sayable, in short, is a function of culture, as exemplified in current shifts in usage such as that from "mankind" to "humankind." Sayability is Lentricchia's basic concern in *Criticism and Social Change*, where he asks, "Can a literary intellectual, to come to the issue that most preoccupies me, do radical work [generic] as a literary intellectual [specific]?" (2). Sayability, finally, can assume ironic forms, as in individualism, which is the discourse of a specific culture, wherein to act generically is to distinguish oneself individually, even to the point of conceiving oneself as autonomous and prior to culture. Crusoe, alone on "his" island, is both hero and *reductio ad absurdum* of individualism.

The Québécois narrative of history, as Charland demonstrates, is another instance of an ultimate terminology (139), one quite different from the Marxist narrative. The parliamentary wrangle that Québécois narrative displaces is that between French and Canadian subject positions in the hyphenated French-Canadian (144). This narrative raises this hyphenated tension between an ethnic subject (French) and a political subject (Canadian) to the level of a mutually exclusive opposition, as it recounts that a people, with its own language and way of life, was subjugated at the hands of British power. To be French-Canadian is to live two identifications, one with the subjugator, the other with the subjugated. In contrast, to be Québécois (specific) is to live an identification with a people exercising the universal right of all peoples to self-determination (generic). As we saw in the last

19 The allusion is to the film *Malcom X*. "Malcolm Little" is Malcolm's "real" name. "Conk" is American slang for a chemical preparation blacks used to straighten their hair – that is, to look more white; this practice was common before the "black is beautiful" slogan of the 1960s. The film begins with Little going to a barber shop for a "conk," indicating that he starts out by selling out to white culture. Later, as Malcolm X, he learns to take pride in his blackness and to fight back.

chapter, selection and logic go hand in hand, as in this case the selection of the discourse of self-determination dictates one and only one political course of action. To be Québécois, Charland observes, "is to be constituted such that sovereignty is not only possible, but necessary. Without sovereignty, this constitutive rhetoric would die and those it has constituted would cease to be subjects, lacking maturity, responsibility, and autonomy" (146).

The rhetorical appeal of acting generically in acting specifically exhibits itself even in the disciplinary autonomy of science (specific) as it sees itself as the agent of humankind's enlightenment (generic). One should, Burke suggests in analyzing his example of the scientist's crisis, be on the lookout for the theologizing of science despite its protestations to the contrary: the liberal apologist for the autonomy of science "vacillates indeterminately between his overt claims for science as sheer method . . . and his covert claims for science as a substance which, like God, would be an intrinsically *good* power" (*RM* 30). From this standpoint, the scientist's crisis is that it's difficult to act generically in acting specifically when one serves a military looking for weapons of mass destruction. To continue to see themselves as agents of enlightenment, scientists are tempted "in varying degrees of deliber-ateness and unawareness," Burke suggests, to "conceal from themselves the true implication of their role" (35). In other words, the utopian unconscious can take the perverse form of self-deception, which risks turning into scapegoating if one yields to the temptation to think that the potential victims of one's acts are not part of humankind and that one therefore serves humankind in eliminating them.

As the multiplicity of ultimate terminologies suggests, what is generic to one person may be specific to another. How can one arbitrate among them? Burke addresses this question in "'Sociology of Knowledge' vs. Platonic 'Myth,'" the chapter following "Ultimate Elements in the Marxist Persuasion." The "sociology of knowledge" is Karl Mannheim's answer, advanced in *Ideology and Utopia*. The range framed by Mannheim's title interests Burke, although for reasons different from Mannheim's. For Mannheim, Burke observes, "the Utopian bias is progressive, futuristic, whereas the ideological bias is conservative or reactionary, designed to maintain a status quo or to reinstate an earlier social order" (199). For Burke, in contrast, the utopian, construed from the standpoint of Platonic myth, points toward an answer altogether different from Mannheim's.

Mannheim broadens Marxist demystification to encompass the

exposure of any bias whatsoever, including the Marxist. "[A] human terminology of motives is necessarily partial," Burke paraphrases, "whatever its claims to universal validity, its 'principles' favor the interests of some group more than others" (198). Mannheim's own terminology is subject to the same test, but according to his method, it can be subjected to this test only from the standpoint of a terminology other than his own (198). Through the repeated exposure of biased division behind the assertion of universal identification, Mannheim's epistemology arrives at knowledge about the relation of terminologies to their nonverbal ground. This epistemology, however, makes Mannheim's text vulnerable to dramatistic deconstruction, as Mannheim seems to recognize. "For he explicitly asks himself," Burke accentuates, "where the zeal of human effort would come from, if it were not for the false promises of our Utopias. And he asks this, even as he aims by scrupulous method to destroy the zeal of such false promises, or mythic Utopian illusions" (201). The methodological problem that Burke finds here is analogous, *mutatis mutandis*, to the one he finds, discussed a few chapters back, in logical positivism, which is caught between the rock of thinking itself to be a good thing and the hard place of having relegated terms such as "good" to the bin of nonsense. As he adds in *RM*, "'Positivism' itself is not a positive term . . . [It is] not in the order of *motion and perception*, but rather in the order of *action and idea*" (184).

The alternative method that Burke proposes is based on a different relationality. Mannheim's method presupposes that the relationality of terminologies to their nonverbal ground is available to objective description, in the classical sense, such that a neutral point beyond any bias can be occupied by a "sociology of knowledge." Burke's alternative presupposes, instead, a relationality among discourses. Instead of eliminating bias, one distinguishes among levels of bias. Ideology and utopia can serve to distinguish these levels, although not when contrasted as forward-looking on one hand and backward-looking on the other:

insofar as [like Mannheim] you correct the bias of both ideology and myth (Utopia), you rob yourself of a motive. But of course, if the myth had been interpreted as figuring a motive beyond the reach of ideology, the motive of the myth would be felt to lie beyond the motivational order treated in the competing ideologies. Its motive would be "ultimate," as the motives of the ideologies were not. (202)

Burke's myth of return is designed to figure such a motive beyond the particular ideologies of particular hierarchies: a utopian motive to subordinate hierarchy through reversals of hierarchy. In Burke's methodology, in other words, "ultimate" is a relational term. Marxist narrative is an ultimate terminology relative to the ideologies of different classes in history, but it is an ideology relative to the ultimate terminology of Burke's myth, a narrative that should be read mythically rather than literally — that is, its return to origins is a figuration of a priority that in literal narratives may be projected into the future (Marxism) or the past (Québécois).

A rhetorical realist, Burke is as convinced as Mannheim that there is a nonverbal realm beyond discourse, but he recognizes that our approach to it is always discursively mediated through the act of language. Mannheim, contradictorily, concedes this mediation on the one hand and refuses it on the other, since his approach to the nonverbal is both mediated, through the exposure of terminological bias, and unmediated, through his epistemological assumption of a point of neutrality beyond the bias inherent in terminology. Mannheim subscribes to the epistemological premise of neutrality without recognizing that the positing of this premise is a verbal act. His methodological blindness evidences itself as he verges on recognizing that he undermines "the zeal of human effort" in the very process of looking for a basis for such effort beyond the partiality of bias. Failing to recognize the act at the basis of his terminology, he can never recognize that his discourse, like any other, is a putting of an "oar" into the Burkean conversation. Mannheim searches for neutrality; Burke, for a utopian motive of action. The utopian is the dramatistic alternative to the neutrality of epistemology. Neutrality is outside human interest. The utopian is collective, or generic, human interest.

This contrast between neutrality and generic human interest may be rewritten as the contrast that Burke draws, noted earlier, between Descartes and Spinoza: knowledge vs. adequate idea. This contrast has been obscured by the enlightenment premise that the Cartesian regime of knowledge is synonymous with generic human interest. But perhaps we are recovering this contrast, ironically with the help of this regime itself, in the difference between a knowledge of power over nature and an adequate idea of living in it. One demonstration that the former needs to be subordinated to the latter is nuclear power, which may prove to be easier to control than other less dramatic, more pervasive demonstrations.

The rhetorical appeal of acting generically as one acts specifically is the motive of motives of hierarchization in the constitutional act. A rhetorical subject is not an impartial, detached observer of the world but an actor in it with a utopian unconscious.

The Burkean conversation reappears in "'Mythic' Ground and 'Context of Situation,'" the chapter following the polemic with Mannheim. "Context of situation" is a borrowing from Bronislaw Malinowski, who uses it to designate the situation that contextualizes a community rather than an individual or a faction. Such a situation frames competing terminologies "as to just what important relationships and situations there are, particularly in the social and political realm, [that] confront one another as competing orators, hence requiring either dialectical compromise or dialectical resolution by reduction to an ultimate order" (206–07). Discourses in a situation struggle rhetorically to define the situation; they contain the situation as they construct it, and they are contained by the situation as it imposes necessitarian imperatives. Mannheim's epistemology thinks it outflanks the conversation, but like any discourse, it is an orator within it.

This term "context of situation" also reminds us that when Burke introduces his conversation, in "PLF," he equates dialectic to drama in conceiving a text as an "answer or rejoinder to assertions current in the situation in which it arose" (109). "[D]ialectical resolution by reduction to an ultimate order" is for Burke dialectical not in the sense of a "grand narrative" of history, a sense that became commonplace in the wake of Hegel, but in the sense that it's a rejoinder in a situation, an assertion of constitutionality that takes into account varying rhetorical weights of competing discourses in the situation. This competition may be resolved through "compromise" – the parliamentary wrangle – or an "ultimate order," as in the Marxist and the Québécois narratives, which see themselves as "grand," but which the dramatistic dialectic sees as acts in the conversation. Dramatistically considered, the utopian motive is to be found *in medias res*, in acts in the Burkean conversation, itself without either origin or telos.

While Burke equates the dramatistic to the dialectical, he acknowledges in "Dialectic in General," *GM*'s last chapter, that he also sometimes conceives dialectic more broadly as formal linguistic operations, particulary division and composition or merger (402). The rhetorical form of composition or merger is identification. These formal operations stand behind Burke's suggestion, quoted earlier, that "the theologian's concerns with Eden and the 'fall' come close to the heart of the rhetorical problem." As he elaborates later in *RM*, "'Eden' and 'the fall' are mythic terms for composition and division. Such terms are concealments ... But they are enigmas of a revealing sort, too, insofar as they sum up, or stand for, a complexity of personal, sexual, social, and universal motives" (176). In other words, these formal operations, like the pentad, are enacted, the enactment both concealing and revealing.

Ethical alternatives involving the operations of merger and division arise from the situation of the act in the conversation. One alternative is taken up in "Courtship" (208–12), the chapter following "'Mythic' Ground and 'Context of Situation,'" and continues as a theme in succeeding chapters, culminating in "Pure Persuasion" (267–94). The other appears in the two chapters immediately preceding "Pure Persuasion" as one of the words in their titles: "kill." The same alternatives appear in Burke's myth in the counterpointing of courtship and scapegoating (141). The situation of the peuple Québécois, a historical episode still in progress, can serve to illustrate these alternatives. In this situation, identification as a Canadian political subject is the identification that the agon of history has rhetorically transformed from an unquestioned assumption that "goes without saying" into an issue structuring rhetorical struggle. The situation tempts the peuple Québécois, to galvanize itself to sever this identification, to paint the Canadian in dark colors. To this divisive temptation in any agon, scapegoating is the extreme response, whereby killing can even become religious if eliminating the victim is seen as acting generically in the service of humankind. Burke calls attention to the example of Hitler's formulation: "By warding off Jews I am fighting for the Lord's work" (RHB 198). At the other ethical extreme, the peuple Québécois could sever its identification with Canada on one level and restore it on another. Refusing to be a Canadian political subject any longer, the peuple Québécois could identify with Canada as one people addressing another in a utopian conversation among peoples. Such a utopian vision is implicit in the Québécois ultimate terminology, built as it is on the premise of the universal right of all peoples to self-determination. In the ultimate terminology of the Marxist narrative, in contrast, there is a different utopia, one that envisions the sacrifice of class for classless subjecthood.

Pure persuasion occurs in acts in the conversation, *in medias res* rather than in a utopia projected into the past or the future. Utopian in the strict sense – it's no place – it is paradoxically also commonplace.

As Burke puts it, "Yet, though what we mean by pure persuasion in the absolute sense exists nowhere, it can be present as a motivational ingredient in any rhetoric, no matter how intensely advantage-seeking such rhetoric may be" (*RM* 269). Methodologically, "the indication of pure persuasion in any activity is in an element of 'standoffishness,' or perhaps better, *self-interference*, as judged by the tests of acquisition. Thus, while not essentially sacrificial, it *looks* sacrificial when matched against the acquisitive" (269).

The persuasive relation of speaker and audience is "in essence 'courtly,' hence involves communication between hierarchically related orders" (285), but this hierarchical relation is reversible in both directions, as in "the artist-entertainer [who] is the servant of the very despot-audience he seeks to fascinate (as the spellbinder can tyrannize over his audience only by letting the audience tyrannize over him, in rigidly circumscribing the range and nature of his remarks)" (286). This speaker defers to his audience to persuade it to defer to him, each in effect taking turns stepping down and stepping up in a game of hierarchical chairs. This two-way street may be counterpointed to the one-way Hegelian master–slave relation, as expounded in Alexander Kojève's influential commentary: "He [the slave] must give up his desire and satisfy the desire of the other: he must 'recognize' the other without being 'recognized' by him. Now, 'to recognize' him thus is 'to recognize' him as his Master."[20] Defoe's Friday, conforming to the letter of this formula, exhibits the emptiness of such recognition. Allegorical commentary on this emptiness appears in J. M. Coetzee's *Foe*, where Friday is tongueless (empty recognition of the master) and Crusoe is hollow (emptied rather than enlarged by slavish recognition). Contrast God's grace in certain forms of Christianity, a recognition one gets by giving up claim to it. That is, one gets it through the self-interference of pure persuasion, the more authentic the stepping down of self-interference, the more likely the stepping up of grace, an irony that makes this authenticity — rhetorical rather than romantic — hard to come by.

One can find faint traces of self-interference in any rhetoric insofar as even the most manipulative, advantage-seeking rhetoric cannot be openly manipulative if it is to succeed. To persuade, there must be self-interference, however diluted. But before God, one cannot be a "thieving lawmaker," which makes God or the rhetorical equivalent

---

20 *Introduction to the Reading of Hegel*, trans. James H. Nichols, Jr. (Ithaca: Cornell University Press, 1980), p. 8.

the ideal audience for pure persuasion. Burke suggests an aesthetic parallel in proposing that "considered as an object of pure persuasion, Dante's Beatrice would be not woman idealized, but rather the absolute audience realized" (*RM* 293–94). There is aesthetic grace as well as religious: pure persuasion "can arise out of expressions quite differently motivated, as when a book, having been developed so far, sets up demands on its own, demands conditioned by the parts already written, so that the book becomes to an extent something not foreseen by its author, and requires him to interfere with his original intentions. We here confront an 'ultimate' motive (as distinct from an 'ulterior' one)" (269). Perhaps one can discern even a political grace in the strategy of passive resistance, as practiced from Gandhi to King, the rhetorical power of which derives from self-interference: the greater the self-interference, the greater the power.

Pure persuasion is communication elevated to a level of rhetorical grace that is utopian in the strict sense:

In its essence communication involves the use of verbal symbols for purposes of appeal. Thus, it splits formally into the three elements of speaker, speech, and spoken-to, with the speaker so shaping his speech as to "commune with" the spoken-to. This purely technical pattern is the precondition of *all* appeal... Rhetorically, there can be courtship only insofar as there is division. Hence, only through interference could one court continually, thereby perpetuating genuine "freedom of rhetoric." (271)

The freedom here is not freedom from interference but freely imposed self-interference. Such perpetual rhetoric, Burke suggests, would be equivalent to the image of courtship on Keats's "Grecian Urn" (275):

Bold Lover, never, never canst thou kiss,
Though winning near the goal – yet, do not grieve;
She cannot fade, though thou hast not thy bliss,
Forever wilt thou love, and she be fair!

As Burke accentuates on the last page of the "Pure Persuasion" chapter, "'Pure persuasion' is as biologically unfeasible as that moment when the irresistible force meets the immovable body... Psychologically it is related to a conflict of opposite impulses... Theologically or politically, it would be the state of intolerable indecision just preceding conversion to a new doctrine" (294). A new doctrine is a new constitution. A new constitution is a transformation, which is the form origination takes in the conversation, where we are always already *in medias res*. As the condition of rhetoricity, pure persuasion is instantiated prior to the rhetoric of any particular constitution. Whatever and wherever the conversion, it passes through pure persuasion.

In pure persuasion, identification and persuasion intersect. Enacting the "technical pattern [that] is the precondition of *all* appeal," pure persuasion is the identification of identifications insofar as it is the primal identification that makes possible the rhetorical activity of communication characteristic of living in any culture. This identification of identifications is a division too, but only in the sense that it divides living as a human being from other modes of living. Acts in the conversation are all built on this primal, generic identification, itself unconscious, as it is the transformation from animal to cultural animal.

Burke finds in pure persuasion "a *symbolically grounded* distrust of acquisitiveness, a feeling that one should not just 'take things,' but should court them, show gratitude for them, or apologize for killing them" (271). Returning to the issue of biological acquisitiveness that he considers in his Veblen chapter, Burke adds, "And for our part, rather than treating the fantastic acquisitiveness of imperialists as a mere 'mental replica' of biological desires, we would explain it thus roundabout, as *the dialectical transformation of self-denial into its opposite*" (272). In *GM*, as we saw earlier, Burke proposes that "a linguistic factor at every point in human experience complicates and to some extent transcends the purely biological aspects of motivation" (318). Pure persuasion is the complication of complications.

The appearance of God in Burke's theorizing of pure persuasion has an analogue in Althusser's theorizing of ideological interpellation, where God appears in a Lacanian mirror phase:

God is thus the Subject, and Moses and the innumerable subjects of God's people, the Subject's interlocutors-interpellates: his *mirrors*, his *reflections*. Were not men made *in the image* of God?... [T]he structure of all ideology...is *speculary*, i.e. a mirror-structure...[T]he Absolute Subject occupies the unique place of the Centre, and interpellates around it the infinity of individuals into subjects...such that it *subjects* the subjects to the Subject.[21]

Althusser thus finds in Lacan's mirror phase a structure with which to theorize a subject ideologically decentered. In the mirror, there is the image of subjecthood, but the image is other, separated from the eyes looking into the mirror. Forgetting this otherness is the condition of being interpellated as a subject. As we saw in chapter 1, Althusser sees

---

21 "Ideology," pp. 179–80.

ideology as the "atmosphere" indispensable to any society, even a communist society, but his theorizing of interpellation suggests that this atmosphere suffocates more than it invigorates. His subject is trapped in the pathos of slavery to a master that subjects.

We may, however, have now reached a point – which thinkers like Althusser helped us to reach – at which such pathos can be recognized as the last breath of a tradition now dead, a last variation on an old theme. Lukács's variation is earlier, an optimistic vision of proletarian epistemology taking us beyond the "atmosphere" of false consciousness. Althusser is contemporary insofar as he sees no exit from the "atmosphere" of culture, but traditional insofar as he imagines the absence of an exit as pathos. These two variations are part of a tradition broader than the Marxist. Lacan offers a variation that is almost a formulaic version of the traditional theme in characterizing "meaning, as it emerges in the field of the Other . . . [as] the disappearance of being, induced by the very function of the signifier."[22] In this tradition, rhetorical sayability – the cultural "atmosphere" sustaining cultural animals – has always been cast as insubstantial, ephemeral, something to put aside in favor of the solid dependability of enlightenment certainty or the uplifting imaginativeness of romantic authenticity. In the long run, however, recognition that there is no exit from culture puts aside this tradition and the pathos that is its dying breath, making possible an epochal reevaluation of culture. Through the possibility of rhetorical grace, sayability acquires a dignity heretofore denied it. This dignity is of our own making, rooted in rhetoric rather than being, but that magnifies rather than diminishes the respect it deserves. Compared to history, being is child's play.

The trade-off of pure persuasion – "simultaneous gain and loss" (286) – is implicit in Aristotle's thesis that the true citizen rules and is ruled, since the ruler who steps down to let another take a turn simultaneously steps up to true citizenship. A similar trade-off appears in Burke's example in *RM*'s "Introduction" – quoted near the end of the present chapter's first section – of the man who may identify with his community to gain personal advantage but who also may step down to step up to "willingly make sacrifices in behalf of such identification." Stepping down in one sense can translate, in short, into stepping up in a rhetorical sense. This hierarchical reversibility is the promise envisioned in Burke's myth. In the nightmare of history,

22 *The Four Fundamental Concepts of Psycho-Analysis*, trans. Alan Sheridan (New York: W. W. Norton, 1981), p. 211.

however, this promise is routinely honored in the breach. The promise is a utopian vision rather than a historical plausibility; power is somewhere, Foucault notwithstanding, and those who are there nearly always use it to keep it. This historical lesson is clear to the creatures from the sea in Burke's myth. Pure persuasion is *in medias res*, but as the myth suggests, it is barely audible. Being free to speak means little without being powerful enough to be heard. Jameson reminds us, "the political thrust of the struggle of all groups against each other can never be immediately universal but must always necessarily be focused on the class enemy."[23] Only the agon of history can build a platform for bracing, full-voiced pure persuasion. This utopian possibility, however remote, stirs the creatures from the sea to open their eyes every morning on a new day.

23 *Political Unconscious*, p. 290.

8

The Rhetoric of Religion: history in eclipse

> Finally, History fell a-dreaming
> And dreamed about Language –   Burke, CP

In the periodization of Burke's career, there is a late phase. How best to characterize late Burke is a live issue, but there is consensus that there is one. In the 1980s, in texts to be considered in the present chapter, Burke himself helped to form this consensus as he proposed his own characterization of the distinctiveness of his later work. An anticipation of Burke's self-characterization appears in William H. Rueckert's 1982 edition of his pioneering 1963 book, *Kenneth Burke and the Drama of Human Relations* – this second edition testifying to the continuing importance of the first. In the chapter added for this new edition – "From Dramatism to Logology" – Rueckert contrasts his initial to his later view of *RR*:

> The book originally seemed like the culmination of dramatism; and in some ways it is. Now, many years later, I see that it also indicated a shift from dramatism to logology... [U]sing one of Burke's own devices, one can say that before 1961 there was *Dramatism* and logology and after 1961 there was dramatism and *Logology*... [I]t now seems quite clear that logology moves beyond dramatism and that *The Rhetoric of Religion* represents a further and almost final state in Burke's long and remarkable development.   (242)

What wasn't initially evident, in short, was that *RR*'s logology was destined to upstage *GM*'s dramatism.

Having published *GM* in 1945 and *RM* in 1950, Burke created the expectation that *SM* would appear in the mid-1950s. Moreover, it seemed to students of his work, Rueckert suggests, that with *SM* Burke's "work would come to some kind of culmination" (*Drama* 230). Instead, his next book didn't appear until 1961, and it was *RR* not *SM*. Seeing *RR* as nonetheless somehow culminative was encouraged by its first chapter, however, for it concludes with an outline of dramatism (38–42), suggesting that "dramatism" is still Burke's titular term and that "logology" is simply another addition to his dramatistic vocabulary (see also 180–81).[1] Only later did it become clear that *RR* marks a reorientation in Burke's thought. *RR* grew in importance, moreover, as it proved to be Burke's last book-length theoretical undertaking – *LSA* collects essays from the 1950s and 1960s; *DD* is a booklet reprinting two talks for the Heinz Werner Lectures. *RR* is the hub of the later work. Some themes in it are developed more extensively elsewhere, before as well as afterwards, but it remains the chief place where they're clustered together. As Rueckert puts it, *RR* is Burke's "last stand" (242).

RR's silences constitute one sign in *RR* itself that it marks a reorientation. In its outline of dramatism, for example, there is not a word about the tripartite structure of grammar, rhetoric, and symbolic repeated routinely in earlier outlines. Even as Burke said somewhat different things about these three from context to context, he always said dramatism consisted of these three parts. Even more surprising is the silence about *SM*. That *SM* was the book expected, not *RR*, would by itself seem to have been reason enough to prompt some comment. This silence speaks even more loudly as one reads further and sees how much *RR* is a theory of the subject, thus seeming to undertake the theme previously assigned to *SM*. Even *RR*'s outline of dramatism introduces this theme in offering a definition of the subject, one revised and expanded in "Definition of Man," reprinted in *LSA*. All these silences come, moreover, after a decade had passed with no book from Burke, a hiatus that is extraordinary after two extraordinarily productive decades. These silences after this hiatus add up to additional evidence that Burke's "last stand" is a new stand.

The logological project in *RR* is to construe words about God as words about words. In the book's "Foreword," Burke justifies his deployment of this analogy: "it is our 'logological' thesis that, since the theological use of language is thorough, the close study of theology and its forms will provide us with good insight into the nature of language itself as a motive" (vi). The key point is methodological: the most "thorough" example is the best example. The thoroughness of theology can be illustrated by the example in chapter 1 of Foucault's critique of Reich, which recognizes that because orthodoxy is a rule that can be broken,

---

1 "Terministic Screens," one of Burke's most widely read essays, conveys the same impression. See TS 44, 47, 53.

deviancy is a part of orthodoxy, not a displacement of it. Burke's logological point would be twofold: (1) language is the condition of such rules; (2) this linguistic condition is exemplified with maximum thoroughness in God's command to Adam and Eve, which creates the possibility of sin just as orthodoxy creates the possibility of deviancy.

RR's concluding "Prologue in Heaven" sums up logology in the form of a one-act dialogue between TL (The Lord) and S (Satan) that is a "prologue" in the sense that it is prior to the emergence on earth of a new species, "the Word-Using Animal" (276). This priority is as logical as it is temporal, TL and S being a function of language as much as the new animal about whom they amuse themselves in the high comedy of their dialogue. Their dependence on language is dramatized at the end, which is left open to two possibilities, one happy and one unhappy. This latter cuts TL off in mid-word as the stage suddenly blackens to music suggesting the finality of extinction (315–16). The logological point: no word-using animal, no TL and S. TL and S are logological – words about words – not theological.

RR's centerpiece is "The First Three Chapters of Genesis," especially the section "Tautological Cycle of Terms for 'Order'" (183–96), a version of which appeared in a 1958 article (FTCG). Burke's logological reading of this biblical text produces *RR*'s theory of the subject, the premise of which is stated concisely: "Logologically, one would identify the principle of personality with the ability to master symbol-systems. Intrinsic to such a personality is the 'moral sense,' that is, the sense of 'yes and no' that goes with the thou-shalt-not's of Order" (208–09). The yes-and-no that goes with verbal prowess makes verbal law vulnerable to the violation of deviance. TL and S contrast this violability to the inviolability of the law dictating a pebble's response to a kick (280–81). Because of this emphasis on yes-and-no, *RR*'s conception of language is analogous to Foucault's of power insofar as Foucault insists, as we saw in chapter 1, that there is a power relationship only when there is the possibility of resistance as well as obedience. The threat of violence may almost erase this possibility, but only actual violence can erase it altogether.

Logologically considered the subject is "de-termined," a point TL makes to clarify things for S:

S. Pray, teach me further, milord... In particular, as regards these two occasions on which I have used the expression, "forced to be free," I can't just see how *they* will contrive to put determinism and free will together.

TL.... [A]s regards the sheer formality of the situation, recall that, though terms in their formality come to a kind of crisis in the "free" choice between Yes and No, there is also the technical fact that terms are by definition "de-terministic."

S. Milord, I swoon! (293–94)

"Forced to be free" in this de-terministic sense is different from the necessitarian sense we saw in *GM*. Necessitarian forcing is in the world; de-terministic, in language. Occasioned by conflicts among voluntaristic principles, the necessitarian is realistic. Occasioned by language, the de-terministic is formalistic.

From the yes-and-no in language, logology derives a psychology that Burke sums up in the form of a poem of three stanzas, the first of which is omitted here:

> Order leads to Guilt
> (for who can keep commandments!)
> Guilt needs Redemption
> (for who would not be cleansed)
> Redemption needs a Redeemer
> (which is to say, a Victim!).
>
> Order
> Through Guilt
> To Victimage
> (hence: Cult of the Kill).... (*RR* 4–5; Burke's ellipsis)

While cleansing can also be inward, in the benign forms of repentance and mortification (200–01), it's the malign alternative, killing a scapegoat, that the poem underlines.

This logological psychology is systematically generated in "Tautological Cycle of Terms for 'Order,'" where God's command to Adam and Eve is the fundamental order, this moral order theologically fused in God with the natural order. "Order" is *RR*'s word for orthodoxy. In this tautological cycle, in addition to the basic sequence leading from God's command to victimage, logology generates traditional psychological categories such as reason, will, and imagination. Burke even supplies a full-page chart of this complete cycle (184). One sign of the attention that this chapter has received is that a number of commentators have reproduced Burke's chart in full (for example, Booth, "Burke's Comedy" 117; Conrad 101; Henderson, *Burke* 143). Burke's logological reading of Genesis thus construes the theological Garden-of-Eden narrative as about language's yes-and-no and its consequences. God's command is violable, even though it comes from God, because it is verbal. Adam and Eve play out the "no" and the guilt and punishment that it entails. The ultimate consequence of sacrificial redemption, Burke concedes, is less evident in the first three chapters of Genesis: "We have tried to argue for its implicit presence by showing that the idea of redemption is a further stage in the idea of punishment, and the idea of a redeemer (hence, of vicarious atonement) is implicit in the idea of redemption" (177).

To conclude this section, we turn to the previously omitted first stanza of Burke's poem on his cycle of terms for order:

> Here are the steps
> In the Iron Law of History
> That welds Order to Sacrifice

Burke, in other words, depicts as history the cycle that the present section depicts as psychology. The deepest tension in *RR*, the present chapter proposes, is between its methodological commitment to the most "thorough" example and its logological project: the method directs attention to history, but the project produces a psychology that puts history into eclipse.

Prior to the chapter on terms for order, there is a different cycle: a "cycle of terms implicit in the idea of a Covenant" (179). The main stages of Burke's sequence from order to victimage, moreover, are initially generated from this term "covenant" before they are generated a second time from the term "order." Each term has its text: Hobbes's *Leviathan* is the one for "covenant." Despite these parallels, however, the two terms do not receive equal treatment. There is no chapter, "Tautological Cycle of Terms for 'Covenant,'" analyzing this cycle as carefully as the other, and "covenant" is explicitly shelved in favor of "order." Burke accentuates the principal difference between the two terms as he shelves "covenant": "However, when putting it ['Order'] in place of the word 'Covenant,' we should try never to forget Hobbes's emphasis upon the severities of *sovereignty* as integral to the kind of Order we shall be studying" (181). Encompassing socio-political structures, the term "covenant" has historical content that its rival lacks, for "order" is formalistically rooted in language's yes-and-no.

This formalism is why the term "order" entails the risk of forgetting the Hobbesian emphasis.[2]

What advantage does "order" possess that persuades Burke to undertake this risk?

the term "covenant" is not wholly convenient for our purposes. Having no opposite in standard usage, it seems as purely "positive" as words like "stone," "tree" or "table," which are not matched by companion words like "counter-stone" ... The term "order," on the other hand, clearly reveals its dialectical or "polar" nature, on its face. "Order" implies "disorder," and vice versa. And that's the kind of term we need.   (181)

"Order" and "disorder," in other words, are like "yes" and "no." The reason for taking the risk, then, seems to be terminological convenience: "order" implies "on its face" the opposite that would have to be manufactured for "covenant." However, considering that Burke heretofore was not one to fear stretching terms to suit his purposes, and that he later uses the term "counter-nature" (e.g., *PC* 297, *IH* 339), it's fair to wonder why he here shies away from "counter-covenant," or even "revolution," a clear polar opposite of "covenant" even if the polarization isn't etched into the terms as in "order" and "disorder."

That something other than terminological convenience is involved becomes more apparent later, when Burke's methodological conviction that the best example is the most "thorough" example prompts a reconsideration of his decision to privilege "order" rather than "covenant":

Methodologically, we might say that we have now come upon the penalties resulting from our earlier decision ... For the idea of a "Counter-Covenant" would have been somewhat different from the idea of such a mere disintegration as is usually suggested by the term "Disorder."

In sum, there is a notable qualitative difference between the idea of a mere "fall" from a position in which one still believes but to which one is at times unequal, and the idea of a deliberate turn to an alternative allegiance. It would be a difference between being "weak in virtue" and being "strong in sin."   (194)

To stay with "order" and "disorder," Burke concedes, would require two kinds of disorder: "(1) a tendency towards failure to obey completely always; (2) disobedience due to an out-and-out enrollment in the ranks of a rival force. We might call this a distinction between mere Disorder and deliberate allegiance to a Counter-Order" (195).

2 As Henderson observes, logology's formalism tends "to ignore act–scene relationships, the reality of action with which words are strongly bound up, the context of situation" (*Burke* 122).

This reconsideration of terminology occurs in the context of Burke's analysis of the cycle of terms for order itself. In this analysis, the step from order (God's command) to obedience–disobedience poses in turn the problem that theology typically conceives as one of free will. Logology, however, is under no obligation "to attempt solving this ultimate theological riddle" (193). Instead, logology need consider only "the conditions of dominion, as they prevail among human symbol-using animals. As seen in this light, the thought of all such issues leads us to revision of our initial dialectical pattern. That is, the Order–Disorder pair is not enough" (193). Burke thus concedes that while obedience and disobedience can be rooted formalistically in language's yes-and-no, they are nonetheless situated in history, in "conditions of dominion." The logological counterpart to free will must have historical content. To find the most "thorough" example of this counterpart, Burke recognizes that he must return to "covenant" and "counter-covenant," his terms for dominion.

In the context of dominion, one can see that language's formalistic "no" is ambiguous, for one may say no to an orthodoxy either through deviance (weak in virtue) or through a turn to an alternative orthodoxy (strong in sin). There is, in short, a big difference between (1) saying yes or no to an orthodoxy and (2) saying yes to this orthodoxy or yes to that one: yes-against-no vs. yes-against-yes. This latter is the choice between covenant and counter-covenant. The more "thorough" of the two, this choice occurs not within an orthodoxy but in the agon of history. It is the choice in a constitutional act, which constitutes an orthodoxy in the context of choice between orthodoxies in the agon of history. In Brown vs. Board of Education, the Supreme Court rejected the old orthodoxy of Plessy vs. Ferguson, "separate but equal," ruling that separation is inherently unequal, and replaced it with a new orthodoxy of integration. This contrast between yes-against-no and yes-against-yes is equivalent to the contrast, discussed in chapter 1, between Foucault's disciplinary agon and the agon of history. Burke's methodological conviction that the best example is the most "thorough" example directs his attention away from the disciplinary agon and toward the agon of history. His privileging of yes-against-yes is the moment when the constitutional act in *GM* reappears in *RR*.

Yes-against-yes is privileged, however, logologically rather than dramatistically. While distinguishing yes-against-yes from yes-against-no directs attention to history, distinguishing it as "strong in sin" is a terminological blinder that prevents attention from getting beyond Foucault's disciplinary yes-against-no. "Weak in virtue" is to "strong in sin" as guilt is to perversion. Perversion is strong sin in the sense that it is sin without guilt, sin that smiles defiantly at orthodoxy. Such sin may be at the outer limit of orthodoxy, almost free of its gravitational pull, but it is not altogether free because its pleasure comes from its defiance of orthodoxy, and to that extent it remains dependent on orthodoxy. "Strong in sin" is equivalent to Reich's sexual liberation – sexual sin without guilt – which Foucault critiques precisely because it ultimately reaffirms rather than displaces the orthodoxy of sexuality. To characterize yes-against-yes as "strong in sin" is, simultaneously, to turn toward history and to put it into terminological eclipse.[3]

The choice of Hobbes also merits scrutiny. For in choosing Hobbes's *Leviathan* to analyze yes-against-yes, Burke in effect substitutes this text for the US Constitution. From the standpoint of *RR*'s logologese, what are the advantages of Hobbes's terminology? First, even though Hobbes's covenant is contrasted to Genesis's order, the Hobbesian terminology defers to the biblical insofar as its "covenant" is a biblical term too. "The First Three Chapters of Genesis" begins with Hobbes, but his terminological overlap with the Bible allows Burke to incorporate biblical references, such as, "The possibility of a 'Fall' is implied in the idea of a Covenant insofar as the idea of a Covenant implies the possibility of its being violated" (174). The second and more important advantage appears in the main Hobbes chapter, "Covenant and 'Counter-Covenant' in Hobbes's *Leviathan*," where this Hobbes text is mapped onto the Genesis text at a level deeper than this terminological overlap.

The *Leviathan*'s antagonist is historical: the Pope in Rome. Just as in *GM* Parkes's antagonist in his new constitution for capitalism is Marxism, Hobbes's antagonist in his new covenant for a "Christian Commonwealth" is popery (198). But Hobbes depicts his antagonist as a "Kingdom of Darkness" run by the prince of darkness himself, who surpasses all others in being "strong in sin":

Hobbes helps us realize that, implicit in the idea of a Covenant is the idea not just of obedience or disobedience to that Covenant, but also of obedience or disobedience to a *rival* Covenant. The choice thus becomes not just a

3 That yes-against-yes is overshadowed by the yes-against-no of *RR*'s rhetoric of order is as evident in commentary on *RR* as in *RR* itself. See Thomas, for example, especially p. 337, where the subject is seen as conforming or not conforming to a community, never as not conforming to one by conforming to another.

difference between seeking the light and not seeking the light, but rather the difference between eagerly seeking the light and just as eagerly seeking darkness (a "Disorder" having an "Order" all its own, however insistent the orthodoxy must be that the Satanic counter-realm can exist only by the sufferance of the One Ultimate Authority). (199)

Burke equates "weak in virtue" to temptation and "strong in sin" to a Faustian pact with the Devil, paralleling this contrast with that in Joyce's *Portrait* "between Stephen's sexual fall despite himself in the second section, and his deliberate choice of a 'proud' aesthetic calling, as 'priest of the imagination,' in section four" (195–96). But does this parallel hold? Stephen's priesthood of the imagination is a genuine new aesthetic yes against the old Catholic yes. A Faustian pact, in contrast, is a perverse no, not a rival yes. *RR* forgets the recognition in "PLF" that the devil is a part of that against which he rebels: "As an angel, Lucifer is in synecdochic relationship with God (i.e., he is a 'messenger'). As a rebel, he is in negatively synecdochic relationship" (59–60). In short, the *Leviathian* theorizes, not yes-against-yes, but yes against the strong no of strong in sin. Or, perhaps more precisely, *RR* forgets until its "Prologue in Heaven," where S remarks to TL at one point, "your positives and my negatives mutually imply each other in perfect dialectic oneness" (291).

Hobbes's text is thus a variation of Genesis's yes-and-no, not the shift away from it that the turn from "order" back to "covenant" appears to promise. Genesis, not the *Leviathan*, displaces the Constitution as Burke's "representative anecdote." Burke says as much, even though he doesn't use this term explicitly, when he remarks that Genesis "is just about *perfect* for the purposes of the 'logologer'" (3).[4] This displacement is not altogether silent, however; the noisy shifts back and forth between the terms "order" and "covenant" are the sounds of Burke moving heavy furniture in his theoretical edifice. On the one hand, his methodological commitment to "thoroughness" recognizes that the yes-against-yes of the agon of history is more thorough than the yes-against-no of the disciplinary agon. On the other hand, his new representative anecdote, by privileging the disciplinary, requires that yes-against-yes be rewritten as yes-against-no. The methodological commitment has to yield: the less thorough example has to be allowed to trump the more thorough – a reversal that puts history into eclipse.

4 Suggestive also is the contrast between *RR*'s first sentence – "Religion has often been looked upon as a center from which all other forms of human motivation gradually diverged" (v) – and *GM*'s: "What is involved, when we say what people are doing and why they are doing it?" (xv).

In *RR*, Burke thus theorizes his way to the disciplinary agon that Foucault never managed to leave altogether behind. We would agree and disagree with Cary Nelson's poststructuralist reading of Burke, which proposes that beginning with *RR* Burke places us, as symbol-using animals, "within a verbal drama that is in a sense already written for us" (157). Agreed, but we would attribute this placement to *RR*'s turn from the agon of history — where the new is possible because the act is never more than partially written in advance — to a Foucauldian disciplinary agon, where, as the cycle of terms for order dictates, the same disciplinary drama is played over and over, and, as Trevor Melia aptly suggests, "symbolic *action* threatens to reduce to symbolic *motion*" (68). Nelson, in contrast, attributes this placement to Burke's recognition that "one cannot write except as an *agent* of the very verbal structures one may want to expose and criticize" (159). But this recognition comes earlier, as evidenced by the pentad, the whole point of which is that we can never get outside its structures, a point that Nelson verges on conceding in a long endnote on the pentad (172–73).

Foucault, we saw in chapter 1, exhibits the underside of orthodoxy, exposing it not as it sees itself in the self-portrait of its own rationality, but as an imposition of power. *RR* inverts Foucault in that it depicts orthodoxy as it sees itself. Deviations from orthodoxy, for late Burke, are "weak in virtue" or "strong in sin," whereas for Foucault, they are honored as "resistance." Foucault, moreover, explicitly identifies resistance as the proper methodological standpoint from which to analyze the operations of power. In Burke, a view from above; in Foucault, from below.

This view from above, however, is qualified by dramatic irony, such that orthodoxy is like a tragic hero: its viewpoint is dignified as dominant but nonetheless seen to err (*hamartia*).[5] Standing with Burke, we see more than the orthodoxy sees, as in the cycles both for order and for covenant, there is vicarious atonement to purge the guilt inherent in order, typically taking the form of victimage (191, 199), as in the lines quoted earlier (p. 220):

> Order
> Through Guilt
> To Victimage
> (hence: Cult of the Kill)....

5 Support for this point appears in Griffin, who equates his dramatistic view of social movements to "the dialectical movement of tragedy" (456). Writing in the 1960s, when *RR*, as Rueckert indicates, "seemed like the culmination of dramatism," Griffin produces an impressive reading of the totality of Burke through the lens of *RR*.

Scapegoating, in other words, seems to be the telos of orthodoxy. The flaw, moreover, seems incurable, as inevitable as death and taxes. All orthodoxies seem equally doomed, the only hope being a reduction of scapegoating through the self-understanding of tragic recognition (*anagnorisis*).[6]

Burke's logological psychology thus raises scapegoating to a new level. A scapegoat temptation arises in the situation of the scientist analyzed in *RM*, but it is projected as an effect of an emergent orthodoxy. Burke explicitly entertains the possibility of an alternative orthodoxy in which this temptation would not arise as he urges scientists to refuse the hierarchization that the emergent Cold War orthodoxy is constituting. In *RM* scapegoating is always a potentiality, but some orthodoxies are more conducive to its actualization than others. In *RR*, in contrast, whatever the differences between this orthodoxy and that one, they are submerged beneath the disciplinary yes-against-no common to all orthodoxies from which scapegoating derives. Viewing the US and the USSR from the standpoint of *RR*, Burke wishes a plague on both their houses:

If we are right in what we take the Creation Myth in Genesis to be saying, then the contemporary world must doubly fear the cyclical compulsions of Empire, as two mighty world orders ... confront each other ... [I]n keeping with the "curative" role of victimage, each is apparently in acute need of blaming all its many troubles on the other, wanting to feel certain that, if the other and its tendencies were but eliminated, all governmental discord (all the Disorder that goes with Order) would be eliminated. (4)

GM, when considering Parkes's agon, sees it as a struggle between orthodoxies whose differences matter. Burke also suggests ways of deploying the notion of circumference to position oneself to judge both from the position of neither (351–55). *GM* presupposes the premise of the agon of history, that historical change is possible. But in *RR*, the possibility of transformation in the agon of history gives way to the disciplinary agon from which there is no exit. All roads are the same: order, guilt, victimage.

While late Burke and Foucault are inversions of one another in one sense, they are identical in privileging the disciplinary agon and its transindividual perspective. Logological psychology is pitched at the level, not of the individual but of the human species, the same level as

---

6 See Carter, who concludes, "Logology in the very strictest Burkean sense is a metalinguistic attempt to decrease the number of sacrificial victims" (18).

the innate forms in Burke's early aesthetic and as the biologism in *PC*. *RR*'s transindividuality may be a reason for its silence about *SM*, which was conceived from the standpoint of the Freudian individualism that emerged in *ATH* and reappeared as "dream" in "PLF" in its tripartite structure of symbolic action – dream, prayer, chart – the precursor of the tripartite structure of dramatism. That *RR* appeared when *SM* was expected exhibits *GM*'s and *RM*'s recognition that individualism is an orthodoxy, a cultural rhetoric, as Burke acknowledges in agreeing with Jameson that individualism is an ideology.

RR may be viewed as a return to Burke's beginnings insofar as logological psychology is a psychology of the human species, but it's a return with a difference. For *RR*'s disciplinary yes-against-no is cultural, historical, rather than innate or biological. Burke's disciplinary agon is innate or biological only in the sense that it involves our inborn capacity to learn language. As is evident in his response to Jameson, late Burke, while insisting on a level of biological individuation, clearly distinguishes this level from the cultural level of the formation of subjects, such as the subject of individualism. Like Foucault, however, late Burke fails, as Marx might say, to rise all the way to the historical concrete. This failure results, in Burke's case, from displacing the abstraction of yes-against-yes in favor of the abstraction of yes-against-no. That this displacement occurs in the face of a clear recognition that yes-against-yes is the more "thorough" of the two – and thus in violation of *RR*'s own methodological prescription – is a sign of *RR*'s resistance to a rhetoric of the subject.

While considering Hobbes's counter-covenant, Burke suggests that it may be considered as a variant

of the Manichaean "heresy," according to which Evil is a power in its own right. As we have observed before, logology must side with Augustine's attacks upon this position. For logology looks upon "evil" as a species of the negative, and looks upon the negative as a sheerly linguistic invention. This would be the logological analogue of Augustine's theological doctrine that *malum* is a *causa deficiens*, a mere deficiency.   (199-200)

This passage merits attention not only as a cross-reference between Burke's new representative anecdote and his reading in *RR* of Augustine's *Confessions*, but also, going outside *RR*, as a link with Burke's theory of the negative, which appears in "A Dramatistic View of the Origins of Language" (DVOL). A major theoretical undertaking published in the early 1950s before its later reprinting in *LSA*, this text may be considered the beginning of the later Burke.

The negative helps to explain Burke's interest in this Augustine text as well as his approach to it. In attacking Manichaeanism, Augustine attacks a former self, of course, since he is a convert from the Manichaean to the Christian orthodoxy. But constitutional analysis of this conversion interests Burke less than the logological match that he finds between his theory of the negative and Augustine's of "the unreality of evil" (89). Constitutional analysis appears briefly as Burke analogizes parenthetically that "Manichaeanism was to him [Augustine] what communism is to an ardent ex-communist" (70), and, more importantly, in a gem of a footnote, as Burke sketches hierarchizing issues in Augustine's debates with not only Manichaeans but also Pelagians and Donatists. All these issues, Burke suggests, center finally on the constitutional act necessary for sustaining Christianity as a church, an ecclesiastical institution (115). These passages are enough to suggest how a constitutional analysis could historically situate Augustine's formation as a Christian subject, but the proportional weight they receive – to apply Burke's proportionalizing method to Burke – relegates them to the status of digressive asides to the main business of logological analysis. Just as Burke recognizes yes-against-yes only to bury it beneath yes-against-no, he recognizes constitutional analysis only to marginalize it in favor of logologically rewriting Augustine's theological doctrine of evil as words about the word "no," such that the alternative to "yes" is not a different "yes" but a version of "no," a "deficiency" rather than "a power in its own right."

Hence, Burke treats Augustine's conversion to Christianity as a shift not from an alternative orthodoxy but from perversion: "we might best point up the chapter on his final conversion by juxtaposing it with the chapter on perversity" (64–65). If counter-covenant is equated to evil, as in Hobbes, and if evil is equated to *causa deficiens*, as in Augustine, and if counter-covenant, evil, and *causa deficiens* are together equated to the negative, as in Burke, then yes-against-yes gives way to yes-against-no, and perversion becomes of interest as the negative taken to the extreme of "strong in sin." Moreover, Burke's reading of Augustine's chapter on perversity – the pear-stealing episode – contains illustrations of perversity that we can cite to substantiate our earlier argument that "strong in sin" never gets beyond the gravitational pull of the orthodoxy from which it deviates because orthodoxy is the condition of the pleasures of perversity. A few examples: "pure dedication to crime for its own sake" (94), "the act was all the more pleasing in that it was illicit" (98), "it was only the crime itself that made them [the pears] taste good" (99).

In theorizing the negative in "Dramatistic View of Origins," dramatism reorients itself as it theorizes the act within the framework of the logological tension between yes and no instead of the constitutional tension between voluntaristic and necessitarian principles. In its narration of this reorientation, the present study gives special attention to a passage near the end of *RM* where Burke first advances and then abandons a proposal that nature must be "super-personal" in the sense that it contains the "personal" found in the human realm in addition to everything outside this realm:

> If you insist, we'll abandon, for argument's sake, the notion that nature is "super-personal." The argument is based on the assumption that there is such a thing as "personality" in the human realm. And when you get through dissolving personality into the stream of consciousness, or into dissociated subpersonalities, or into "conditioned reflexes," or into appearances of substance that derive purely from such extrinsic factors as status and role, there may not seem to be any intrinsic core left. So we'll retreat to our more easily defendable position: that nature must be more-than-verbal. For in its totality it encompasses verbal and nonverbal both; and its "nonverbal" ground must have contained the "potentiality" of the verbal, otherwise the verbal could not have emerged from it.   (290)

If there is no "intrinsic core" to the personal, there is no theoretical basis for the unique individual that *SM* was to theorize. Burke, however, seems to have been unwilling to leave the formation of the subject as open to the agon of history as a rhetoric of the subject proposes. Instead, having in *GM* and *RM* theorized the personal out from under himself, Burke repositioned the personal, shifting it from the unique individual to the transindividual yes and no in language that is in all individuals by virtue of the linguistic prowess of the human species. *RR* theorizes the personal "by equating human personality with the ability to use symbol-systems (centering in the feeling for the negative, since 'reason,' in its role as the 'sense of right and wrong,' is but a special case of the 'sense of yes and no')" (192; see also 208–09, a passage quoted earlier). By deriving personality from the verbal and the verbal from the more-than-verbal, Burke finds a ground for personality that is humanistic in the sense that it's prior to history (DVOL 456).

"Dramatistic View of Origins" fleshes out this *RM* passage by positing the negative as the line between the nonverbal, in the narrow sense of less-than-verbal, and the verbal. Burke italicizes this thesis: *"The essential distinction between the verbal and the nonverbal is in the fact that language adds the peculiar possibility of the Negative"* (453–54). In advancing this thesis, Burke undertakes some lines of analysis that are inconclusive but informative as illustrations of the difficulties he encounters as he tries to use the negative to drawn a bright line between the nonverbal and the verbal. In a section entitled "Behavioristic Pre-Language," he argues, "The senses classify, when they 'translate' some vibrations into terms of sound, others into terms of color, or record still others as smell, etc." (425). Such an argument implies that linguistic classification can be derived behavioristically, an implication that this section's title reinforces. To silence the smoke alarm that such an implication sets off in his theoretical edifice, Burke qualifies his argument: "to say that the principles of abstraction, classification, generalization, and specification (or division) are present in prelinguistic behavior is not the same as saying that their linguistic analogues are 'nothing but' more complicated versions of the pre-linguistic" (427). He adds, "we must be on guard lest, in our zeal to make much of the negative, we give too much credit to it in particular ... as a peculiarity of language" (427). Going in the other direction, he concedes that "behavioristic pre-language" also includes the negative in the sense that "either infant or animal in effect 'says no' when turning the head away from something that it does not want" (427).

Burke draws his line most cleanly with the aid of the terms "idea" and "image": *"the negative is an idea*; there can be no image of it. *But in imagery there is no negative"* (430). Later in his text, Burke refines this thesis with a more technical analysis, one that distinguishes sensory from linguistic imagery:

In saying that one cannot say no in imagery, we certainly did not mean that one cannot *imply* no. If, when a would-be thief is eyeing some valuable property that is not his, you pointedly show him a picture of a jail, you have pictorially implied, "Don't steal, or else ... [Burke's ellipsis]." But it is not the mere *physical* aspects of the image that make such implication possible. It is the *idea* of a jail that implies the negative ...

Images, in their role as verbal counters, are on the side of idea ... [T]his is their bond with the realm of *action*. In their reference to physical sensation as such, they are "primitive-positive" — and this aspect of their nature connects them with the no-less realm of sheer motion, where everything can be only what it is. (460)

This distinction between idea and image also appears in *RM* – Burke consistently writes against trends in social science that overemphasize the empirical image – but there he finds its paradigmatic form in the rhetorical distinction between "'infinite' (or 'general') and 'definite' (or 'specific') questions" (85). To illustrate, he quotes from Thomas Wilson's *Art of Rhetoric*: "Those questions are called infinite which generally are propounded without the comprehension of time, place, or person... As thus, whether it be best to marry, or to live single... These questions are called definite, which set forth a matter, with the appointment and naming of place, time, and person" (85). Here in *RM* "idea" and "image" thus refer to what are in effect different places in the Burkean conversation. In "Dramatistic View of Origins," in contrast, "image" and "idea" replicate the distinction in the Kantian epistemological tradition between "phenomenon" and "noumenon." The phenomenon is equivalent to the image, considered as pure intuition of the sensory "in the no-less realm of sheer motion"; the noumenon, to the linguistic negative, the condition of action in Burke's reorientation of dramatism.

Kant appears extensively in "Dramatistic View of Origins," proportionally more extensively than anywhere else in Burke. Kant serves in effect as Burke's point of departure for his reorientation of dramatism. This new dramatism retains this epistemological imprint even as later texts gravitate away from more rigorously Kantian formulations to be found in this one. A good example is a categorization of words, which appears in *RR* before being developed even more thoroughly in "What Are the Signs of What?" (*WW*). The categories are "(1) words for the sheerly natural (in the sense of the less-than-verbal...); (2) words for the verbal realm itself...; (3) words for the sociopolitical realm...; (4) words for the 'supernatural' (*WW* 373–74). In this fourfold, the first three are grouped together as "the three empirical worldly orders" (374). This tripartite empirical realm corresponds by analogy to the phenomenality of the sensory image. The supernatural, in contrast, corresponds to the noumenality of the idea beyond the image. Empirically inaccessible, the supernatural is described with words "necessarily borrowed from our words for the three worldly orders: Thus, a metaphor for God's power, such as the 'arm' of God, would be taken from the natural order; the notion of the divine creative Fiat... from the verbal order; and the reference to God as father or lord... from the sociopolitical order" (374; see also *RR* 37–38). The supernatural and the negative come together explicitly in negative theology whereby God, empirically indescribable, is defined negatively: "The simplest route to negative theology is to make negatives of all terms that designate positive availability to sensory perception (as *invisible, unknowable, boundless*)" (DVOL 457; see also *RR* 22–23). This epistemological world of phenomenality and noumenality is quite different from the world whose substance is formed through the use of pentadic categories in constitutional acts.

Natural, verbal, and sociopolitical imagistic metaphors for God – depending on one's God – may be positive, a carrot rather than the stick behind the image of a jail before a would-be thief. In other words, the negative in a God's thou-shalt-not may be positivized: "no" can negate itself to become a positive "yes." Such positivizing of the negative is a major preoccupation throughout "Dramatistic View of Origins." In Kant's text, Burke observes, "the thou-shalt-not's of moral law retreat behind the positive accents of noble righteousness" (441). By virtue of positivizing the negative, there is a "no" behind a "yes," so that the logological yes-and-no is really no and no-no (negating no). Analogous to Foucault's "power is everywhere" is logology's "no is everywhere." Further, in the positivizing of the negative, there is also an analogue to Foucault's conception of power as positive or productive, that is, power that prompts submission through the carrot of empowerment rather than the stick of prohibition. Burke's Kantian reorientation of dramatism translates readily into a Foucauldian disciplinary agon in which negativity penetrates the body insofar as cultural codes circumscribe sensory experience, such that the sensory can never be simply itself. As Burke explains,

Within the Dramatistic scheme, any reference to the "senses" must be examined for possible motivations not specifically "sensory" at all . . . Why? Because the "senses" as such are not a fit for any one social order . . . [C]ontrol (the code of thou-shalt-not's) is not "positive" until it contains its fulfillment in the citizens' will freely to practice self-control; . . . such self-control is synonymous with control over "the senses," insofar as "the senses" are credited . . . with all the tendencies to deviate from the *ideals* that go with the given social order.   (442–43)

In Burke's reorientation of dramatism, the dramatistic act is thus forged in the disciplinary agon between no and no-no.

This act substitutes in late Burke for *GM*'s constitutional act, which is forged in the agon of history, where necessitarian imperatives require hierarchizing of competing voluntaristic "wishes," or constitutional clauses, each a motivational discourse in competition with other discourses. In the cauldron of this agon, a new orthodoxy can emerge. This possibility of the new, we recall from chapter 6, prompts Burke to select the Act of Creation as his model for the act. In "Dramatistic View of Origins," in contrast, Burke finds his model not in the Act of Creation but in the Ten Commandments (422). History is marginalized as this new model directs our attention away from historical differences to the process common to all commandments: order, guilt, victimage.

In his self-characterization in the 1980s of the distinctiveness of the logological phase of his career, Burke deploys an analogy: "'dramatism' and 'logology' are analogous respectively to the traditional distinction... between ontology and epistemology" (DL83; see also DL85). Burke is not, of course, saying anything new in equating dramatism to ontology, albeit a rhetorical ontology. This equation appears in *GM* itself, as we saw at the end of chapter 6, and reappears in a 1955 text:

We shall look upon language-using as a mode of conduct and shall frame our terms accordingly. We could call this position "dramatistic" because it thus begins with a stress upon "action." And it might be contrasted with idealistic terminologies, that begin with considerations of perception, knowledge, learning. In contrast with such *epistemological* approaches, this approach would be *ontological*, centering upon the *substantiality* of the *act*." (LAPE 259)

Also reappearing here is the contrast between dramatism and epistemology that Burke uses, as we saw in chapter 5, in introducing dramatism during the 1940s. In the context of this contrast, Burke's equation of logology to epistemology amounts to a handshake with an old antagonist — that is what is new in his self-characterization. In this handshake, moreover, Burke is acknowledging that logology is not, as *RR* seems to imply, a mere satellite of dramatism. He confirms Rueckert's judgment, noted earlier, that logology is a theoretical center with its own satellites, equivalent in status to dramatism.

Burke's distinction between his ontological and epistemological phases appears initially in the unusual form of a letter to the editor, one occasioned moreover by a review not of his own work but of Rueckert's book, from which we quoted at the beginning of the present chapter. Burke writes to correct the reviewer's remark that "dramatism" and "logology" are simply different names for the same theory of language (DL83). Two years later, in 1985, Burke expands on this correction (DL85). The reviewer's remark, in short, seems to have provided an occasion for Burke to speak about something already on his mind. One suspects that Burke was motivated, at least in part, by his participation, at the 1982 conference of the Eastern Communication Association, in a symposium where he responded to papers on his work (DOES 17). The periodization of his career was not an issue on the symposium agenda, but it became one in the wake of Burke's response to Bernard L. Brock's paper. What started out as a discussion of how best to define dramatism turned into a discussion of how best to characterize the shift from middle to late Burke. Brock's paper, Burke's response, and some of the symposium discussion, which continued through the mails after the conference, were all published in 1985 (DOES).

In his response to Brock's paper, Burke quotes from "Dramatism" (D68), which he wrote for the *International Encyclopedia of Social Sciences*, from a section that begins with a question, "Is dramatism merely metaphorical?" and that answers with an unequivocal "no" (DOES 23; see also D68 448). Burke designed this section to refute the claim that dramatism is rooted in a metaphor, a claim encouraged, he concedes, by *PC*'s thesis that all language is metaphorical. Brock's iteration of this claim prompts Burke's return to this text, and in turn, the symposium becomes a debate over whether dramatism, considered as a terminology, speaks literally or metaphorically.

At the symposium, which occurred before Burke's 1983 letter to the editor, Burke's analogy of dramatism to ontology and logology to epistemology does not appear. It had appeared, however, by the time the symposium was published, as an editor's introduction acknowledges as it mentions Burke's letter (DOES 18) and in effect adds this analogy to the symposium: "The central issue which emerges here is whether or not dramatism should be viewed as: (1) an ontological system which offers literal statements regarding the nature of the human being as a symbol-user and the nature of language as an act, or (2) an epistemological system which posits but one way of viewing human beings and human activities such as language-using" (DOES 17). Further, also in 1985, Brock revises his 1982 paper to periodize Burke's career in a narrative in which dramatism begins as a metaphor and later, in "Dramatism," becomes literal, a shift Brock depicts as one from epistemology to ontology ("Epistemology"). By 1985, the question thus changed from how best to define dramatism to how best to periodize Burke.

Brock's periodization, however, reverses Burke's insofar as Burke narrates a shift from ontology (dramatism) to epistemology (logology), whereas Brock narrates one from epistemology (dramatism is metaphor) to ontology (dramatism is literal). Brock's narrative is based on a marriage of literality to ontology and metaphor to epistemology – the same marriage that occurs in the symposium editor's introduction – such that Burke's argument in "Dramatism" that dramatism is literal becomes the beginning of his final phase. Notably, Brock's narrative effectively marginalizes logology, mentioning it only once and then inconclusively ("Epistemology" 103).

The marriage that occurs in Brock and the editor's introduction does not occur in Burke. Brock and the editor leave unexplored the possibility that ontology–epistemology is to be preferred to metaphor–literal as a framework within which to periodize Burke. Burke doesn't explicitly address the issue, but he does suggest at the symposium, in characterizing *PC*'s language-is-metaphor thesis as using "rhetoric and ontological as synonymous terms" (DOES 22), that ontology can be equated to metaphor as well as the literal. Ontology and the literal, in other words, need not be automatically identified. Further, and more importantly, Burke introduces his ontology-epistemology periodization in his letter after the symposium, implicitly preferring ontology-epistemology to metaphor–literal as a periodizing framework. Before considering additional reasons for preferring the ontology–epistemology framework, however, the periodization depicting Burke as moving from rather than toward epistemology merits more attention. We differ with this periodization but the difference is in part merely semantic.

Brock's 1985 periodization narrates a shift from one dramatism to another: from (1) dramatism = metaphor = epistemology; to (2) dramatism = literal = ontology. In this narrative, as noted earlier, logology is marginalized. In contrast, logology is more prominent in James W. Chesebro's periodization, as it is included in his basic equations: from (1) logology = metaphor = epistemology; to (2) dramatism = literal = ontology. Chesebro agrees with Brock, however, that Burke moves away from epistemology not toward it. In Chesebro's narrative, logology is epistemology, and it appears not only in *RR* but also well before: "Burke's logological or epistemic inquiries are amply illustrated in his *Grammar, Rhetoric,* and *Rhetoric of Religion*" ("Epistemology" 181). Brock returns to the discussion in 1993 with a new narrative that gives more prominence to logology than his earlier one and that periodizes Burke's whole career into three main stages. In this narrative, as in Chesebro's, logology appears *avant la lettre*: "'Logology,' developed during Burke's first and second stages, embodies his concern for epistemology... 'Dramatism,'... [for] the ontology of [his] third stage..." ("Evolution" 326).[7]

This periodization of Burke as moving from rather than toward epistemology may be attributed to a discursive framework in the field of speech that functions as a Burkean terministic screen — a screen perhaps more apparent to someone outside the field rather than to scholars inside it, since it's no doubt easier to see someone else's screen than one's own. Writing in 1988, Chesebro lays out this discursive framework as he contextualizes his periodization of Burke by first recollecting the seminality of Robert L. Scott's 1967 conceptualization of "epistemic rhetoric" and then listing limitations to this conception noted more recently by various scholars in the field. This shift in the discourse in the field frames Chesebro's claim that prior to Burke's late phase, his work "was flagrantly grounded in an epistemic orientation" ("Epistemology" 179). The shift in Burke thus anticipates the shift in the field.

One must therefore ask, what kind of epistemology is epistemic rhetoric? Scott looks at rhetoric in broad historical sweep going all the way back to Plato. The tendency for over two millennia has been to see rhetoric as a handmaiden to a truth that is immutable and prior to its operations. Always needing to fight the suspicion that it sought only to manipulate unsuspecting audiences, the best rhetoric could hope for was to win applause for a brilliant ornamentation of truth. In other words, at best rhetoric was second class. Scott re-hierarchizes rhetoric by questioning the possibility of such a truth and thereby giving rhetoric a constitutive role:

[T]ruth is not prior and immutable but is contingent. Insofar as we can say that there is truth in human affairs, it is in time; it can be the result of a process of interaction at a given moment. Thus rhetoric may be viewed not as a matter of giving effectiveness to truth but of creating truth... [T]ruth can arise only from cooperative critical inquiry.[8]

Epistemic rhetoric, in short, is a historicizing of epistemology. As such it is far removed from the Cartesian epistemology that Burke has in mind in the 1940s when he introduces dramatism by contrasting it to

---

7 Brock and Chesebro are major Burkeans in the field of speech. Brock's work on Burke has been widely read in the field for two decades. Chesebro served on the steering committee that established the Kenneth Burke Society in 1984, and he was the chief planner for its 1993 convention. See Chesebro, *Extensions* 342.

8 "On Viewing Rhetoric as Epistemic." *Central States Speech Journal* 18 (1967): 13, 14.

epistemology. Insofar as Brock and Chesebro depict late Burke as turning away from a historicizing of epistemology – which is what dramatism effected in the 1940s in its subordination of epistemological concerns to action – their periodization is not as different from the present chapter's as might appear at first blush.

Returning to Burke's ontology–epistemology distinction, one can find an additional reason for preferring it as a periodizing framework by looking closely at the passage from "Dramatism" that Burke quotes at the symposium. What one finds is a repetition of the argument that we saw earlier, in chapter 5, in considering the term "representative anecdote" that Burke uses in *GM* in his polemic with behaviorism. In both places, Burke makes his case for the reality of rhetoric by contrasting scientists' relation to things in the realm of motion to their relations with colleagues in the realm of action. First, the argument from "Dramatism," which appears in 1968:

Is dramatism merely metaphorical? Although such prototypically dramatistic usages as "all the world's a stage" are clearly metaphors, the situation looks quite otherwise when approached from another point of view. For instance, a physical scientist's relation to the materials involved in the study of motion differs in quality from his relation to his colleagues. He would never think of "petitioning" the objects of his experiment or "arguing with them," as he would with persons... Implicit in these two relations is the distinction between the sheer motion of things and the actions of persons.

In this sense, man is defined literally as an animal characterized by his special aptitude for "symbolic action," which is itself a literal term. (D68 448)

Second, the 1945 precedent appearing in *GM*:

A representative case of human motivation must have a strongly linguistic bias... The very man who, with a chemical experiment as his informing anecdote, or point of departure, might tell you that people are but chemicals, will induce responses in people by talking to them, whereas he would not try to make chemicals behave by linguistic inducement. (59)

An argument stated in 1945 and repeated in 1968 is not a basis on which to build a periodizing shift during the intervening decades. The most one can say is that there is a terminological shift from "representative anecdote" to "literal."

Further, while Burke does say at the symposium that this 1968 text is where he first addresses this issue of whether dramatism is "merely metaphorical" (DOES 22), in doing so he forgets the 1955 text quoted at the beginning of the present section, for immediately after this passage, Burke adds, "Also, a 'dramatistic' approach, as so conceived, is *literal*, not *figurative*. Man *literally* is a symbol-using animal" (LAPE 259–60). Finally, and most importantly, as we saw in chapter 5, Burke's conception of language as action effectively demotes the metaphor–literal distinction to at best second-tier status. What remains consistent in Burke from the 1940s through the 1960s and beyond is the core thesis that the human being is uniquely "an animal characterized by . . . [a] special aptitude for 'symbolic action.'" His final variation on this formulation appears in his afterword for the 1984 edition of *PC*: "When viewing us as the only animal, to my knowledge, that seeks to define itself, I have finally reduced the tenor of my concerns with the nature of human relations to this four-word formula: We are 'Bodies That Learn Language'" (*PC* 295). In this sense, Burke's thought is consistently dramatistic. In the periodization of his career, the change that distinguishes his middle from his late phases is his theorizing of the act – the shift from the Act of Creation to the Ten Commandments. The distinction that defines this shift is not metaphor–literal, but ontology–epistemology. Middle Burke needed *GM* and *RM* to theorize the act. Late Burke needed only logology.

What kind of epistemology is logology? Logology is a handshake with epistemology in one sense, but not in another, as suggested by Burke's privileging of the hortatory rather than the propositional negative in "Dramatistic View of Origins." Literality in Burke is never the literality of the classical philosophical "is." Burke's "Definition of Man" may seem to promise such an "is" in its title, but it begins, "First, a few words on definition in general. Let's admit it: I see in a definition the critic's equivalent of a lyric" (DM 3). The tension between literality in the philosophical sense and literality in the sense of Austin's "Lord Raglan won the battle of Alma" is resolved in rhetoric by making the former an instance of the latter writ large.

Classical epistemology is preeminently concerned with the comprehension of truth. Burke does not become an epistemologist in this sense. He never subscribes to the classical correspondence theory of truth. As he says in the 1967 version of "Dramatism," a longer version of the 1968 text from which he quotes at the symposium: "Once we choose a generalized term for what people do, it is certainly as literal to say that 'people act' as it is to say that they 'but move like mere things.' Yet the Dramatistic critique of language does not require the acceptance of this distinction as 'true'" (D67 337). Similarly, in "Terministic Screens":

Even the behaviorist, who studies man in terms of his laboratory experiments, must treat his colleagues as *persons*... I should make it clear: I am not pronouncing on the metaphysics of this controversy. Maybe we are but things in motion... I need but point out that, whether or not we are just things in motion, we think of one another...as *persons*... For the sake of argument, I'm even willing to grant that the distinction between *things moving* and *persons acting* is but an illusion. All I would claim is that, illusion or not, the human race cannot possibly get along with itself on the basis of any other intuition. The human animal, as we know it, *emerges into personality* by first mastering whatever tribal speech happens to be its particular symbolic environment.   (TS 53)

One might say, in short, that Burke is a "metaculturalist" rather than a metaphysician. In such "for the sake of argument" argument, Burke fights an uphill rhetorical battle to establish rhetorical sayability against the tradition descending from enlightenment certainty and romantic authenticity that has, as noted near the end of our last chapter, relegated rhetoric to second-class status. Burke's work anticipates the epochal reevaluation of culture now under way that promises to recognize rhetorical sayability as the "natural" habitat of the human being, who is if not a political animal, as Aristotle thought, at least a rhetorical animal.

But if Burke's epistemology is not classical, what qualifies it as an epistemology? The answer that interests us is the one that bears on the issue of the subject. What is distinctive about what the human subject becomes in an epistemology?

Consider the example of the imagination and its relation to other human faculties. What distinguishes the imagination is that it can deal with images independently of direct sensory experience. For centuries this capacity, as Burke observes, ranked "quite low in the scale of mental functions, being next to brute sensation, and the highest faculty of which brutes were thought capable. In human beings, according to this hierarchy, it stood midway between sensation and intellect" (*RM* 78). During the romantic period, in contrast, imagination was often radically re-hierarchized, elevated from this lowly position all the way to the top of the ladder of human faculties. Far from being brutish, imagination became the essence of being human. From the standpoint of a rhetoric of the subject, such re-hierarchizing is an effect of the agon of history. Hierarchizing is an act with real effects such that its occurrence is a function of struggle between opponents and supporters of these effects. An epistemology, in contrast, takes one such hierarchization and seeks to immunize it from this struggle by positioning it outside history. Late Burke constructs such a standpoint with the new representative anecdote that he locates in his tautological cycle of terms for order.

Order, guilt, sacrifice – together with all the additional refinements in the analysis of the tautological cycle, including positioning of "reason," "will," and "imagination" – constitute Burke's logological epistemology (*RR* 184). The shift from middle to late Burke is a shift from a history of subjects to a subject prior to history, one rooted in the more-than-verbal. This priority is nowhere more evident than in "Prologue in Heaven," where it is the premise of the dialogue between TL and S. TL's first speech recounts the origins of words from the more-than-verbal: "In the first chaotic swirl, the eventual emergence of the Word-Using Animal was implicit. And I shall not interfere with those processes that, having led to beautiful gardens can now, as it were, people the loveliest of them with this cantankerous animal" (276). From the position of this originary moment, TL and S look forward at this animal's destiny as the subject of history.

The reorientation in Burke's thought effected by his logological epistemology is most evident when TL and S take up the historical phenomena of injustice and inequality. Defenders of these, TL foretells, will require sanctions – "In the course of 'proving' that such inequities are 'right,' sanctions will pile up like bat dung in a cave" (287) – that in turn will be challenged: "The range of language being what it is, the very propounding and treasuring of such sanctions will lead in turn to the equally persuasive questioning of them. And all these matters will come to a head in man's theology, metaphysics, political theory and the like, in short the higher criticism that grows out of such venerable piles" (287). At the site of "these matters," the ontology of the constitutional act and the epistemology of the negative meet, but only to look past one another.

From the standpoint of the act, "these matters" involve hierarchizing issues among competing discourses, resolution of which is determined in the agon of history, where hierarchizations compete: yes-against-yes. In this struggle, the real appears in the form of the necessitarian principle by virtue of which doing this precludes doing that. Constitutional acts are in the world. They have real effects that are the stakes in agons of history. Struggle is a function of the real. In contrast, from the standpoint of logological epistemology, agonistic struggle over such issues recedes from view, giving way to the epistemological paradoxes attendant upon the negative being noumenal. Conceding that the "higher criticism" arising from debate over sanctions wanders far from the phenomenal, TL goes on, "True, by definition their speech will not be able to express the ineffable, any more than their eyes will be equipped to see the invisible. Even so, this persistent creature can reasonably assert: 'Here's what you could say about the ineffable if it could be talked about. Here's what eternity would look like if it did have visibility'" (287–88). Epistemology reorients attention away from acting in the world to knowing the world.

Burke comes closest to classical epistemology in his Kantian concerns with the visible (image) and the invisible (idea). But for Burke the visible world of positive imagery is subordinated to the negative of the cultural thou-shalt-not's that police the sensory and penetrate to their greatest depth when they positivize themselves to assume imagistic form. As S laughs, "I see it! I see it! And implicit in their supposedly objective versions of what is and is not, they will have concealed a set of shall's and shall not's, which they will then proceed methodically to 'discover'! What better comedy!" (279). Burke's epistemology, in short, is Foucauldian: knowing the world is fundamentally not a matter of cognition but of discipline. TL sums up:

But, to quick summation, and the perfect symmetry: In their societies, they will seek to keep order. If order, then a need to repress the tendencies to disorder. If repression, the responsibility for imposing, accepting, or resisting the repression. If responsibility, then guilt. If guilt, then the need for redemption, which involves sacrifice, which in turn allows for substitution. At this point, the logic of perfection enters. (314)

With a few words about this logic, this section can conclude.

TL introduces this logic early, promising S much more about it as the dialogue progresses (281). As the above passage suggests, TL's principal example of perfection is inscribed in the phase of the disciplinary agon in which one returns to the fold after a lapse into deviance: "here enters the principle of perfection. The Earth-People will consider themselves so guilt-laden, that only a perfect sacrifice would be great enough to pay off the debt" (295). This sacrifice is, of course, Christ. The logic of perfection, however, extends beyond this example, turning out to have a future in Burke's later discourse. In this sense, its prominence in *RR*'s closing pages is prophetic. It later becomes most prominent, as we'll see, in the guise of a different term: not "perfection" but one that appears in *RR* in an aside, as TL, in one of his references to this logic, foretells, "A bright Greek will treat of it in terms of what he will call the 'entelechy'" (300).

With the help of Wilma R. Ebbitt, I received a copy of Burke's unpublished *Poetics, Dramatistically Considered (PDC)* from Henry W. Sams, who in a letter to me from 1973 indicates that Burke wrote it in 1957–58, during his year at Stanford's Center for Advanced Study in the Behaviorial Sciences. Burke must, however, have started writing it years before, for he refers to it in 1952 in "Form and Persecution in the *Oresteia*" (FPO), which is drawn from a chapter in *PDC*.[9] In any case, the manuscript is book-length, though not quite complete – see table of contents below.

Rueckert cites this manuscript as evidence that Burke achieved a clear, nearly final conception of *SM*: "The 'Symbolic' has never been brought into coherent final form by Burke, though it was clearly in coherent form in his head as he was writing the different parts of it in the fifties and when he assembled 'Poetics, Dramatistically Considered,' a 391-page, incomplete first draft manuscript of the 'Symbolic'" (*Drama* 231). Rueckert leaves one question unaddressed, however: why the change in title? While authors change titles in the course of writing a book, *SM* was entitled in advance to parallel *GM* and *RM*. There is no denying that there is a relation between *PDC* and *SM*. Burke started writing *PDC* about the time it was expected that he would start *SM*. Further, in *GM*, in identifying the different kinds of texts that he planned to consider in the different parts of his trilogy, he indicated that literature, his focus in *PDC*, would be his focus in *SM*. But whatever the relation between *PDC* and *SM*, this title change indicates that it is not one of flat identification.

Much of the manuscript has appeared in published articles. Articles publishing portions of it are listed, in the table of contents reproduced below, by abbreviations to the left of chapter titles. One article incorporates material from multiple chapters.

9 The reference appears in both the reprinting of this article in *LSA* and the 1952 version in the *Sewanee Review*, volume 60. The only difference is that in 1952 the manuscript is "a book now in progress" (377), whereas in the 1966 reprinting it is "a book that has since undergone much revision" (125).

(Still missing: Section on Comic Catharsis; further references to individual works, illustrating various observations by specific examples; batch of footnotes indicating various other developments; appendix reprinting various related essays by the author, already published in periodicals.)

The articles generally follow the manuscript closely. The article on the *Oresteia* is an exception in being considerably shorter than the corresponding chapter.

Rueckert attributes the fact that no *SM* ever saw print to a "deliberate withholding" from publication on Burke's part (*Drama* 233), a withholding "for reasons that are clear to no one, not even Burke, I think" (231).[10] Rueckert proposes that *SM* receded in importance for Burke as a shift in the place of literature occurred in his thinking: "It is not that Burke abandoned literature ... it is just that he moved to a higher level of generalization, to a set of ideas which included poetry along with other symbolic actions and made all of them subject to the same logological principles" (236). Perhaps, however, there is a move "to a higher level of generalization" even in *PDC* itself, as appears to be the case when one contrasts the kind of literature it analyzes to that examined in "PLF." As we noted in chapter 5, the tripartite structure of the symbolic act proposed in "PLF" — dream, prayer, chart — is a precursor of the tripartite structure of the dramatistic trilogy proposed a few years later in *GM. SM*'s precursor

10 This mystery has prompted speculation ranging as far as Jay's that the effect on Burke of the loss of his wife in 1969 is perhaps the reason *SM* was never published (*SCBC* 360).

is the dream, or cluster, analysis that is the principal focus in "PLF," where Burke returns repeatedly to psychoanalysis to contrast it to his own dream analysis. The subject of his analysis is, of course, the unique individual, specifically Coleridge, a focus consistent with the emphasis, which we saw at the end of chapter 4, on the individualistic, "pre-forensic" level that Burke privileges in theorizing the acceptance and rejection, at the deepest level, of symbols of authority. Logology, in contrast, as we saw earlier, is transindividualistic. *PDC* is closer to this later perspective than the earlier one.

In contrast to "PLF," *PDC*'s principal subject-matter is tragedy: Aristotle's *Poetics* is Burke's point of departure, as indicated at the outset of "On Catharsis, or Resolution" (CR 337), which is based on the first of *PDC*'s chapters on catharsis. As we noted in considering *ATH* in chapter 4, Burke sees ambiguity in tragedy insofar as it may either discipline by punishing deviance to reaffirm orthodoxy, or rebel by introducing a new orthodoxy to come, if only in an anticipatory way. But *ATH* does, finally, place tragedy on the acceptance, or disciplinary, side of its range of poetic categories, indicating that the genre is primarily disciplinary rather than revolutionary. That the emphasis is similarly on the disciplinary in *PDC* is evident in its extensive attention to catharsis. This attention, considered retrospectively, is a precursor of logology's attention to the redemptive value of victimage. Tragedy, moreover, is civic or forensic, rather than pre-forensic, a point Burke makes in "On Catharsis, or Resolution" as he contrasts tragic catharsis to the Freudian catharsis in the psychoanalytic process (CR 337). Catharsis in the disciplinary agon of tragedy purges not the deviation from the norm in the unique individual but the deviations pervading a community that threaten to tear it apart. The redemptive function of the tragic hero is civic and thus on the slope toward the redemptive function of Christ, who died for everyone.

In sum, *PDC*'s transindividuality is a departure from the unique individuality originally projected as *SM*'s project. In one comment in which Burke still envisions completing *SM*, he indicates that part of his difficulty is that the project threatens to split into two, a poetics and an ethics, such that the trilogy would become a tetralogy (*CS* 222). Burke gives us a glimpse of this tetralogy in "On Catharsis, or Resolution":

Poetics as here considered is part of a scheme involving what I take to be the four aspects of language. Besides Poetics there are: Logic (or "Grammar"), the universal principles of linguistic placement; Rhetoric, language as addressed, as hortatory, and as designed for the stimulating or transcending of partisanship; Ethics, language as a medium in which, willy nilly, writer and reader express their identities, their characters, either as individuals or as members of groups. The Poetic dimension of language concerns essentially the exercise of linguistic resources in and for themselves, by an animal which loves such exercise because it is the typically language-using animal. (CR 340)

The category Ethics in this scheme is closest to the original conception of *SM*. That the Poetics got written rather than the Ethics confirms *PDC*'s status as a step in the abandonment of *SM*, a transitional moment on the way to *RR*.

In this poetic concern with "the exercise of linguistic resources in and for themselves," one can detect late Burke's theme of entelechy, particularly because this exercise is identified as a distinctive characteristic of "the typically language-using animal." For Burke, as Rueckert observes, "entelechy [becomes] the most basic human motive intrinsic to all symbol-using" (*Drama* 236).

Tracing the rise of this term is difficult because Burke sometimes uses synonyms as alternatives to it, as suggested by TL's aside, noted earlier, that explicitly identifies "perfection" as a synonym for "entelechy." Other synonyms are "culmination" and "consummation." Sometimes even the same examples are used to illustrate "entelechy" in one context and another term in a different context. Applying Burke's method of cluster analysis, one could say that "entelechy" is part of a cluster of terms and examples such that whenever any member of the cluster appears, one should be on the lookout for the entelechial theme.

Indebted to Aristotle for the notion of entelechy, Burke sometimes tries to draw a fine line between himself and Aristotle, who, he explains, "uses the term 'entelechy' to designate the efforts of each thing to fulfill the potentialities of its kind — a fish aiming to be perfectly or thoroughly a fish, a tree to evolve in keeping with its nature as a tree, etc."; whereas

logological realism would restrict this notion to an incentive in language; namely: "the tracking down of implications." The nomenclature of physics, for instance, suggests certain possibilities of further development. The nomenclature of psychology suggests possibilities in another direction, economics in another, politics in another, etc... I call this an "entelechial" aspect of symbolic motivation. It involves all sorts of strivings after "perfection." (SRM 33; see also PAC 404–05)

But in other passages, it's difficult to see this line:

There is a sense in which the sheer exercising of the symbol-using faculty, in and for itself and without respect to further benefits, should gratify a symbol-using animal, quite as a bird must be gratified in being "free" to fly or a fish in being "free" to swim (and not just to the ends of "survival," but first of all because such are the ways whereby these different natures can most fully "be themselves"). (PM 55)

This latter passage is from "The Poetic Motive," a notable text because it is based on *PDC*'s concluding chapter.

A study of Burke's notion of entelechy could begin with a 1952 essay, "A 'Dramatistic' View of 'Imitation'" (DVI), which argues that starting at least as far back as Sidney's *Apology for Poetry*, the meaning of imitation lost the entelechial sense that Burke would have us recover. The essay's introduction concludes: "we try to show how the *culminative* emphasis in his [Aristotle's] notion of the 'entelechy' was obscured by a notion of representation that is nearer to the stress upon the average or 'statistical'... Othello, for instance, would be a 'culminative' or 'entelechial' depiction of a jealous husband. He is not the statistical average" (DVI 229). From its position here in the context of poetics, entelechy is in subsequent decades generalized to encompass all discourses. Entelechy's progress from a particular discourse to a universal principle of all discourse can be traced from the standpoint of Burke's notion of "the tracking down of implications": just as the implications of the idea of a jealous husband can be tracked to the discovery of the character Othello, the implications of the discourse of physics can be tracked to the discovery of further developments in physics. The state of the discourse frames the discovery that modifies the discourse. Apples fall on a lot of heads, but when one fell on Newton's a discovery occurred because Newton inhabited a discourse that gave the event its meaning. At the core of the process of tracking implications are the linguistic resources, as Burke puts it, "whereby, once you have such a word as 'ruler,' you can advance to the idea of a 'perfect ruler'" (PAC 404–05; see also *DD* 59).

Consideration of entelechy's progress suggests reasons for modifying Rueckert's proposal, noted earlier, that Burke's attention, in his final phase, shifts from literature in particular to discourse in general. Whatever shift occurs, Burke carries literature along with him as he makes it. Entelechy becomes, as Rueckert observes, the most basic motive of the human species, but it is a motive with a distinctive poetic coloration. In Burke's later discourse, entelechy wanders far from its beginnings in Aristotle's *Poetics*, but it never severs itself from its poetic roots.

Entelechy is thus another variant of a recurrent theme in the present study, where we've seen Burke repeatedly anchor his discourse in artistic activity. Theorizing this activity in different ways at different points in his career

> chapter 2: eloquence rooted in innate ideas, or in formal and symbolic effects combined
> chapter 3: a biological will to eloquence
> chapter 4: a Freudian eloquence expressing individualizing "pre-forensic" experience
> chapter 8: entelechial eloquence

Burke habitually returns to this activity even as he repeatedly transforms his discourse in radical ways. Michael Feehan may go too far in asserting that "Burke will *always* take the artist's work as the definitively human activity" ("Oscillation" 324; italics added), but there is no doubt that Burke began his career inside aesthetic humanism and that he may never have moved altogether outside its gravitational field.

The possible exception is Burke's use of the Constitution, the theoretical gesture in his career that seems most clearly to escape the gravitational force of the aesthetic. The constitutional act serves in the present study as the basis for a rhetoric of the subject (chapters 5–7), but in his final phase Burke turned away from the Constitution to theorize a logological subject driven by an entelechial motive. In retrospect, the Constitution seems more exceptional than ever, yet whether Burke was ever prepared to take the step from the constitutional act to a rhetoric of the subject remains an open and perhaps unanswerable question.

Entelechy is like the negative in that both motives are transindividual. In both cases, Burke finds a motive in language that he attributes to the human species as an effect of its linguistic prowess. Both, in other words, exhibit the decided shift from the individualist perspective of the projected *SM* to the transindividualist perspective of logology. Is there a tension between entelechy and the negative? The negative, especially when one considers its policing role, could be the basis for a theory of "civilization and its discontents." Entelechy, on the other hand, seems resoundingly positive: word-using as a telic, natural fulfillment rather than as an alien intruder on natural contentment.

Nonetheless, entelechy and the negative can work together, as in the redemptive sacrifice of Christ that TL discusses. Such sacrifice functions in a disciplinary agon, purging guilt to reaffirm the thou-shalt-nots of orthodoxy that fostered the guilt in the first place. In this reaffirmation, the negative seems more honorific, while entelechy, in its role in perfecting the sacrificial victim, seems perhaps less.

Burke sees such sacrifice, as noted earlier, as analogous to the sacrifice of a tragic hero, as he effectively illustrates in *"Coriolanus —* and the Delights of Faction" (CDF), featured in *LSA* as the last of the essays constituting the book's first part: "Five Summarizing Essays." What impresses Burke most about this tragedy is "how perfectly the chosen victim's virtues and vices work together, in fitting him for his sacrificial function" (CDF 83). Most of Burke's attention is devoted to analyzing the entelechial perfecting of Coriolanus for this function. Analysis of this perfecting expands to detailed attention to virtually the entire cast of characters, an expansion methodologically justified thus: "A character cannot 'be himself' unless many others among the dramatis personae contribute to this end, so that the very essence of a character's nature is in large measure defined, or determined, by the other characters who variously assist or oppose him" (CDF 84). In this analysis, in short, poetic perfection and the disciplinary thou-shalt-not become inextricably tied.[11]

Entelechy is most positive, echoing the innate forms in Burke's early aesthetic, when it appears to be the telos of the body as well as language in a dialectic analogous to Schiller's, where opposition between the material drive (*Stofftrieb*) and the formal drive (*Formtrieb*) is transcended in play (*Spieltrieb*). Entelechy is less positive when Burke, as in a passage quoted earlier, distinguishes himself from Aristotle by limiting entelechy to a strictly linguistic incentive that is apart from the body and could conceivably even be antagonistic to it. That there is an unbridgeable gap between body and language is a thesis that Burke develops at some length in a late essay, "(Nonsymbolic) Motion / (Symbolic) Action" (M/A), which posits a principle of "duplication"

11 This analysis of the disciplinary agon also marginalizes the yes against yes agon of history. Hans Jürgen Weckermann's *"Coriolanus:* The Failure of the Autonomous Individual" suggests by its title the rival "yes" that is ultimately defeated; Weckermann's text is included in *Shakespeare: Text, Language, Criticism: Essays in Honour of Marvin Spevack,* eds. Bernhard Fabian and Kurt Tetzeli (Hildesheim: Georg Olms AG, 1987): 334–49. Burke examines briefly the motivations involved in the agon of history under four headings: individual, family, class, nation (CDF 90–91), but "this motivational tangle (individual-family-class-nation)" interests Burke only to the extent that Shakespeare's narrative untangling of it is itself cathartic "in the Crocean sense rather than the Aristotelian" (91).

such that body and language may mirror one another but nothing more: on the side of motion, "an unchartable complexity of behavings among the cells of the body may add up ... to an overall 'unitary' sense of well-being" (M/A 815–16), whereas on the side of action, "the gratification of ... a purely symbolic symmetry can rise to an ecstasy of conviction that we call 'mystical'" (817–18). But in such duplication, the two sides are not only independent of one another but also incomplete without each other. On the one hand, the symbolically induced ecstasy is vulnerable to sloth (*acedia*) because of its "underlying emptiness as tested by a similarly structured physiological counterpart" (818); on the other hand, there is "a kind of sloth implicit in the sheer failure to take delight in the wonders of purely symbolistic enterprise" (818). The symbol-using animal is driven by an entelechial promise of unification that can never be realized: instead of Schilleresque wholeness, a whole person manqué.

Finally, in the context of Burke's concerns with ecology, entelechy becomes more antagonist than protagonist. These concerns are prominent enough to prompt Rueckert to entitle one section of his analysis of late Burke "Entelechy and Technology: Burke's Eco-Logo-Logical Vision" (*Drama* 273). In this context, entelechy sometimes becomes a subject of history heading for catastrophe:

And the mere tracking down of the implications in any specific scientific nomenclature would be an example of such a poetic or entelechial "compulsion" – and all the more insistently so when any such "craving" has been massively potentiated by the accumulation of technological resources constructed in its image, a fateful duplication whereby many men of great skill and enterprise must strive like demons to track down the manifold implications of Technologism, with its labyrinthine entanglements of progress, pollution, and war.   (PAC 410)

In "Toward Helhaven: Three Stages of a Vision" (TH), Burke depicts this entelechial subject of history leaving the planet to start over elsewhere. Tracking the implications of technology to their terminus, Helhaven is a bubble on the moon that provides artificial substitutes for all the wonders that nature once provided in abundance on earth. For self-congratulatory moods, there is even a telescope powerful enough to offer a graphic view of the unfortunates left behind on earth to gasp for life.[12]

A compulsion from beyond history destined to obliterate it, this

---

12 To illustrate Burke's "eco-logo-logical-vision," Rueckert analyzes in detail "Toward Helhaven" and its companion "Why Satire, with a Plan for Writing One" (WS) (*Drama* 273–87).

entelechial subject is immune to the agon of history. Considered from the standpoint of Burke's constitutional act, by contrast, the implications of technology that one might entelechially track would be one voluntaristic principle proportionally mixed with others, some of which would be at odds with these implications. The necessitarian imperative would call for an act to resolve the competition among the principles, and the agon of history would be the ultimate arbiter of which act among the various possibilities prevailed. The picture is otherwise with the entelechial "compulsion," which decides every issue in advance. The implications are essentialized; anything that might retard their realization must stand aside to allow the entelechial subject of history to march to its destiny. This subject is a theoretical dead-end: it defeats in advance any strategy devised from any standpoint within history.

A few years before his death, Burke appears to have envisioned returning to the Constitution as a theoretical model. "The 'watershed moment,'" Feehan writes in "Kenneth Burke's Dualistic Theory of Constitutions," "came sometime in 1989 with a leap backwards to the 1940s. Burke returned to *A Grammar of Motives,* to the concept of 'The Dialectic of Constitutions' ... Now, however, Constitutions must be viewed as dualistic" (42). Burke writes, in a letter from which Feehan quotes at length,

Try tentatively seeing how things work out if you look for a "dualistic theory of our Constitution's language." The technological side is marked by an annual measure of the goods and services collectively available to us all in our identities as tax-paying U.S. citizens. Fittingly, this measure, called a Gross National Product, is a device itself technological, as a useful kind of "artificial intelligence," by which we can compare the ups and downs of technological productivity from year to year. Our political Constitution, on the other hand, sets the conditions for factional disputes between parties which in effect distribute the rewards and taxes differently, with correspondingly different rhetorical platforms and rationales. (42)

In this "dualistic theory," Feehan proposes, one can see Burke attempting to comprehend the relationship between the "personal" and the "instrumental" that he explores in other texts from the mid–1980s, particularly "In Haste" and the "Afterwords" to the new editions of *ATH* and *PC.* "In Haste," in its consideration of this relationship, includes an episodic historical narrative in which the future is left to the agon of history to decide.

Our linguistic prowess makes for two dimensions, writes Burke in the *ATH* "Afterword," "One encompasses the vast complex of social relationships, properties, authorities that centers in the principle of *personality*. The other starts from the kinds of transformations in the conditions of living (departures from a primitive state of nature) due to the technological development of *instruments*" (378). Prompted by Burke's proposal, Feehan translates these two dimensions into the language of the Constitution such that this one document authorizes "simultaneously both the kinds of citizens we wish for and the kinds of instruments necessary for sustaining those citizens":

For instance, the US Constitution implicitly defines maturity among the citizens as beginning at age twenty-five and deepening progressively to some presumed plateau at thirty-five, when we achieve Presidential potential. The Constitution also requires that the Congress create a Navy and a Post Office to insure the safe, consistent and efficient movement of governmental and commercial instruments.

(42)

Neither Feehan nor Burke, however, addresses the question of the extent to which the 1989 "dualistic theory" overlaps the dualism in the 1945 theory. This latter evidences itself in the notion of a "Constitution-Behind-the-Constitution," which even serves as the title of a section in "The Dialectic of Constitutions" (*GM* 362). A constitutional act, *GM* stresses repeatedly, becomes the scenic environment of subsequent acts. From the standpoint of the constitution-behind-the-constitution, constitutional practice in the US adds up to "a capitalist Constitution" (*GM* 388).

Burke did not live to develop his dualistic theory to a point that would indicate clearly whether it's a return with a difference to the earlier theory, or a straightforward return. A third possibility is that Burke's 1989 proposal is less a new theory in general than a new constitution in particular, one suited to the situation of the 1980s. As Burke interprets this situation, the ecological crisis overrides all others, carrying more rhetorical weight than any other ingredient in any proportional mix of ingredients in the situation. Considered from the standpoint of this third possibility, Feehan's derivation of the personal–instrumental dualism from clauses in the US Constitution identifies the voluntaristic principles that Burke selects as his focus.

The strategy informing Burke's selection is particularly evident in "In Haste," the text that Feehan discusses at greatest length as he interprets Burke's letter. Particularly notable are lines Burke quotes from one of his poems:

> How walk faster, except by working harder?
> Likewise how run, or speed up a bike,
> except by greater effort? . . .
> Ever so lightly press the pedal down a fraction farther
> And your massive technologic demon
> spurts forward like a fiend.
>
> Tell them that.
> Talk of such brutal disproportion
> between decision and consequences.
> "Might we not here, my friends,
> confront the makings of a madness,
> an unacknowledged leap
> from *This is mine*
> to *By God, this is ME!* . . . ?
> (IH 356, spaced periods do not represent ellipses; see also *CP* 282)

These lines suggest the logic of Burke's equation, noted in chapter 3, of the technological psychosis with the Nietzschean will to power. Like money, technology is empowerment, but unlike money, sufficient technological empowerment can be had on the cheap – even a kid can get a hot car – for it to be widespread enough to form a hegemonic mode of subjecthood in a technological culture. Constitutionally considered, this subject of technology is a constitutional precedent that Burke wants the culture to overturn.

"In Haste" characterizes this subject of technology not as an effect of an entelechial compulsion rooted in language such that it is predestined – something that can be contemplated from the standpoint of a "Prologue in Heaven" – but as a historical construction, an identification of the personal and the instrumental constituted at one point in history that can be reconstituted at another. The episodic history that "In Haste" constructs is designed to uncover different ways that this identification was constituted in different historical episodes. Overturning the precedent of this subject of technology will not, however, come easily, as Feehan shows after accentuating that *GM* sees constitutions as engaged in agonistic struggle ("Dualistic" 43, 54–55). But overturning it is the aim. That Burke's 1989 "dualistic theory" points ultimately toward a new subject is confirmed by Feehan when he observes in his concluding paragraph, "Burke's theory argues that repair of the world requires a re-visioning of PERSON" (58).

Finally, however, from the standpoint of the concerns of the present study, how one construes Burke's final turn to the constitutional theme is less important than the turn itself. By design, our narrative ends with this 1989 Burke after beginning with the 1918 Burke who devoted himself to art with Flaubertian zeal. Engaged in rhetorical struggle to melt down one subject to clear the ground for a new one, the Burke with which we conclude is at the molten core of a rhetoric of the subject where the final arbiter of subjecthood is the agon of history. This is a place, our narrative suggests, to which he did and did not want to go.

This is also the place where one finds rhetorical humanism, if we might venture a phrase that may sound oxymoronic, especially when rhetoric, as in these pages, is married to history. Humanism and history do not mix to eyes trained to see history as never more than alienation from a transcendental human essence. But perhaps humanism is not a place in advance of history and thus for all time. Perhaps it is, rather, changing what it means to be human in the high stakes game of historical struggle. The often maligned anti-humanists of recent decades may be the real humanists of our time, since it is they who have forced us to rethink the question of the human subject.

If the human subject is not given but, for better or worse, decided in history, then we all, whether we wish or not, make for a subject that is better or worse. *In medias res*, like Burke's creatures from the sea, we alone can keep utopian hope alive.

Index

Index

Index

Index

Index

Newton, I. 247
Nietzsche, F. 1, 6, 61, 65, 66, 68, 74–75,
   76–78, 81, 106

Ohmann, Richard 55

Parkes, Henry Bamford 142, 148–49, 157,
   186–87, 224, 227
Pater, Walter 41
Pavlov, I. 69 n.22, 110–12
Perot, Ross 133
Petrey, Sandy 140, 162–63, 165
Plato 16, 48, 84, 121, 177, 207, 237, 244
Plessy v. Ferguson 223
Ponge, Francis 160 n.25
Popper, Karl 15 n.42, 172 n.41
Popular Front 57, 58
postmodernism 19, 25, 29, 85, 120, 132,
   133, 134, 154, 157, 185, 198
Pound, Erza 39, 40

Quayle, Dan 98

Ransom, John Crowe 123, 137
Read, Herbert 142, 143
Reagan, Ronald 178–79
Reich, Wilhelm 32–33, 34, 218, 224
rhetoric of the subject 25–28, 139, 147–48,
   164, 228, 230
   and agon of history 27, 35–36, 54, 126,
      130, 132, 134, 148, 154–55, 157–58,
      161–62, 200, 230, 233–34, 240–41,
      253–54
   and transhistorical 22–23, 26–27, 156
   in Althusser 10
   in Burke 5, 26–27, 108, 121–27, 129–30,
      132, 134, 145, 154, 155–58, 166,
      195–200, 233–34, 248, 253–54
   in Defoe 28, 35–36
   in Derrida 161–62
   in Foucault 35, 154
   in Richardson 36, 175
   in Therborn 8, 18–21, 23, 26–27
   versus individualism 23, 25–26, 27, 136,
      146–48, 157–62
   versus Lukács's transcendental subject 8,
      9, 17, 18–21, 25, 153, 175, 196,
      205–06
rhetorical commensurability 31 n.68, 172,
   174, 182
   versus epistemological
      commensurability 172
rhetorical humanism 254
rhetorical realism 19, 23, 27, 38, 109, 121,
   122, 135, 163, 167–75, 177

and agon of history 27
and transhistorical 17–21
   in Althusser 12, 13
   in Burke 6, 12, 24, 112, 115, 119–20,
      121, 127, 133, 154, 173–75
   in Derrida 6, 162, 166, 170–71
   in Foucault 31 n.68
   in Jameson 5–6, 109
   in Therborn 21, 23
   versus Lukács 37
   versus rhetorical idealism 6, 11, 23–24,
      70, 99, 111, 133, 142, 162–66, 172,
      209
rhetorical sayability 31, 109, 113 n.5, 154,
   174, 206
   and agon of history 27, 96, 133, 147,
      148, 152, 154, 198, 200, 211, 216
   in Burke 12, 93, 98, 103–04, 132, 152,
      174, 193–94, 206, 240
   in Coleridge 126
   in Defoe 126
   in Foucault 31
   in Lentricchia 206
   versus Kant 172, 174
   versus romantic authenticity and/or
      enlightenment certainty 4, 12, 109,
      119, 212, 215, 240
Richards, I. A. 44, 70–71, 74–75, 114
Richardson, S. 36, 175, 178
Ricoeur, Paul 85 n.3
Roig, Charles 138 n.4
Rorty, Richard 3, 113, 118, 119, 133, 153,
   155, 172, 182
Rosenfeld, Isaac 137
Rousseau, J. J. 164
Rueckert, William H. 65 n.20, 88 n.6, 124
   n.22, 138, 217–18, 226 n.5, 234,
   243–44, 246, 247, 250

Said, Edward 1–2
Sams, Henry W. 243
Sanders, Jane 56 n.3
Saussure, F. 120–21
Schiappa, Edward 119 n.17
Schiller, F. 249–50
Schlauch, Margaret 87–88, 92, 93, 98, 102
Schlesinger, Arthur 37
Schrecker, Ellen W. 56 n.3
Schwartz, Lawrence H. 57, 58 n.13
Scott, Robert L. 237
Searle, John 167–72, 174, 176
Shakespeare, W. 64, 98, 114
   Coriolanus 249
   Falstaff 47
   Macbeth 96–97, 99

Index

Shaw, G. B.   134
Shi, David   56
Sidney, Sir P.   247
Simons, Herbert W.   2 n.7
Skinner, B. F.   69 n.22
Smith, Adam   187
Smith, Paul   13–14
Southwell, Samuel B.   2 n.5, 138 n.4, 184
Spinoza, B.   147, 186–87, 209
Spivak, Gayatri Chakravorty   146, 169, 170
Sprinker, Michael   2, 164 n.31
Spurgeon, Caroline   122
Stalinists versus Trotskyites   92 n.8
Staten, Henry   72 n.27
Stein, Gertrude   43
Stevens, Wallace   37, 39
Stuart, Charlotte L.   138 n.4
Swift, J.   97

Tate, Allen   94
Therborn, Göran   7–8, 9, 10, 18, 19, 20–21,
      23–24, 26–27, 78, 85, 125, 143, 153,
      161, 189, 195–96
Thomas, Douglas   224 n.3
topos, topoi   170–77, 181–82, 183, 190, 198
Tournier, Michel   182
transhistorical   13–17, 25, 26, 28, 36, 156,
      167
   and nature/culture binary   91
   and negative hermeneutics of
      suspicion   37–38
   in Althusser   13, 14–15, 22
   in Burke   26–27, 36–37, 86–87, 93, 95,
      106, 131–33, 185
   in Foucault   31

in Marx   16
in Therborn   23, 26–27, 85, 153
in Wood   15–16, 203
versus transcendental   13, 16–17, 17–21,
      24–25, 85, 131–32, 153
Twain, M.   40, 47

University of Washington   56 n.3 and n.4
Urgo, Joseph   189

Valesio, Paolo   149
Veblen, Thorstein   67, 192, 214
Vico, G.   118 n.14, 171 n.38
Vietnam   55, 179

Wald, Alan   92 n.8
Warren, Austin   137
Watson, Jr., J. S.   40 n.3
Watt, Ian   28
Weber, Max   86
Weckermann, Hans Jürgen   249 n.11
Wellbery, David E.   2, 189–90
Wellek, René   137
Wess, Robert   6 n.17, 7 n.20, 10 n.29, 13
      n.37, 23 n.58, 147 n.16, 186 n1, 187
      n2
Williams, David Cratis   173 n.42, 184 n.49
Williams, Raymond   13, 96, 102
Williams, William Carlos   39, 40
Wilson, Thomas   232
Wittgenstein, Ludwig   70, 115 n.9
Wolfe, Cary   76 n.29
Wood, Ellen Meiksins   15–16, 203–04

Zabel, Morton D.   39